Public-Private Partnerships in the European Unior

Public-Private Partnerships in the European Union aims to be a reference point for academics, researchers and policy makers. The book intends to capture the spirit and pulse of discourse by disseminating outstanding research on strategic multi-disciplinary issues of public- private partnerships as a distinctive feature of public sector management, including privatisation, regulation, procurement, outsourcing, insourcing and service sharing, from legal, economic and public policy perspectives and aims to influence current and future debate in public sector management in the European Union and its member states and across other continents.

Christopher Bovis, *FRSA*, is Professor of International Business at the Business School of the University of Hull. He is Editor-in-Chief of the *European Procurement & Public Private Partnership Law Review,* published by Lexxion.

Routledge Critical Studies in Public Management

Edited by Stephen Osborne

The study and practice of public management has undergone profound changes across the world. Over the last quarter century, we have seen

- increasing criticism of public administration as the over-arching framework for the provision of public services,
- the rise (and critical appraisal) of the 'New Public Management' as an emergent paradigm for the provision of public services,
- the transformation of the 'public sector' into the cross-sectoral provision of public services, and
- the growth of the governance of inter-organizational relationships as an essential element in the provision of public services

In reality these trends have not so much replaced each other as elided or co-existed together—the public policy process has not gone away as a legitimate topic of study, intra-organizational management continues to be essential to the efficient provision of public services, whist the governance of inter-organizational and inter-sectoral relationships is now essential to the effective provision of these services.

Further, whilst the study of public management has been enriched by contribution of a range of insights from the 'mainstream' management literature it has also contributed to this literature in such areas as networks and inter-organizational collaboration, innovation and stakeholder theory.

This series is dedicated to presenting and critiquing this important body of theory and empirical study. It will publish books that both explore and evaluate the emergent and developing nature of public administration, management and governance (in theory and practice) and examine the relationship with and contribution to the over-arching disciplines of management and organizational sociology.

Books in the series will be of interest to academics and researchers in this field, students undertaking advanced studies of it as part of their undergraduate or postgraduate degree and reflective policy makers and practitioners.

Public-Private Partnerships in the European Union

Christopher Bovis

Routledge
Taylor & Francis Group

NEW YORK AND LONDON

First published 2014
by Routledge
711 Third Avenue, New York, NY 10017

Simultaneously published in the UK
by Routledge
2 Park Square, Milton Park, Abingdon, Oxon OX14 4RN

First issued in paperback 2018

*Routledge is an imprint of the Taylor & Francis Group,
an informa business*

© 2014 Taylor & Francis

The right of Christopher Bovis to be identified as the author of the
editorial material has been asserted in accordance with sections 77 and 78
of the Copyright, Designs and Patents Act 1988.

All rights reserved. No part of this book may be reprinted or reproduced or
utilized in any form or by any electronic, mechanical, or other means, now
known or hereafter invented, including photocopying and recording, or in
any information storage or retrieval system, without permission in writing
from the publishers.

Trademark Notice: Product or corporate names may be trademarks or
registered trademarks, and are used only for identification and explanation
without intent to infringe.

Library of Congress Cataloging-in-Publication Data

Bovis, Christopher.
    Public-private partnerships in the European Union / by Christopher Bovis.
        pages cm. — (Routledge critical studies in public management ; 16)
    Includes bibliographical references and index.
    1. Public-private sector cooperation—European Union countries.
2. Public contracts—European Union countries.   I. Title.
    HD3872.E85B68 2013
    338.8'7—dc23
    2013012685

ISBN 13: 978-1-138-34001-5 (pbk)
ISBN 13: 978-0-415-34993-2 (hbk)

Typeset in Sabon
by Apex CoVantage, LLC

Contents

Acknowledgements

It would have been very difficult to complete this project without the involvement of a number of people to whom here I record my great indebtedness. First of all, my thanks go to the publishers for their professionalism and the assistance they provided.

It is also with deep appreciation that I express my gratitude to H. J. Lamar, Y. J. Lamar, Solomon Holtz, Howard Jacobson, Morris Laxman, Kurt Lipstein, Gomez Da Silva Texteira, Terrence Bramall, Richard Watson and David Blunt.

I also profoundly thank Professor Terry Williams, Professor Alan Rosas, Professor Walter van Gerven, Professor Alan Dashwood, Professor Takis Tridimas, Professor Harry Arthurs and Professor Surya Subedi.

Finally, I am eternally indebted to Dr Christine Bovis-Cnossen for her invaluable support and inspiration.

Christopher Bovis
May 2013

Foreword

The current political and economic environment has witnessed a rethink of public services, the way in which they are financed, the way in which they are delivered and the way the state is accountable for them. Many systems across the world, as well as many international organisations, have accepted the axiom that the private sector has a major role to play in the delivery of public services.

The expectations of citizens have been raised; not only have the economic results of globalisation been widely felt, but the transformation of the global market place has posed fundamental questions about the role and responsibilities of the state, international organisations, multinationals and the citizens as end-users and the recipients of public services.

The term *public service* often refers to a service which is offered to the general public, or highlights that a service has been assigned a specific role in the public interest, or refers to the ownership or status of the entity which provides the service. In the latter situation, public service fuses with the concept of *public sector* which covers the state and its organs and undertakings controlled by public authorities.

Two models for the assessment of public services have been developed, based on different theoretical and conceptual values. On the one hand, public services which capture general needs of the public are delivered through market-based mechanisms where the public sector interfaces or competes with private sector undertakings; on the other hand, public services which are described as essential facilities are sheltered from competition in order to ensure the integrity of their delivery.

Discourse has propelled the axiom that the delivery of public services takes place in a *sui generis* market place. A number of pertinent questions have subsequently arisen. Do we except the principles of competition, transparency and accountability and equality to be present within such market place? Do we expect the state to fund public services and how? Do we expect the private sector to be rewarded for the delivery of public services, over and above contractual obligations for taking risks or offering innovative solutions? Do we expect a governance mechanism to control the deliverables in terms of quality and price? And finally, do we believe that Public-Private

Partnerships can make a real difference in delivering public services in the twenty-first century?

The rhetoric of governments across the world surrounding public-private partnerships eulogises the attributes of the relations between the public and private sectors in delivering public services in an effective and efficient manner. The concept of public-private partnerships denotes a collaborative effort between the public sector, which comprises the government, its organs and its agencies, and the private sector which includes the financial services sector. Such effort is based on long-term, complex contractual arrangements and in all cases requires the provision of private finance. It replicates the traditional role of the state as owner and provider of public services. The concept of public-private partnerships registers a shift in theoretical and conceptual dynamics earmarking an era of new public sector management where the state "steers" regulation into markets, public and private, and assumes an enabling capacity distancing itself from ownership and direct involvement in the delivery of public services.

The appetite of governments for such relationships with the private sector originates in the transition from traditional public management theories to a modern thinking of public governance which reveals demonstrable advantages based on strategic collaboration between public and private sectors. The often-referred to as infrastructure deficit in both developed and developing countries augments and necessitates a different intellectual approach to public service delivery, particularly when the technological advances of the twentieth century have pushed citizens' expectations to ever higher levels for standards in public services. The attraction of public-private partnerships to deliver public services rests on some fundamental perceptions which alarmingly reflect reality; budget constraints confronting national governments and the widespread assumption that private sector know-how will improve the delivery of public services appear as the main policy drivers for selecting the public-private partnership route. In addition, the preferential accountancy treatment of public-private partnerships benefits national governments as the assets and debt involved in a public-private partnership are classified as nongovernment assets, and therefore are recorded off-balance sheet for public accountancy purposes.

From a different prism, the public-private interface allows both sectors to combine their skills and know-how based on a partnership approach. This feature would be difficult to occur in traditional contractual relations. The reasons for such assumption are the ever important risk allocation and the ensuing risk management, which bring together the optimal incentivisation of the parties on the one hand and the pursuit of public interest on the other hand. A common theme across the world is the severe budgetary constraints governments are faced with alongside their persistent devotion to the welfare state. The public-private partnership offering, not surprisingly, offers a balanced approach of risk and delivery, not only in infrastructure but also in any aspect of public services. It is common to expect a public-private partnership arrangement to provide for a single platform for both the public and private sector to work together for the delivery of public services. The public-private partnership offering also expands into an industrial policy dimension where it occupies choices for investment, strategic growth of sectors, internationalisation and competitive advantages. The industry (the private sector which includes the financial sector) has viewed the public-private partnership agenda as a credible solution to long-term economic growth with high market visibility and potential for sustainable earnings.

A common definition on public-private partnerships does not exist. However, common characteristics exist. The relatively long duration of the relationship, the method of financing and the risk transfer from the public to the private sector are common features in different jurisdictions across the world. These features reflect on and reveal the expected role of the private sector, who participates in different stages, varying from the design, financing, completion, implementation and refinancing. The role of the public sector relates to defining the objectives to be attained in terms of pursuing public interest, the quality of services and pricing policy as it takes responsibility for monitoring compliance with these objectives. The precise distribution of risk is determined in accordance with the respective ability of the parties to assess, control and manage risk.

The principal benefit from involving the private sector in the delivery of public services through a public-private partnership format has been attributed to the fact that the public sector does not have to commit its own capital resources in funding the delivery of public services, and that substantial transfer of risks to the private sector offers value-for-money for the public sector and the taxpayers.

As a result of the private sector incentivisation and the appropriately managed risks, there is significant probability of large-scale infrastructure projects delivered on time and within budget. On a more strategic approach, public-private partnerships promote a service culture in the delivery of public services which has increased innovation and competition, optimise design and focus the procurement exercise on achieving life cycle costs and also on transferring life cycle risks. A change of focus by the public sector on outcomes rather than inputs, in particular with a concentration on value-for-money over the longer term as opposed to concentrating on short-term capital expenditure, is also registered. In theory, PPPs offer innovative ways of privately sourced finance, which allow the public sector to concentrate its funding on priority areas. Finance innovation also creates the potential for revenue-based projects which deliver public services as a credible and viable alternative asset class for pension funds by providing the opportunity to match long-term liabilities with relatively low-risk and index-linked revenue streams.

The principal criticism directed on the public-private partnerships agenda and its offerings focusses on the proposition as an expensive and inflexible way to engage with the private sector, on the grounds that real risk transfer

does not take place and that always the government will be the guaran-
tor of the delivery of the project. Other points reflect on the false appetite
to use public-private partnerships on the assumption that it is a legitimate
way for governments to evade international accounting standards on public spending rules by excluding public-private partnerships financing and
liabilities from their respective borrowing requirements. Finally, another
criticism is that public-private partnerships allow the private sector to make
supra-competitive profits from what should ordinarily be a contract for
the delivery of public services in addition to the potential of profits from
refinancing and attracting secondary investments throughout the life of the
public-private partnership.

This book has a single focus; to touch upon the concept of public-private
partnerships within the EU legal system and link its function and features
with the elements of public sector integration.

In the Introduction, the remit of the relevant market place is set by defining the notion of public markets and the concept of public services, and
by opening the debate on public services in the EU offering an analytical
exposition of their features and characteristics such as public service obligations, universal service obligations and services of general economic interest.
These features reveal the economic assessment and the legal treatment of
the financing of public services and the engagement options on the part
of the public sector. The Introduction sets the fundamental platform upon
which contractualised governance has emerged and assisted the evolution
of public-private partnerships as a phenomenon of public service delivery in
the EU and its Member States.

Chapter 1 explores the remit of public sector regulation in the EU context by analysing its economic policy dimension in public sector regulation
in the delivery of public services. The economic policy dimension of the
EU public sector also reveals its links with antitrust and the public policy
dimension in public sector regulation, which in turn reflect on the industrial policy dimension in public sector regulation and the close relation of
public sector regulation with public procurement and state aid control.
Chapter 2 covers concepts in public sector regulation, starting with public
contracts and concessions. Such relation reflects on the nexus of the state
with the private sector and the compensatory and remunerative approach
by the state in the delivery of public services which delineates the regulatory
treatment of the contractual interfaces between public and private sectors.
Chapter 3 examines the notion of contracting authorities and the emanations of the state which are contracting with the private sector in order
to deliver public services. The chapter reflects on significant developments
from the European judiciary which have offered a wide spectrum of flexibility for stretching the notion of contracting authorities to actors within
the private sector. Chapter 4 focusses on the evolution of public-private
partnerships as a global phenomenon and covers its influencing factors and
the application of public-private co-operation in delivering public services.

It appraises recent legal, policy and judicial developments that have emerged as a result of the involvement of the private sector in the delivery of public services and in particular their financing. Chapter 5 analyses the development of public-private partnerships in the European Union. The concept of public-private partnerships has become synonymous with growth strategies at EU Institutional levels as EU policy and law makers are keen to see the model as a credible and effective delivery mechanism for public services in an era of economic crisis. The chapter examines the features of public-private partnerships, provides for taxonomy of legal and operational characteristics of public-private partnerships and identifies the two most important features, the relevant implications arising from methods of financing and the risk allocation in such arrangements between the public and private sector. Chapter 6 covers the procurement regulation of public-private partnerships. Considerable emphasis has been placed on observing the principles of transparency and accountability, competitiveness and value-for-money during the procurement process of public-private partnerships. This chapter demonstrates that the procurement of public-private partnerships must adhere to the enshrined principles of transparency, objectivity and nondiscrimination that underlie the public sector regulation. Chapter 7 analyses the development of public-public partnerships in the European Union, in policy and legal terms. The chapter examines the features and dynamics of long-term arrangements between public sector bodies in pursuit of public interest functions, the characteristics and organisational features of the types of public-public partnerships, the legal and corporate treatment between the parties and the boundaries for public task allocation in such undertakings. Chapter 8 explores future trends in public-private partnerships. This chapter reflects on the legal and regulatory mapping of public-private partnerships and elaborates on the current and future legal trends within which the regulation of public-private partnerships will be developed. Furthermore and in conjunction to the emergence of legal trends, the analysis reflects on societal needs which need calibrating in terms of expectation, but mostly perception when faced with the modality of public-private partnerships for the delivery of public services. The chapter casts a conceptual map of the challenges for the development of the law in relation to public-private partnerships, by depicting their interface as public services instrument, as investment instruments and as growth instruments. Conclusions sum up the efforts of the book to provide for a comprehensive set of conceptual directions in modern EU public sector governance by supporting the intellectual credibility of the notion of public-private partnerships in delivering public services.

Professor Christopher H. Bovis JD, MPhil, LLM, FRSA

Introduction
Public Markets and Public Services in the EU

THE CONCEPT OF PUBLIC MARKETS

The paradigm of New Public Management (NPM) in public administration[1], influenced by public choice theory, has been pointing towards a mixed economy where the public sector would manage the relevant markets and the private sector and other stakeholders would provide public services.[2] The division of roles would bring about substantial efficiency gains and quality improvements from the use of market and quasi-market competitive mechanisms as a result of externalisation and unbundling in the delivery of public services. The state and its organs enter the market place in pursuit of public interest.[3] However, the activities of the state and its organs do not display the commercial characteristics of private entrepreneurship, as the aim of the public sector is not the maximisation of profits but the observance of public interest.[4] This fundamental difference emerges as the ground for the creation of *public markets* where public interest substitutes profit maximisation.[5] However, further variances distinguish private from public markets. These focus on structural elements of the market place, competitiveness, demand conditions, supply conditions, the production process, and finally pricing and risk. They also provide for an indication as to the different methods and approaches employed in their regulation.[6] The main reason for regulating public sector, the utilities and network industries is to bring their respective markets in parallel to the operation of private markets.[7] European policy makers have recognised the distinctive character of *public markets* and focused on establishing conditions similar to those that control the operation of private markets through a sophisticated and detailed framework of procurement regulation.[8] The public markets reflect an economic equation where the demand side is represented by the public sector at large and the utilities, whereas the supply side covers the industry.

Private markets are generally structured as a result of competitive pressures originating in the interaction between buyers and supplier and their configuration can vary from monopoly or oligopoly conditions to models operating under advanced competition. Demand arises from heterogeneous buyers with a variety of specific needs, is based on expectations and is multiple for each product. Supply, on the other hand, is offered through various product ranges, where products are standardised using known technology, but constantly improved through research and development processes. The production process is based on mass-production patterns and the product range represents a large choice including substitutes, whereas the critical production factor is cost. The development cycle appears to be short to medium term and finally, the technology of products destined for the private markets is evolutionary. Purchases are made when an acceptable balance between price and quality is achieved. Purchase orders are multitude and at limited intervals. Pricing policy in private markets is determined by competitive forces and the purchasing decision is focused on the price-quality relation, where the risk factor is highly present.

On the other hand, public markets tend to be structured and to function in a different way. The market structure often reveals monopsony characteristics. Monopsony is the reverse of monopoly power. The state and its organs often appear as the sole outlet for a sector's or an industry's output. In terms of its origins, demand in public markets is institutionalised and operates mainly under budgetary considerations. It is also based on fulfilment of tasks linked with the pursuit of public interest and it is single, in contrast to the multitude nature of demand in private markets, for many products. Supply in public markets also has limited origins, in terms of the establishment of close ties between the public sector and industries supplying it and there is often a limited product range. Products are not innovative and technologically advanced and pricing is determined through tendering and negotiations. The purchasing decision is primarily based upon the whole-life cycle, reliability, price and political considerations. Purchasing patterns follow tendering and negotiations and often purchases are dictated by policy rather than price/quality considerations.

The intellectual support of public procurement regulation in the European Union draws inferences from economic theories[9], and mainly neo-liberal theories. Although procurement regulation aims primarily at the purchasing patterns of the demand side, it is envisaged that the integration of public markets through enhanced competition could bring about beneficial effects for the supply side. These effects focus on the optimal allocation of resources within European industries, the rationalisation of production and supply, the promotion of mergers and acquisitions and the creation of globally competitive industries. Public procurement has cyclical dynamics and its regulation purports to change both behavioural and structural perceptions as its effects will be applied to both the demand and supply sides.

The integration of the public markets of the European Union is achieved primarily by reference to the regulation of the purchasing behaviour of the demand side (the contracting authorities). The behaviour of the supply side is not the subject of procurement regulation, although it is of equal importance to the integration of public markets in the European Union. The supply side in the public procurement equation is subject to the competition law and policy of the European Union, although there is a lack of an integral mechanism in the public procurement legislation to allow the introduction of the antitrust rules to the supply side. *Stricto sensu,* anticompetitive behaviour of undertakings or collusive tendering do not appear as reasons for automatic disqualification from the selection and award procedures of public contracts in the European Union.

European Institutions have assumed that by encouraging the public and the utilities sectors in the European Union to adopt a purchasing behaviour which is homogenous and is based on the principles of openness, transparency and nondiscrimination, the public sector would achieve efficiency gains and savings and industrial restructuring in the supply side would be stimulated. Economic inefficiencies caused by the nonexternalisation of public tasks and services range from 10 per cent to 30 per cent of the contract value.[10]

The European Commission has claimed that the procurement regulation throughout the European Union and the resulting elimination of nontariff barriers arising from discriminatory and preferential purchasing patterns of Member Sates could bring about substantial savings.[11] Combating discrimination on grounds of nationality in the award of public procurement contracts and eliminating domestic preferential purchasing schemes could result in efficiency gains at European and national levels through the emergence of three major effects which would primarily influence the supply side. These include a *trade effect,* a *competition effect* and a *restructuring effect.*[12]

The trade effect[13] represents the actual and potential savings that the public sector will be able to achieve through lower cost purchasing. The trade effect is a result of the principle of transparency in public markets (compulsory advertisement of public contracts above certain thresholds). However, the principle of transparency and the associated trade effect in public markets do not in themselves guarantee the establishment of competitive conditions in the relevant markets, as market access—a structural element in the process of integration of public markets in Europe—could be subsequently hindered by the discriminatory behaviour of contracting authorities in the selection stages and the award stages of public procurement.[14] The trade effect has a static dimension, since it emerges as a consequence of enhanced market access in the relevant sector or industry.[15]

The competition effect relates to the changes of industrial performance as a result of changes in the price behaviour of national firms which had previously been protected from competition by means of preferential and discriminatory procurement practices.[16] The competition effect derives also from the principle of transparency and appears to possess rather static characteristics.[17] Transparency in public procurement breaks down information and awareness barriers in public markets, and as mentioned above, it brings a trade effect in the relevant sectors or industries by means of price competitiveness. The competition effect comes as a natural sequence to price competitiveness and inserts an element of long-term competitiveness in the relevant industries in aspects other than price (e.g. research and development, innovation, customer care).

The competition effect will materialise in the form of *price convergence* of goods, works and services destined for the public sector. Price convergence could take place both nationally and Community-wide, inasmuch as competition in the relevant markets would equalise the prices of similar products.

Finally, the restructuring effect reveals the restructuring dimension and the re-organisational dynamics in the supply side, as a result of increased competition in the relevant markets. The restructuring effect is a dynamic one and refers to the long-term industrial and sectoral adjustment within industries that supply the public sector. The restructuring effect will encapsulate the reaction of the relevant sector or industry to the competitive regime imposed upon the demand and supply sides, as a result of openness and transparency and the sequential trade and competition effects.[18] The response of the relevant sector or industry and the restructuring effect itself would depend on the efficiency of the industry to merge, diversify, convert or abort the relevant competitive markets and would also reflect upon contemporary national industrial policies.[19]

THE PUBLIC SERVICES IN THE EU

The term *public service* in the EU often refers to a service which is offered to the general public, or highlights that a service has been assigned a specific role in the public interest, or refers to the ownership or status of the entity providing the service. In the latter situation, public service fuses with the concept of *public sector* which covers the state and its organs, bodies governed by public law and undertakings controlled by public authorities.[20]

Art 106 TFEU represents the legal cornerstone[21] of the competence of Member States to provide, organise and deliver public services. Two models for the treatment of public services have been developed in the EU, based on different theoretical and conceptual values. On the one hand, public services which capture general needs of the public are delivered through market-based mechanisms where the public sector interfaces or competes with private sector undertakings; this model is based on Art 106 TFEU, sectoral primary and secondary legislation, as well as state aid rules. On the other hand, public services which are described as essential facilities (e.g. defence, policing) should be sheltered from competition in order to ensure the integrity of their delivery.[22] The provision of these types of public services is the prerogative of the state and not affected by the thrust of EU law.[23]

Although the term *public services* does not feature in the *acquis communautaire* relevant to Art 106 TFEU, surrogate concepts have attributed in constructing a notion where the state is expected or even obliged[24] to enter the market place in order to deliver directly or organise the delivery of public services. These surrogate concepts are reflected in the terms of *public service obligations* and *universal service obligations*, which have supported the liberalisation process of sectoral policies of the European Union.[25] The

term *public service obligations* refers to specific quality and price requirements that are imposed by public authorities on the provider of the service
in order to ensure that certain public interest objectives applicable at Community, national or regional level are met.[26] The term *universal service
obligations* denotes contractual or regulatory requirements imposed by public authorities upon undertakings with a view to maintaining regularity and
affordability[27] in the provision of the relevant services.[28] Alongside public
service obligations and universal service obligations, Art 106(2) TFEU has
introduced the term of *services of general economic interest,* a term which its
significance has been augmented by virtue of Art 16 EC.[29] The term *services
of general economic interest* is not defined further in the Treaty or in secondary legislation. The term refers to services of an economic nature which the
Member States or the Community subject to specific public service obligations or universal service obligations by virtue of a general interest criterion.
Thus, services of general economic interest cover services provided by utilities or network industries such as transport, water, postal services, energy
and communications but also extend to any other economic activities which
may be subject to public service obligations.

The characteristics of public services are multitude.[30] One of the fundamental characteristics of public services is their economic nature. The
funding of public services, which may emerge through different formats
such as payment or remuneration under a contract, payment of annual subsidies, preferential fiscal treatment or lower social security contributions
to an entrusted undertaking, reveals such characteristic.[31] This means that
public services have a cost and a value attached to them. Cost reflects upon
capital considerations, whereas value reflects upon revenue considerations.
Even the provision of *social services of general interest*[32] which include
health services, long-term care, social security, employment services, and
social housing is compatible with their economic character assessment.[33]

However, public services lack industrial or commercial character. The
European Court of Justice ruled[34] that the noncommercial or industrial
character of a service is a necessary criterion intended to clarify *needs in the
general interest.* The Court recognised that there might be needs of general
interest, which have an industrial and commercial character and that it is
also possible private undertakings can meet needs of general interest, which
do not have industrial and commercial character. Nevertheless, the test for
needs in the general interest which do not possess industrial or commercial
character is that the state or other public authorities choose themselves to
meet these needs or to have a decisive influence over their provision.[35] In
parallel, the Court indicated[36] that if an activity which meets general needs
is pursued in a competitive environment, there is a strong indication that it
possesses commercial characteristics.

The absence of commerciality from a public service or the absence of
competitive forces within the markets it is delivered represents a strong
indication of the *sui generis* market place public services are delivered or

organised.[37] The first implication of such nature is the nonapplicability of general competition law. In addition to the provisions of Art 106 TFEU, sector-specific regulation has removed the treatment of financing public services from the general provisions of competition law and placed it within the state aid regime.[38] Furthermore, the *sui generis* nature of public service markets provide the conceptual bridge to engage the public procurement regime as a guardian of the principles of accountability and transparency in the delivery of services of '*general interest having non industrial or commercial character*'.[39]

State aid *acquis* and jurisprudence have validated that services of general economic interest, which embrace the specific concept of public service obligations[40] project certain characteristics, such as the compensatory nature of their reimbursement and the need for market-oriented prerequisites for the selection of the entrusted undertaking for their delivery. These characteristics coincide conceptually with the repercussions of the *sui generis* market place of public services: their placement within state aid regulation and the need of the existence of public procurement as a competition benchmark.

This is reflected in the European Commission's vision to utilize state aid regulation as a platform for the provision of essential public services through public service contracts.[41] The *Liikenne*[42] ruling verifies the above approach, as the essential character of public service obligations for the provision of adequate services must be assessed by reference to elements that exceed the *stricto sensu* commerciality of the venture and instead must demonstrate a combination of factors which include the public interest, substitutability of services, price comparisons and the competitive environment in the relevant market. The leap from the commercial assessment of a venture which embraces public service obligations to the elaborate appraisal of substitutability assessment under a public service contract reveals that the competent authorities of Member States will choose the lowest cost service, if all available services can be offered under equivalent conditions. Such observation brings into play the compensatory characteristics of services of general economic interest and public service obligations.[43]

The compensatory element of public service contracts is clearly demonstrable in air transport services, where public service obligations[44] can only be conferred to operators by reference to a specific procedure, which links their compensation with a selection process based on a public tender.[45] The significance of this process is such as to allow Member States to determine the value for a public service by taking into account both the users' interests and costs incurred by the relevant operator. The criteria for calculating the compensation involve only factors relevant to the operating deficit incurred on a specific route[46], including a reasonable remuneration for capital employed.[47] Thus, a public service contract to perform public service obligations is awarded to the operator which requires the lowest financial compensation.[48] The compensation in the form of a public service contract awarded through the tendering process reveals a neutral commercial operation between the relevant Member State and the selected air carrier. The neutrality of such transaction is based on the reimbursement limited solely to losses sustained because of the operation of a specific route and does not bring about any special benefit for the air carrier.[49] Compensation of costs incurred by a carrier which has not been selected according to the tendering process or compensation which is not calculated on the basis of the lowest cost criterion would be assessed under the general state aid rules.[50] Compensation will be considered state aid if it diverts significant volumes of traffic or allows carriers to cross-subsidize routes on which they compete with other Community air carriers.[51]

1 The Public Sector Regulation in the EU Context

The public sector regulation within the context of the European integration process reveals the significance of public services and their delivery as instruments of policy from an economic, antitrust and industrial perspective. In the history of European integration and throughout the Treaties which bind together different legal, economic and political regimes, the public sector has emerged as the persistent nontariff barrier that creates the most prolific obstacles to the function of a genuinely competitive market across the Member States of the European Union. The regulation of public sector through an *integrationist* approach and the involvement of the private sector in delivering public services aims at the observance of fundamental principles of the EU, such as transparency and accountability and objectivity in order to establish the necessary conditions and the appropriate environment for competitive forces to rein the relevant markets.[1]

The establishment of the common market, as the core objective envisaged by the Treaty of Rome as the treaty creating the European Economic Communities and reinforced by the Treaty of Maastricht as the treaty creating the European Union and all the amending Treaties leading to the Treaty of Lisbon on the Functioning of the European Union, is to be achieved through the progressive approximation of the economic policies of the Member States. The concept of the common market embraces the legal and economic dynamics of the European integration process, with clear political ambitions from its accomplishment, and presents the characteristics of a genuine integral market.[2] Such a market is a place where unobstructed mobility of factors of production is guaranteed and where a regime of effective and undistorted competition regulates its operation. These characteristics reflect on the four fundamental freedoms of a customs union (free movement of goods, persons, capital and services) and, to the extent that the customs union tends to become an economic and a monetary one, on the adoption of a common economic policy and the introduction of a single currency. The adherence by Member States to the above-mentioned fundamental principles of European economic integration will result in the removal of any restrictions or obstacles to interstate trade. The level of success of economic integration in the European Union would determine the level of success of political integration among member states, which is the ultimate objective stipulated in the Treaties. It is maintained that a fifth freedom, the free movement of payments[3], reflects a complementary dimension of the free mobility of capital as a production factor and plays an extremely important role in the process of integration of public markets, and in particular in financing public projects either through indirect or direct investment.

The law and policy of the European Union have conceived the creation of a supranational legal system alongside existing domestic legal systems, where the supremacy of the former over national laws has been declared by the Court system of the European Union.[4] The economic integration of the European Union requires the assistance of a legal order that can facilitate its functioning and observe its evolutionary progress. The new legal order is a conglomerate of mutual rights and duties between the European Union and its subjects, both Member States and private persons, and provides for the procedures which are necessary for adjudicating infringements of the law of the European Union. The new legal order does confer rights and obligations not only to Member States but also to individuals, either physical or legal persons.[5]

Two strategic plans have facilitated the economic integration of the EU Member States.[6] These plans were enacted by European institutions and have been subsequently transposed into national laws and policies by Member States. The first plan included a series of actions and measures aiming at the abolition of all tariff and nontariff barriers to intracommunity trade. The second plan has focussed on the establishment of an effective, workable and undistorted regime of competition within the common market, in order to prevent potential abuse of market dominance and market segmentation, factors which could have serious economic implications in its functioning. The first plan, the abolition of all tariff and nontariff barriers to intracommunity trade, reveals a static effect which aimed at eliminating all administrative and legal obstacles to free trade and had as its focal point Member States and their national administrations. The second plan, the establishment of an effective, workable and undistorted regime of competition within the common market, has been implemented at industry level and has a rather ongoing and dynamic effect.

All tariff barriers were abolished by the end of the first transitional period[7], so customs duties, quotas and other forms of quantitative restrictions could no longer hinder the free flow of trade amongst member states. Nontariff barriers, however, have proved more difficult to eliminate, as they involve long-established market practices and patterns that could not change overnight. Nontariff protection represents a disguised form of discrimination and can occur through a wide spectrum of administrative or legislative frameworks relating to public monopolies, fiscal factors such as indirect taxation, state aid practices and subsidies, technical standards and public sector procurement. Nontariff barriers are by no means confined to the European integration process. The existence of nontariff barriers is a common phenomenon in world markets and their elimination is the main objective of regulatory instruments of international trade. It has been maintained that nontariff barriers could seriously distort the operation of the common market and its fundamental freedoms and derail the process of European integration.

The European Commission's White Paper for the Completion of the Internal Market[8] identified existing nontariff protection and provided the framework for specific legislative measures[9] in order to address the issue at national level. The enactment of a range of Directives was deemed necessary for the completion of the internal market by the end of 1992, and the time table was set out in the 1986 Single European Act, which in fact amended the 1957 Treaty of Rome by introducing *inter alia* the concept of the internal market. The internal market, in quantifiable terms, could be considered as something less than the common market but, perhaps the first and most important part of the latter, as it 'would provide the economic context for the regeneration of the European industry in both goods and services and it would give a permanent boost to the prosperity of the people of Europe and indeed the world as a whole'.[10]

The internal market, as an economic concept, could be described as an area without internal frontiers, where the free circulation of goods and the unhindered provision of services, in conjunction with the unobstructed mobility of factors of production, are ensured. The concept of the internal market is a reinforcement of the principle of the customs union as the foundation stone of the common market. The internal market embraces, obviously, less than the common market to the extent that the economic and monetary integration elements are missing. The 1986 Single European Act, as a legal instrument amending the Treaty of Rome, revealed strong public law and public policy characteristics, since the regulatory features of its provisions promote the importance of certain areas that had been previously overlooked. As a result, there has been both centralised and decentralised regulatory control by European Institutions and Member States over environmental policy, industrial policy, regional policy and the regulation of public sector procurement. The above areas represented the priority objectives in the process of completing the internal market. Public sector integration was specifically pointed out as a significant nontariff barrier and a detailed plan was devised to address the issue. The European Commission based its action on two notable studies.[11] Those studies provided empirical proof of the distorted market conditions in the public sector and highlighted the benefits of the regulation of public procurement.

The entire regulation of public sector in the European Union has been significantly influenced by the internal market project. The White Paper for the Completion of the Internal Market[12] and the 1986 Single European Act reflected upon the conceptual foundations of the regulation of public markets of the Member States. Firstly, the identification of public procurement as a significant nontariff barrier has offered ample evidence on the economic importance of its regulation.[13] Savings and price convergence appeared as the main arguments for liberalising the trade patterns of the demand (the public and utilities sectors) and supply (the industry) sides of the public procurement equation.[14] The regulation of public procurement exposes an economic and a legal approach to the integration of public markets in the European Union. Secondly, the economic approach to the regulation of public procurement has aimed at creating an integral public market across the European Union. Through the principles of transparency, nondiscrimination and objectivity in the award of public contracts, it has been envisaged that the public sector regulatory system will bring about competitiveness in the relevant product and geographical markets, will increase import penetration of products and services destined for the public sector, will enhance the tradability of public contracts across the common market, will result in significant price convergence and finally it will be the catalyst for the needed rationalisation and industrial restructuring of the European industrial base.[15]

The legal approach to the regulation of public sector in the EU, on the other hand, has reflected on a medium which facilitates the functions of the common market. In parallel with the economic arguments, legal arguments emerged supporting the regulation of public procurement as a necessary ingredient of the fundamental principles of the Treaties, such as the free movement of goods and services, the right of establishment and the prohibition of discrimination of nationality grounds.[16] The legal significance of the regulation of public procurement in the common market has been well documented through the Court's jurisprudence. The liberalisation of public procurement indicates the wish of European institutions to eliminate preferential and discriminatory purchasing patterns by the public sector and create seamless intracommunity trade patterns between the public and private sectors. Procurement by Member States and their contracting authorities is often susceptible to a rationale and a policy that tend to favour indigenous undertakings and *national champions*[17] at the expense of more efficient competitors (domestic or European Union–wide). As the relevant markets (product and geographical) have been sheltered from competition, distorted patterns emerge in the trade of goods, works and services destined for the public sector. These trade patterns represent a serious impediment in the functioning of the common market and inhibit the fulfilment of the principles enshrined in the European Treaties.[18]

Legislation, policy guidelines and jurisprudence have all played their role in determining the need for integrated public markets in the European Union[19], where sufficient levels of competition influence the most optimal patterns in resource allocation for supplying the public sector as well as the public utilities with goods, works and services. Procurement regulation was declared as a milestone of the vision of the European Union in becoming the most competitive economy in the world by 2010.[20] The significance of such a liberalised and integrated public sector as an essential component of the Single Market has been documented[21] by European institutions and prompted the European Commission to launch a Green Paper[22] to revise the public procurement Directives.[23]

THE REMIT OF PUBLIC SECTOR REGULATION IN THE EU

Whereas the regulatory weaponry for private markets is dominated by antitrust law and policy, public markets are *fora* where the structural and behavioural remedial tools of competition law emerge as rather inappropriate instruments of a regulatory framework.[24] The applicability of competition law to public markets is limited, mainly due to the fact that antitrust often clashes with monopolistic structures which exist in public markets. State participation in market activities is regularly assisted through exclusive exploitation of a product or a service within a geographical market. The market activities of a public entity are protected from competition by virtue of laws on trading and production or by virtue of delegated monopolies. Another reason for the limited applicability of antitrust law and policy in public markets is the fact that conceptual differences appear between the two categories of markets—private and public—in the eyes of antitrust, which could be attributed to their different nature. In private markets, antitrust law and policy seek to punish cartels and abusive dominance of undertakings. The focus of the remedial instruments is the supply side, which is conceived as the commanding part in the supply/demand equation due to the fact that it instigates and controls demand for a product. In private markets, the demand side of the equation (the consumers in general) is susceptible to exploitation and the market equilibria are prone to distortion as a result of collusive behaviour of undertakings or abusive monopoly position. On the other hand, the structure of public markets reveals a different picture. In the supply/demand equation, the dominant part appears to be the demand side (the state and its organs as purchasers), which initialises demand through purchasing, whereas the supply side (the industry) fights for access to the relevant markets. Although this is normally the case, one should not exclude the possibility of market oligopolisation and the potential manipulation of the demand side.[25] These advanced market structures can occur more often in the future, as a result of well-established trends of industrial concentration.

Another argument which has relevance to the different regulatory approach of public and private markets reflects on the methods of possible market segmentation and abuse. It is maintained that the segmentation of private markets appears different than the partitioning of public ones. In private markets, market segmentation occurs as a result of cartels and collusive behaviour, which would lead to abuse of dominance, with a view to driving competitors out of the relevant market, increasing market shares and ultimately increasing profits. Private markets can be segmented both geographically and by reference to product or service, whereas public ones can only be geographically segmented. This assumption leads to the argument that the partition of the public markets would be probably the result of concerted practices attributed to the demand side. As such concerted practices focus on the origin of a product or a service or the nationality of a contractor, and then the only way to effectively partition the relevant market would be by reference to its geographical remit. In contrast, as far as private markets are concerned, the segmentation of the relevant market (either product or geographical) can only be attributed to the supply side. The argument goes further to reveal the fact that the balance of powers between the supply and the demand side are reversed in public markets. In the latter, it is the demand side that has the dominant role in the equation by dictating terms and conditions in purchases, initiation of transactions, as well as by influencing production trends.

In public markets, concerted practices of the demand side (e.g. excluding foreign competition, application of buy-national policies, and application of national standards policies) represent geographical market segmentation, as they result in the division of the European public markets into different national public markets. It could also be maintained that public markets are subject to protection—rather than restriction—from competition, to the extent that the latter are quasi-monopolistic and monopsonistic in their structure. Indeed, the state and its organs, as contractors possess a monopoly position in the sense that no one competes against them in their market activities.[26] Even in cases of privatisation, the monopoly position is shifted from the public to private hands. The situation is different in cases of an open privatised regime pursuing an operation of public interest. In that case, it would be more appropriate to refer to oligopolistic competition in the relevant market. Also in privatised regimes, interchangeability of supply is very limited, to an extent that monopoly position characteristics survive the transfer of ownership from public to private hands. The state and its organs also possess a monopsony position, as firms engaged in transactions with them have no alternatives to pursue business. Access barriers to geographical public markets are erected by states as a result of exercising their discretion to conclude contracts with national undertakings. This type of activity constitutes the partition of public markets in the European Union, whereas undertakings operating in private markets must enter into a restrictive agreement between themselves in order to split up the relevant markets. Due to their different integral nature, private and public markets require different control. The control in both cases has a strong public law character, but while antitrust regulates private markets, it appears rather inappropriate for public ones. Antitrust law and policy is a set of rules of a negative nature; undertakings must *restrain* their activities to an acceptable range predetermined in due course by the competent authorities. On the other hand, public markets require a set of rules that have positive character. It should be recalled that the integration of public markets is based on the abolition of barriers and obstacles to national markets; it then follows that the type of competition envisaged for their regulation is mainly *market access competition*. This primarily indicates that price competition is expected to emerge in European public markets, only after their integration.[27]

It appears, however, that in both private and public markets, two elements have relevance when attempting their regulation. The first element is the *price differentiation* of similar products; the second element is *access* to the relevant markets.[28] As the European integration is an economic process which aims at dismantling barriers to trade and approximating national economies, the need to create acceptable levels of competition in both public and private markets becomes more demanding. In fact, a regime of genuine competition in public markets would benefit the public interest as it will lower the price of goods and services for the public, as well as achieve substantial savings for the public purse.

The evolution of public procurement regulation in the European Union points towards a strategy for eliminating discriminatory public procurement amongst member states which have posed significant obstacles to the fundamental principles of free movement of goods, the right of establishment and the freedom to provide services. That strategy has been based on two principal assumptions: the first assumption acknowledged the fact that in order to eliminate preferential and discriminatory purchasing practices in European public markets, a great deal of *transparency* and *openness* was needed; the second assumption rested on the premise that the only way to regulate public procurement in the Member States in an effective manner was through the process of *harmonisation* of existing laws and administrative practices which had been in operation, and not through a *uniform* regulatory pattern which would replace all existing laws and administrative practices throughout the Community. The latter assumption indirectly recognised the need for a decentralised system of regulation for public procurement in the European Union.[29]

Since harmonisation was adopted as the most appropriate method of regulation of public procurement in the common market, and the decentralised character of the regime was reinforced through legislation, the onus then was shifted to the national administrations of the Member States, which had to implement the Community principles into domestic law and give a certain degree of clarity and legitimate expectation to interested parties. Occasionally, the European Commission is criticised for not reserving for itself or other Community institutions central powers, other than those already available and in its disposal as the guardian of the Treaty, in relation to the enforcement of and compliance with public procurement rules. The critics often refer to the applicability of competition law and policy of the European Union and the regime which legally implements it through specific Regulations.[30] However, although in principle competition law of the European Union may apply to the award of public contracts[31], the *effectiveness* and *efficiency* of a regulatory regime in the public markets through basic antitrust remedies remains a challenge for the law and policy maker.[32] A rigid regime in its application through a uniform way across the common market would not take into account national particularities in public procurement and a highest common denominator would probably eliminate any elements of *flexibility* in the system. Public procurement, as the *nexus* of transactions in the supply chain of the public sector, does not differ in principle with the management of purchasing practices in the private sector, which remains unregulated. Public procurement has the tendency to create anticompetitive frictions in the market place. The paradox is that although the pursuit of public interest underpins public procurement as an instrument of public sector regulation, social welfare and alocative efficiencies are not always promoted by such a system. The primary reason has been the structure and dynamics of the public markets and the limited ability of antitrust to regulate them.[33]

THE ECONOMIC POLICY DIMENSION IN PUBLIC SECTOR REGULATION

Viewing public procurement from the prism of an economic exercise, its regulation displays strong neoclassical influences.[34] Such influences embrace the merit of efficiency in the relevant market and the presence of competition, mainly price competition, which would create optimal conditions for welfare gains. The connection between public procurement regulation and the neoclassical approach to economic integration in the common market is reflected upon the criterion for awarding public contracts based on the lowest offer. This feature of the public procurement legal framework focusses on price competition being inserted into the relevant markets, and assisted by the transparency requirement to advertise public contracts above certain thresholds[35] it would result in production and distribution efficiencies and drive the market towards an optimal allocation of resources.[36]

The lowest offer as an award criterion of public contracts is a quantitative method of achieving market equilibrium between the demand and supply sides. The supply side competes in costs terms to deliver standardised (at least in theory) works, services and goods to the public sector. Price competition is bound to result in innovation in the relevant industries, where through investment and technological improvements, firms could reduce production and/or distribution costs. The lowest-offer criterion could be seen as the necessary stimulus in the relevant market participants in order to improve their competitive advantages.

The lowest-offer award criterion reflects on, and presupposes, low barriers to entry in a market and provides for a type of predictable accessibility for product or geographical markets. This is a desirable characteristic in a system such as public procurement regulation which is charged with integrating national markets and creating a common market for public contracts which is homogenous and transparent. In addition, the low barriers to enter a market, together with the competitive and transparent price benchmarking for awarding public contracts through the lowest-offer criterion, would inevitably attract new undertakings in public procurement markets. This can be seen as an increase of the supply-side pool, a fact which would provide the comfort and the confidence to the demand side (the public sector) in relation to the competitive structure of an industry. Nevertheless, the increased number of participants in public tenders could have adverse effects. Assuming that the financial and technical capacity of firms is not an issue[37], the demand side (the public sector) will have to bear the cost of tendering and in particular the costs relating to the evaluation of offers. The demand side often omits risk assessment tests during the evaluation process. The Directives remain vague as to the methods for assessing financial risk, leaving a great deal of discretion in the hands of contracting authorities. Evidence of financial and economic standing may be provided by means of references including: i) appropriate statements from bankers; ii) the presentation of the firm's balance sheets or extracts from the balance sheets where these are published under company law provisions; and iii) a statement of the firm's annual turnover and the turnover on construction works for the three previous financial years. The more participants enter the market for the award of public contracts, the bigger the costs attributed to the tendering process would have to be borne by the public sector.

However, competitiveness in an industry is not reflected solely by reference to low production costs.[38] Efficiencies which might result through production or distribution innovations are bound to have a short-term effect on the market for two reasons: if the market is bound to clear with reference to the lowest price, there would be a point where the quality of deliverables is compromised (assuming a product or service remains standardised). Secondly, the viability of industries which tend to compete primarily on cost basis is questionable. Corporate mortality will increase and the market could revert to oligopolistic structures.

The welfare gains emanating from a neoclassical approach of public procurement regulation encapsulate the actual and potential savings the public sector (and consumers of public services at large) would enjoy through a system that forces the supply side to compete on costs and price. These gains, however, must be counterbalanced with the costs of tendering (administrative and evaluative costs borne by the public sector), the costs of competition (costs related to the preparation and submission of tender offers borne by the private sector) and litigation costs (costs relevant to prospective litigation borne by both aggrieved tenderers and the public sector). If the cumulative costs exceed any savings attributed to lowest-offer criterion, the welfare gains are negative.

A neoclassical perspective of public procurement regulation reveals the zest of policy makers to establish conditions which calibrate market clearance on price grounds. Price competitiveness in public procurement raises a number of issues with antitrust law and policy. If the maximisation of savings is the only (or the primary) achievable objective for the demand side in the public procurement process, the transparent/competitive pattern cannot provide any safeguards in relation to underpriced (and anticompetitive) offers.

The price-competitive tendering reflects on the dimension of public procurement regulation as an economic exercise. On the one hand, when the supply side responds to the perpetually competitive purchasing patterns by lowering prices, the public sector could face a dilemma: *What would be the lowest offer it can accept?* The public sector faces a considerable challenge in evaluating and assessing low offers other than 'abnormally low' ones.[39] The European rules provide for an automatic disqualification of an 'obviously abnormally low offer'. The term has not been interpreted in detail by the judiciary at European and domestic levels and serves rather as a 'lower bottom limit'. The contracting authorities are under duty to seek from the tenderer an explanation for the price submitted or to inform him that his tender appears to be abnormally low and to allow a reasonable time within which to submit further details, before making any decision as to the award of the contract. The Court has ruled[40] that the contracting authorities must give an opportunity to tenderers to furnish explanations regarding the genuine nature of their tenders, when those tenders appear to be abnormally low. Unfortunately, the Court did not proceed to an analysis of the wording 'obviously'. It rather seems that the term 'obviously' indicates the existence of precise and concrete evidence as to the abnormality of the low tender. The wording 'abnormally' implies a quantitative criterion left to the discretion of the contracting authority. However, if the tender is just 'abnormally' low, it could be argued that it is within the discretion of the contracting authority to investigate the genuine offer of a tender. *Impresa Lombardini*[41], followed the precedence established by *Transporoute* and maintained the unlawfulness of mathematical criteria used as an exclusion of a tender which appears abnormally low. Nevertheless, it held that such criteria may be lawful if used for determining the abnormality of a low tender, provided an *inter partes* procedure between the contracting authority and the tenderer that submitted the alleged abnormal low offer offers the opportunity to clarify the genuine nature of that offer. Contracting authorities must take into account all reasonable explanations furnished and avoid limiting the grounds on which justification of the genuine nature of a tender should be made. Both the wording and the aim of the public procurement rules direct contracting authorities to seek explanation and reject unrealistic offers. In *ARGE*[42], the rejection of a tender based on the abnormally low pricing attached to it got a different twist in its interpretation. Although the Court ruled that directly or indirectly subsidised tenders by the state or other contracting authorities or even by the contracting authority itself can be legitimately part of the evaluation process, it did not elaborate on the possibility of rejection of an offer, which is appreciably lower than those of unsubsidised tenderers by reference to the 'of abnormally low' disqualification ground. In *ARGE* the Court adopted a literal interpretation of the Directives and concluded that if the legislature wanted to preclude subsidized entities from participating in tendering procedures for public contracts, it should have said so explicitly in the relevant Directives.[43]

It is difficult to identify dumping or predatory pricing disguised behind a low offer for a public contract. On the other hand, even if there is an indication of anticompetitive price fixing, the European public procurement rules do not provide for any type of procedure to address the problem. The antitrust rules take over and the suspension of the award procedures (or even the suspension of the contract itself) would be subject to a thorough and exhaustive investigation by the competent antitrust authorities.[44]

Evidence of the neoclassical approach in public procurement regulation can be traced in the Guidelines[45] issued by the European Commission. The Commission adopted a strict interpretation of the rules and focussed Member States on an economic approach in the application of the public procurement Directives. The Commission has championed the neoclassical approach for two reasons: first, to bring an acceptable level of compliance of Member States with the public procurement regime and secondly, to follow the assumptions made through the internal market process that procurement represents a significant nontariff barrier and its regulation can result in substantial savings for the public sector.

It is interesting to follow the Commission's approach[46] in litigation before the European Court of Justice, where as an applicant in compliance procedures, or as an intervening party in reference procedures, it consistently regarded public procurement regulation as an economic exercise. The backbone of such approach has been the price approach to the award of public contracts, predominately through the lowest-offer award criterion, but also through the most economically advantageous offer criterion, where factors other than price can play a role in the award process. Even in the latter category, where some degree of flexibility is envisaged by the legal regime, the Commission has been sceptical of any attempts to apply so-called qualitative factors in the award process. Along these lines, the European Court of Justice pursued a neoclassical approach of public procurement regulation through its rulings relating to i) compliance procedures against Member States for not observing the publicity and mandatory advertisement requirements, ii) procedures concerning standardisation and technical specifications[47] and iii) procedures relating to the notion of abnormally low offers.[48]

THE ANTITRUST AND THE PUBLIC POLICY DIMENSION IN PUBLIC SECTOR REGULATION

The regulation of private markets is based upon antitrust law and policy, where the influence of the neoclassical economic approach has been evident.[49] Public markets are *fora* where the structural and behavioural remedial tools of competition law also apply. However, they focus on the supply side (the industry) which *ipso facto* is subject to the relevant rules relating to cartels and abusive dominance.

There is a conceptual difference relating to the application of antitrust in public markets. The demand side (the public sector, the state and its organs) can hardly be embraced by its remit, except in the case of state aid and illegal subsidies. In private markets, antitrust law and policy seek to punish cartels and the abusive dominance of undertakings. The focus of the remedial instruments of antitrust is the supply side, which is conceived as the commanding part in the supply/demand equation due to the fact that it instigates and often controls demand for a product. In private markets, the demand side of the equation (the consumers at large) is susceptible to exploitation and the market equilibria are prone to distortion as a result of collusive behaviour of undertakings or abusive monopoly position. On the other hand, the structure of public markets reflects the dominance of the state and its organs in the supply/demand equation, whereby demand is initiated by the purchasing intentions of the public sector. The supply side of the equation, which is reflected by the industry and the private sector, seeks accessing the relevant markets through procurement processes and tendering procedures to meet the demand initiated by the public sector.

In public markets, market segmentation occurs as a result of concerted practices attributed to the demand side. Since such concerted practices of Member States and their contracting authorities (e.g. excluding foreign competition, application of buy-national policies, and application of national standards policies) focus on the origin of a product or a service or the nationality of a contractor, market segmentation in public markets tends to possess geographical characteristics and results in the division of the European public market into different national public markets. The public procurement regime creates a quasi-competitive environment that facilitates collusion despite transparency and objectivity featuring as its main principles.[50]

The regulation of public markets requires more than the control of the supply side through antitrust. The primary objective is *market access* and the abolition of barriers and obstacles to trade. Therefore, the regulation aims at the demand side, which effectively controls access and can segment the relevant market. Whereas price competition is the main characteristic of antitrust[51], public procurement regulation pursues firstly market access. This perspective reflects on the *sui generis* nature of public markets and has provided ground for developing a regulatory system which is strongly influenced by neoclassical economics, whilst at the same time integrating the relevant market. Such a system has also strong public law characteristics, to the extent that it has been branded as public competition law (*droit public de la concurrence*).[52]

The vehicle of harmonisation has been entrusted to carry the progress of public procurement regulation. Directives, as legal instruments, have been utilised to provide the framework of the *acquis communautaire,* but at the same time afford the necessary discretion to the Member States as to the forms and methods of their implementation. This is where the first deviation of antitrust from the traditional economic approach of public procurement occurs. Antitrust law and policy is enacted through the principle of uniformity across the common market, utilising directly applicable regulations. By allowing for discretion to the Member States, an element of public policy is inserted in the equation, which often has decentralised features. Traditionally, discretion afforded by Directives takes into account national particularities and sensitivities as well as the readiness of domestic administrations to implement *acquis* within a certain deadline. In addition, individuals, who are also subjects of the rights and duties envisaged by the Directives, do not have access to justices, unless provisions of Directives produce direct effect.

However, the public policy dimension of public procurement regulation is not exhausted in the nature of the legal instruments of the regime. The genuine connection of an ordo-liberal perspective[53] with public procurement regulation is reflected in the award criterion relating to the most economically advantageous offer. The public sector can award contracts by reference to 'qualitative' criteria, in conjunction with price, and thus can legitimately deviate from the strict price competition environment set by the lowest-offer criterion.[54] There are three themes emanating from such an approach: one reflects on public procurement as a complimentary tool of the European Integration process; the second regards public procurement as an instrument of contract compliance; last, the ordo-liberal perspective can reveal a rule of reason in public procurement, where the integration of public markets in the European Union serves as a conveyer belt of common policies, such as environmental policy, consumer policy, social policy, industrial policy and takes into account a flexible and wider view of national and community priorities, and a type of 'European public policy'.[55]

Policy makers at both European and national levels have not overlooked the effects of public procurement on the formulation of the industrial policy of the European Union. The objective of the public procurement regulation has to a large extent acquired an industrial policy background, which mainly focuses on the achievement of savings for the public sector and the much desired restructuring and adjustment of the European industrial base. However, public spending in the form of procurement is indissolubly linked with adjacent policies and agendas in all member states. The most important policy associated with public purchasing is social policy. Such an argument finds justification in two reasons: the first relates to the optimal utilisation of human resources in industries supplying the public sector; the second reason acquires a strategic dimension, in the sense that public purchasing serves aims and objectives stipulated in the European Treaties, such as social cohesion, combating of long-term unemployment, and finally the achievement of acceptable standards of living. The underlying objectives of the European

regime on public procurement relating to enhanced competition and unobstructed market access in the public sector at first sight appear incompatible
with the social dimension of European integration, particularly in an era
where recession and economic stagnation have revealed the combating of
unemployment as a main theme of European governance.

The award of public contracts can be based on two criteria: i) the lowest
price or ii) the most economically advantageous offer. Contracting authorities have absolute discretion in adopting the award criterion under which
they wish to award their public contracts. The lowest-price award criterion
is mostly used when the procurement process is relatively straightforward.
On the other hand, the most economically advantageous offer award criterion is suited for more complex procurement schemes.

The most economically advantageous offer as an award criterion represents a flexible framework for contacting authorities wishing to insert a
qualitative parameter in the award process of a public contract. Needless to
say, price, as a quantitative parameter plays an important role in the evaluation stage of tenders, as the meaning of 'economically advantageous' could
well embrace financial considerations in the long run. So, if the qualitative
criteria of a particular bid compensate for its more expensive price, potential
savings in the long run could not be precluded. It is not clear whether the
choice of the two above-mentioned award criteria has been intentional with
a view to providing contracting authorities a margin of discretion to take
into account social policy objectives when awarding their public contracts,
or if it merely reflects an element of flexibility which is considered necessary
in modern purchasing transactions. If the most economically advantageous
offer represents elements relating to quality of public purchasing other than
price, an argument arises here supporting the fact that the enhancement
of the socioeconomic fabric is a 'qualitative' element which can fall into
the framework of the above criterion. This argument would take away the
assumption that the award of public contracts is a pure *economic exercise*.
On the other hand, if one is to insist that public procurement should reflect
only *economic choices*, the social policy considerations that may arise from
the award of public contracts would certainly have an economic dimension
attached to them, often in public service activities which are parallel to public procurement. To what extent contracting authorities should contemplate
such elements remains unclear.

The regulation of public procurement and the integration of the public
markets of the Member States do not operate in a vacuum. Irrespective of
the often-publicised nature of public procurement as the most significant
nontariff barrier for the functioning of the common market and the clini-
cal presentation of the arguments in favour of an integrated public market
across the European Union[56], public purchasing is indissolubly linked with
national policies and priorities.[57] In the history of European economic integration, public procurement has been an important part of the Member
States' industrial policies. It has been utilised as a policy tool[58] in order to

support indigenous suppliers and contractors and protect national industries and the related workforce.

The regulation of the public sector markets can also accommodate *contract compliance* through its award criteria and in particular the most economically advantageous offer. The most economically advantageous offer as an award criterion has provided the Court for the opportunity to balance the economic considerations of public procurement with policy choices. Although in numerous instances the Court has maintained the importance of the economic approach[59] to the regulation of public sector contracts, it has also recognised the relative discretion of contracting authorities to utilise noneconomic considerations as part of the award criteria.

The term *contract compliance*[60] could be best defined as the range of secondary policies relevant to public procurement, which aim at combating discrimination on grounds of sex, race, religion or disability.[61] When utilised in public contracts, contract compliance is a system whereby, unless the supply side (the industry) complies with certain conditions relating to social policy measures, contracting authorities can lawfully exclude tenderers from selection, qualification and award procedures. The potential of public purchasing as a tool capable of promoting social policies has been met with considerable scepticism. Policies relevant to affirmative action or positive discrimination have caused a great deal of controversy, as they practically accomplish very little in rectifying labour market equilibria. In addition to the practicality and effectiveness of such policies, serious reservations have been expressed with regard to their constitutionality,[62] since they could limit, actually and potentially, the principles of economic freedom and freedom of transactions.[63]

Contract compliance is familiar to most European Member States, although the enactment of public procurement Directives has changed the situation dramatically.[64] The position of European Institutions on contract compliance has been addressed before the European Court of Justice.[65] The Court maintained that contract compliance with reference to domestic or local employment cannot be used as a selection criterion in tendering procedures for the award of public contracts. The selection of tenderers is a process which is based on an exhaustive list of technical and financial requirements expressly stipulated in the relevant Directives and the insertion of contract compliance as a selection and qualification requirement would be considered *ultra vires*. The Court ruled that social policy considerations can only be part of award criteria in public procurement, and especially in cases where the most economically advantageous offer is selected, provided that they do not run contrary to the basic principles of the Treaty and that have been mentioned in the tender notice.

The Court's approach has also opened an interesting debate on the integral dimensions of contract compliance and the differentiation between the *positive* and *negative* approaches. The concept of positive approach within contract compliance encompasses all measures and policies imposed by contracting authorities on tenderers as suitability criteria for their selection in public procurement contracts. Such positive action measures and policies intend to complement the actual objectives of public procurement which are confined in economic and financial parameters and are based on a transparent and predictable legal background. Although the complementarity of contract compliance with the actual aims and objectives of the public procurement regime was acknowledged, the Court (and the European Commission) were reluctant in accepting such an overflexible interpretation of the Directives and based on the literal interpretation of the relevant provisions disallowed positive actions of a social policy dimension as part of the selection criteria for tendering procedures in public procurement.

However, contract compliance can incorporate not only unemployment considerations, but also promote equality of opportunities and eliminate sex or race discrimination in the relevant market.[66] Indeed, the Directives on public procurement stipulate that the contracting authority may require tenderers to observe national provisions of employment legislation when they submit their offers. The ability to observe and conform to national employment laws in a Member State may constitute a ground of disqualification and exclusion of the defaulting firm from public procurement contracts.[67] In fact, under such interpretation, contract compliance may be a factor of selection criteria specified in the Directives, as it contains a *negative approach* to legislation and measures relating to social policy.

There are arguments in favour and against incorporating social policy considerations in public procurement.[68] The most important argument in favour focuses on the ability of public procurement to promote parts of the Member States' social policy, with particular reference to long-term unemployment, equal distribution of income, social exclusion and the protection of minorities. Under such a positively oriented approach, public purchasing could be regarded as an instrument of policy in the hands of national administrations with a view to rectifying social equilibria. Contract compliance in public procurement could also cancel the stipulated aims and objectives of the liberalisation of the public sector. The regulation of public markets focusses on economic considerations and competition. Adherence to social policy factors could derail the whole process, as the public sector will pay more for its procurement by extra or hidden cost for the implementation of contract compliance in purchasing policies.[69]

The nomination of regional or national firms in the award process of public contracts, as well as the promotion of socioeconomic considerations relevant to policies of Member States under such premises could, legitimately, elevate preferential procurement as an instrument of industrial policy. This might shift the debate from the potential violation of internal market provisions, such as state aid and the free movement principles towards the overall compatibility of the regime with national or common market-wide industrial policies, thus positioning preferential public procurement in the remit of antitrust.[70]

Secondly, there is a fundamental change in perceptions about the role and responsibilities expected from governments in delivering public services.[71]

The public sector not only initiates and facilitates the delivery of public services but also can actively be involved in the actual delivery process. Such changes, in practical terms viewed through the evolution of public-private partnerships[72], are translated into a new contractual interface between public and private sectors[73], which in turn encapsulates an era of *contractualised governance.*[74]

THE STATE AID DIMENSION IN PUBLIC SECTOR REGULATION

The nature of public procurement as the most significant nontariff barrier for the functioning of the common market[75] and the presentation of the arguments in favour of an integrated public market across the European Union[76] have contributed to the debate that public purchasing is indissolubly linked with national policies and priorities.[77] In the history of European economic integration, public procurement has been an important part of the Member States' industrial policies. It has been utilised as a policy tool in order to support indigenous suppliers and contractors and preserve national industries and the related workforce. The legislation on public procurement in the early days clearly allowed for 'preference schemes' in less-favoured regions of the common market which were experiencing industrial decline. Such schemes required the application of award criteria based on considerations other than the lowest price or the most economically advantageous offer, subject to their compatibility with European law inasmuch as they did not run contrary to the principle of free movement of goods and to competition law considerations with respect to state aid. Since the completion of the internal market in 1992 they have been abolished, as they have been deemed capable in contravening directly the basic principle of nondiscrimination on grounds of nationality.

There has been a great deal of controversy over the issue of the compatibility of preferential procurement with European law. The justification of preference schemes as a ground to promote regional development policies has revealed the interaction of public procurement with state aid.[78] Preferential procurement reflects protectionism, and as such is regarded as nontariff barrier. However, protectionist public procurement, when strategically exercised, has resulted in the evolution of vital industries for the relevant state.[79] Preferential public procurement can be seen through a multidimensional prism. First, it appears in the form of an exercise which aims at preserving some domestic sectors or industries at the expense of the principles of the European integration process. Impact assessment studies undertaken by the European Commission showed that the operation of preference schemes had a minimal effect on the economies of the regions where they had been applied, both in terms of the volume of procurement contracts, as well as in terms of real economic growth attributed to the operation of such schemes.[80] Thus, in such format, preferential public procurement perpetuates the suboptimal allocation of resources and represents a welfare loss for the economy of the relevant state. On the other hand, preferential purchasing in the format of strategic investment to the sustainability of selected industries might represent a viable instrument of industrial policy, to the extent that the infant industry, when specialised and internationalised, would be in a position to counterbalance any welfare losses during its protected period. In the above format, preferential public procurement, as an integral part of industrial policy, could possibly result in welfare gains.[81]

Preference schemes have been indissolubly linked with regional development policies, but their interpretation by the European Court of Justice has always been restrictive.[82] Although the utilisation of public procurement as a tool of regional development policy may breach directly or indirectly primary Treaty provisions on free movement of goods, the right of establishment and the freedom to provide services, it is far from clear whether the European Commission or the Court could accept the legitimate use of public procurement as a means of state aid. Prior notification to the European Commission of the measures or policies intended to be used as state aid apparently does not legitimise such measures and absolve them from adherence to the judicially well-established framework of the four freedoms. The parallel applicability of rules relating to state aid and the free movement of goods, in the sense that national measures conceived as state aid must not violate the principle of free movement of goods, renders the thrust of regional policies through state aid practically ineffective. It appears that the Court has experimented with the question of the compatibility between state aid and free movement of goods in a number of cases where, initially, it was held that the two regimes are mutually exclusive, to the extent that the principle of free movement of goods could not apply to measures relating to state aid.[83] The acid test for such mutual exclusivity was the prior notification of such measures to the European Commission. However, the Court departed from such a position, when it applied free movement of goods provisions to a number of cases concerning state aid, which had not been notified to the Commission.[84] Surprisingly, the Court also brought notified state aid measures under the remit of the provision of free movement of goods and reconsidered the whole framework of the mutual exclusivity of states aid and free movement of goods.[85]

State aid jurisprudence has revealed the catalytic position of public procurement in the process of determining whether subsidies or state financing of public services represent state aid. The significance of the subject is epitomised in the attempts of the European Council[86] to provide for a policy framework of greater predictability and increased legal certainty in the application of the state aid rules to the funding of services of general interest. Along the above lines, public procurement rules have served as a yardstick to determine the nature of an undertaking in its contractual interface when delivering public services. The funding of services of general interest by the state may materialise through different formats, such as the payment of remuneration for services under a public contract, the payment of annual subsidies, preferential fiscal treatment or lower social contributions. The most common format is the existence of a contractual relation between the state and the undertaking charged to deliver public services. The above relation should, under normal circumstances pass through the remit of public procurement framework, not only as an indication of market competitiveness but mainly as a demonstration of the nature of the deliverable services as services of 'general interest having non industrial or commercial character'.

The compensatory nature of the reimbursement for the provision of public services reflects on two main elements: the deficit-based calculation method for their value and, as a result, the noncommercial nature of the markets within which such services are delivered. It is assumed that public services regarding public or universal obligations or services of general economic interest have minimal commercial value. Market forces cannot provide for the needs of the public, as a number of factors deter entry into the relevant market (profitability, set-up costs, risk, volume and levels of demand, intramode competition). Thus the markets within which public service obligations are dispersed are *sui generis*. The most important repercussion of such finding is the true relevance of tools used to compare the value of a relevant service such as the private investor principle. The lack of a reliable comparator, the noncommercial nature of public service obligations and the calculation method for their reimbursement might pose problems in determining an objective and uniformly acceptable value for their delivery. It appears that there are difficult elements surrounding demand structure, infrastructure investment and costs, scale economies and revenue levels.

On the other hand, the market-oriented character of their award, as depicted in the tendering process intends to establish a transparent and objective framework for their delivery. Interestingly, the competitive process for award of public service obligations to the lowest offer reflecting the costs and revenue (viz. the deficit) generated by the service runs in parallel with the application of public procurement rules for the delivery of services of noncommercial nature. The *homogenous* treatment of the relation between Member States and undertakings (public or private) entrusted with the delivery of public services reveal a 'commissioning' role in the part of Member States. Such commissioning role has the intention to remove the regulation of the relevant services from the remit of the general competition rules and place it within the framework of the state aid regime.[87]

There are three approaches under which the European judiciary and the Commission have examined the financing of public services: *the state aid approach, the compensation approach* and *the quid pro quo approach*. The above approaches reflect not only conceptual and procedural differences in the application of state aid control measures within the common market, but also raise imperative and multifaceted questions relevant to the state funding of services of general interest.

The state aid approach[88] examines state funding granted to an undertaking for the performance of obligations of general interest. It thus, regards the relevant funding as state aid within the meaning of Article 107(1) TFEU[89] which may however be justified under Article 106(2) TFEU[90], provided that the conditions of that derogation are fulfilled and, in particular, if the funding complies with the principle of proportionality. The state aid approach provides for the most clear and legally certain procedural and conceptual framework to regulate state aid, since it positions the European Commission in the centre of that framework.

The compensation approach[91] reflects upon a 'compensation' being intended to cover an appropriate remuneration for the services provided or the costs of providing those services. Under that approach state funding of services of general interest amounts to state aid within the meaning of Article 107(1) TFEU, only if and to the extent that the economic advantage which it provides exceeds such an appropriate remuneration or such additional costs. European jurisprudence considers that state aid exists only if, and to the extent that, the remuneration paid, when the state and its organs procure goods or services, exceeds the market price.

The *quid pro quo* approach distinguishes between two categories of state funding; in cases where there is a direct and manifest link between the state financing and clearly defined public service obligations, any sums paid by the state would not constitute state aid within the meaning of the Treaty. On the other hand, where there is no such link or the public service obligations were not clearly defined, the sums paid by the public authorities would constitute state aid.[92]

A hybrid assessment method between the compensation and the *quid pro quo* approaches has been introduced by the Court in *Altmark*[93], where subsidies are regarded as compensation for the services provided by the recipient undertakings in order to discharge public service obligations and do not amount to state aid. Nevertheless for the purpose of applying that criterion, four conditions must be satisfied: first, the recipient undertaking is actually required to discharge public service obligations and those obligations have been clearly defined; second, the parameters on the basis of which the compensation is calculated have been established beforehand in an objective and transparent manner; third, the compensation does not exceed what is necessary to cover all or part of the costs incurred in discharging the public service obligations, taking into account the relevant receipts and a reasonable profit for discharging those obligations; fourth, where the undertaking which is to discharge public service obligations is not chosen in a public procurement procedure, the level of compensation needed has been determined on the basis of an analysis of the costs which a typical undertaking, well run and adequately provided with appropriate means so as to be able to meet the necessary public service requirements, would have incurred in discharging those obligations, taking into account the relevant receipts and a reasonable profit for discharging the obligations.

The choice between the state aid approach and the compensation approach does not only reflect upon a theoretical debate; it mainly reveals significant practical ramifications in the application of state aid control within the common market. Whilst it is generally accepted that the pertinent issue of substance is whether the state funding exceeds what is necessary to provide for an appropriate remuneration or to offset the extra costs caused by the general interest obligations, the two approaches have very different procedural implications. Under the compensation approach, state funding which does not constitute state aid escapes the clutches of EU state aid rules and need not be notified to the Commission. More important, national courts have jurisdiction to pronounce on the nature of the funding as state aid without the need to wait for an assessment by the Commission of its compatibility with *acquis*. Under the state aid approach the same measure would constitute state aid, which must be notified in advance to the Commission. Moreover, the derogation in Article 106(2) EC is subject to the same procedural regime as the derogations in Article 107(2) and (3) EC, which means that new aid cannot be implemented until the Commission has declared it compatible with Article 106(2) EC. Measures which infringe that stand-still obligation constitute illegal aid. Another procedural implication from the compensation approach is that national courts must offer to individuals the certain prospect that all the appropriate conclusions will be drawn from the infringement of the last sentence of Article 108(3) EC, as regards the validity of the measures giving effect to the aid, the recovery of financial support granted in disregard of that provision and possible interim measures.

The *quid pro quo* approach[94] positions at the centre of the analysis of state funding of services of general interest a distinction between two different categories; i) the nature of the link between the financing granted and the general interest duties imposed and ii) the degree of clarity in defining those duties. The first category would comprise cases where the financing measures are clearly intended as a *quid pro quo* for clearly defined general interest obligations, or in other words where the link between, on the one hand, the state financing granted and, on the other hand, clearly defined general interest obligations imposed is direct and manifest. The clearest example of such a direct and manifest link between state financing and clearly defined obligations are public service contracts awarded in accordance with public procurement rules. The contract in question should define the obligations of the undertakings entrusted with the services of general interest and the remuneration which they will receive in return. Cases falling into that category should be analysed according to the compensation approach. The second category consists of cases where it is not clear from the outset that the state funding is intended as a *quid pro quo* for clearly defined general interest obligations. In those cases the link between state funding and the general interest obligations imposed is either not direct or not manifest or the general interest obligations are not clearly defined.[95]

The *quid pro quo* approach appears at first instance consistent with the general case law on the interpretation of Article 107(1) EC. Also it gives appropriate weight to the importance of services of general interest, within the remit of Article 16 TFEU and of Article 36 of the EU Charter of Fundamental Rights. On the other hand, the *quid pro quo* approach presents a major shortcoming: it introduces elements[96] of the nature of public financing into the process of determining the legality of state aid. According to state aid jurisprudence, only the effects of the measure are to be taken into consideration[97], and as a result of the application of the *quid pro quo* approach legal certainty could be undermined.

The application of the state aid approach creates a *lex and policy lacuna* in the treatment of funding of services of general economic interest and normal services. In fact, it presupposes that the services of general economic interest emerge in a different market, where the state and its emanations act in a public function. Such markets are not susceptible to the private operator principle[98] which has been relied upon by the Commission and the European Courts[99] to determine the borderline between market behaviour and state intervention.

European jurisprudence distinguishes the economic nature of state intervention and the exercise of public powers. The application of the private operator principle is confined to the economic nature of state intervention[100] and is justified by the principle of equal treatment between the public and private sectors.[101] Such treatment requires that intervention by the state should not be subject to stricter rules than those applicable to private undertakings. The noneconomic character of state intervention[102] renders immaterial the test of private operator, for the reason that profitability, and thus the *raison d'être* of the private investment, is not present. It follows that services of general economic interest cannot be part of the same demand/supply equation, as other normal services the state and its organs procure.[103] Along the above lines, a convergence emerges between public procurement jurisprudence and the state aid approach in the light of the reasoning behind the *BFI*[104] and *Agora*[105] cases. Services of general economic interest are *sui generis,* having as main characteristics the lack of industrial and commercial character, where the absence of profitability and competitiveness are indicative of the relevant market place. As a rule, the procurement of such services should be subject to the rigor and discipline of public procurement rules and in analogous ratione, classified as state aid, in the absence of the competitive award procedures. In consequence, the application of the public procurement regime reinforces the character of services of general interest as noncommercial or industrial and the existence of public markets.[106]

The compensation approach relies heavily upon the real advantage theory to determine the existence of any advantages conferred to undertakings through state financing. Thus, the advantages given by the public authorities and threaten to distort competition are examined together with the obligations on the recipient of the aid. Public advantages thus constitute aid only if their amount exceeds the value of the commitments the recipient enters into. The compensation approach treats the costs offsetting the provision of services of general interest as the base line over which state aid should be considered. That base line is determined by the market price, which corresponds to the given public/private contractual interface and is demonstrable through the application of public procurement award procedures.

The real advantage theory runs contrary to the apparent advantage theory which underlines Treaty provisions[107] and the approach that relies on the economic effects and the nature of the measures in determining the existence of state aid. The borderline of the market price, which will form the conceptual base above which state aid would appear, is not always easy to determine, even with the presence of public procurement procedures. The state and its organs as contracting authorities (state emanations and bodies governed by public law) have wide discretion to award public contracts under the public procurement rules.[108] Often, price plays a secondary role in the award criteria. In cases when the public contract is awarded to the lowest price, the element of *market price* under the compensation approach could be determined. However, when the public contract is to be awarded by reference to the most economically advantageous offer[109], the market price might be totally different than the price the contracting authority wish to pay for the procurement of the relevant services. The mere existence of public procurement procedures cannot, therefore, reveal the necessary element of the compensation approach: the market price which will determine the 'excessive' state intervention and introduce state aid regulation.[110]

An indication of the application of the compensation approach is reflected in the *Stohal*[111] case, where an undertaking could provide commercial services and services of general interest, without any relevance to the applicability of the public procurement rules. The rationale of the case runs parallel with the real advantage theory, up to the point of recognising the different nature and characteristics of the markets under which normal (commercial) services and services of general interest are provided. The distinction begins where, for the sake of legal certainty and legitimate expectation, the activities undertakings of dual capacity are equally covered by the public procurement regime and the undertaking in question is considered as *contracting authority* irrespective of any proportion or percentage between the delivery of commercial services and services of general interest. This finding might have a significant implication for the compensation approach in state aid jurisprudence: irrespective of any costs offsetting the costs related to the provision of general interest, the entire state financing could be viewed under the state aid approach.

Finally, the *quid pro quo* approach relies on the existence of a direct and manifest link between state financing and services of general interest, existence indicative through the presence of a public contract concluded in accordance with the provisions of the public procurement Directives. Apart from the obvious criticism the *quid pro quo* approach has received, its interface with public procurement appears as the most problematic facet in its application. The procurement of public services does not always reveal a public contract between a contracting authority and an undertaking.

Altmark has created a number of problems. The first condition, which requires the existence of a clear definition of the framework within which public service obligations and services of general interest have been entrusted to the beneficiary of compensatory payments, runs consistently with Article 106(2) EC jurisprudence, which requires an express act of the public authority to assign services of general economic interest.[112] However, the second condition, which requires the establishment of the parameters on the basis of which the compensation is calculated in an objective and transparent manner, departs from existing precedent,[113] as it establishes an *ex post* control mechanism by the Member States and the European Commission. The third condition, that the compensation must not exceed what is necessary to cover the costs incurred in discharging services of general interest or public service obligations, is compatible to the proportionality test applied in Article 106(2) EC. Nonetheless, there is an inconsistency problem, as the European judiciary is rather unclear as to the question of whether any compensation for public service obligations may include a profit element.[114] Finally, the fourth condition, which establishes a comparison of the cost structures of the recipient and of a private undertaking, which is well run and adequately provided to fulfil the public service tasks, in the absence of a public procurement procedure, inserts elements of subjectivity and uncertainty that will inevitably fuel controversy.[115]

Public services require state intervention for their provision, organisation and delivery. This thesis has two implications: firstly, competition law has limited use in their regulation, mainly because of Art 106(2) EC; secondly, what can bring the provision, organisation and delivery of public services in line with competition policy is state aid regulation. However, assessment instruments and methods under state aid policy, such as the private investor principle, show that public services which include public obligations, universal obligations and services of general economic interest, function in *sui generis* markets.[116] They also reveal the noncommercial character of public services, inasmuch as the latter lack profitability, a character which points toward the *compensatory nature* of the reimbursement of public service by the state and its organs.[117] This finding exposes the deficit-based calculation method for their cost and value, which in turn renders their funding compatible with the EU Treaties, provided that the calculation method reflects market conditions and that the selection of the entrusted undertaking is transparent and based on objective criteria. Public procurement is the regime that can provide for transparency, objectivity and nondiscrimination as well as insert elements of competition in the provision, organisation and delivery of public services.

THE INDUSTRIAL POLICY DIMENSION IN PUBLIC SECTOR REGULATION

The implementation of industrial policies through public purchasing focuses on either the sustainability of strategic national industries, or the development of infant industries. In both cases, preferential purchasing patterns can provide the economic and financial framework for the development of such industries, at the expense of competition and free trade. Although the utilisation of public procurement as a means of industrial policy in Member States may breach directly or indirectly primary Treaty provisions on free movement of goods and the right of establishment and the freedom to provide services, it is far from clear whether the European Commission and the European Court of Justice could accept public procurement as legitimate state aid.

The industrial policy dimension of public procurement is also reflected in the form of strategic purchasing by public utilities. Public utilities in the European Union, which in their majority are monopolies, are accountable for a substantial magnitude of procurement, in terms of volume and in terms of price.[118] Responsible for this are the expensive infrastructure and high technology products that are necessary to procure in order to deliver their services to the public. Given the fact that most of the suppliers to public utilities depend almost entirely on their procurement and that, even when some degree of privatisation has been achieved, the actual control of the utilities is still vested in the state, the first constraint in liberalising public procurement in the European Union is apparent. Utilities, in the form of public monopolies or semiprivate enterprises, appear prone to perpetuate long-standing overdependency purchasing patterns with certain domestic suppliers. Reflecting the above observations, it is worth bearing in mind that until 1991 utilities were not covered by European legislation on procurement.[119] The delay of their regulation can be attributed to the resistance from Member States in privatising their monopolies and the uncertainty of the legal regime that will follow their privatisation.

Nevertheless, the public procurement legal framework is positively in favour of strategic subcontracting.[120] Subcontracting plays a major role in the opening up of public markets as it is the most effective way of small- and medium-sized enterprises' participation in public procurement. All Directives on Public Procurement, influenced by Commission's Communications on subcontracting and small and medium enterprises, encourage the use of subcontracting in the award of public contracts. For example, in public supplies contracts, the contracting entity in the invitation to tender may ask the tenderers on their intention to subcontract to third parties part of the contract. In public works contracts, contracting authorities awarding the principal contract to a concessionaire may require the subcontracting to third parties of at least 30 per cent of the total work provided for by the principal contract.[121]

The industrial policy dimension of public procurement evolves around public monopolies in the Member States which predominately operate in the utilities sectors (energy, transport, water and telecommunications) and have been assigned with the exclusive exploitation of the relevant services in their respective Member States. The legal status of these entities varies from legal monopolies, where they are constitutionally guaranteed, to delegated monopolies, where the state confers certain rights on them. During the last decade they have been the target of a sweeping process of transformation from underperforming public corporations to competitive enterprises. Public monopolies very often possess a monopsony position. As they are state-controlled enterprises, they tend to perform under different management patterns than private firms. Their decision making responds not only to market forces but mainly to political pressure. Understandably, their purchasing behaviour follows, to a large extent, parameters reflecting current trends of domestic industrial policies. Public monopolies in the utilities sector have sustained national industries in Member States through exclusive or preferential procurement. The sustainability of 'national champions', or in other terms, strategically perceived enterprises, could only be achieved through discriminatory purchasing patterns. The privatisation of public monopolies, which absorb, to a large extent, the output of such industries will most probably discontinue such patterns. It will also result in industrial policy imbalances as it would be difficult for the 'national champions' to secure new markets to replace the traditional long dependency on public monopolies. Finally, it would take time and effort to diversify their activities or to convert to alternative industrial sectors.[122]

The protected and preferential purchasing frameworks between monopolies and 'national champions' and the output dependency patterns and secured markets of the latter have attracted considerable foreign direct investment, to the extent that European Union institutions face the dilemma of threatening to discontinue the investment flow when liberalising public procurement in the common market. However, it could be argued that the industrial restructuring following the opening up of the procurement practices of public monopolies would possibly attract similar levels of foreign direct investment, which would be directed towards supporting the new structure. The liberalisation of public procurement in the European Union has as one of its main aims the restructuring of industries suffering from overcapacity and suboptimal performance.[123] However, the industries supplying public monopolies and utilities are themselves, quite often, public corporations. In such cases, procurement dependency patterns between state outfits, when disrupted, can result in massive unemployment attributed to the supply side's inadequacy to secure new customers. The monopsony position when abolished could often bring about the collapse of the relevant sector.

Industrial policies through public procurement can also be implemented with reference to defence industries, particularly for procurement of military equipment. The Procurement Directives cover equipment of dual-use purchased by the armed forces, but explicitly exclude from their ambit the procurement of military equipment. It should be also mentioned here that every Member State in the European Union pursues its own military procurement policy. The creation of a framework within which a common

European Defence Policy should be established, should harmonise the procurement of defence contracts and the procurement of military equipment by Member States, to the extent that a centralised mechanism regulating them would replace independent national military procurement practices.

Attempts have been made to liberalise, to a limited extent, the procurement of military equipment at European level under the auspices of European Defence Equipment Market (EDEM). This initiative is a programme of gradual liberalisation of defence industries in the relevant countries and has arisen through the operation of the Independent European Programme Group, which has been a forum of industrial co-operation in defence industry matters amongst European NATO members. The programme has envisaged, apart from collaborative research and development in defence technology, the introduction of a competitive regime in defence procurement and a modest degree of transparency. Award of defence procurement contracts, under the EDEM should follow a similar rationale with civilian procurement, particularly in the introduction of award criteria based on economic and financial considerations and a minimum degree of publicity for contracts in excess of 1 million euro.

The establishment of a Common European Defence Policy could possibly bring about the integration of defence industries in the European Union and this will inevitably require a change in governments' policies and practices.[124] Competitiveness, public savings considerations, value for money, transparency and nondiscrimination should be the principles of the centralised mechanism regulating defence procurement in Europe. The establishment of a centralised defence agency with specific tasks of *contractorisation, facilities management* and *market testing* represent examples of new procurement policies which would give an opportunity to the defence industry to adopt its practices in the light of the challenges, risks, policy priorities and directions of the modern era. In particular, risk management and contracting arrangements measuring reliability of deliveries and cost compliance, without penalising the supply side, are themes which could revolutionise defence procurement and play a significant role in linking such strategic industries with national and European-wide industrial policies. Public procurement as a discipline expands from a simple internal market topic to a multifaceted tool of European regulation and governance covering policy choices and revealing an interesting interface between centralised and national governance systems.[125]

The Defence Procurement Directive[126] which was enacted in August 2009 gave an implementation period to Member States until 21 August 2011. The Directive attempts to regulate the procurement of armaments and other security supplies, services, and works, worth about Euro 30 billion annually, which so far have been often treated as falling outside the field of application of the EC Treaty, and the Public Sector Procurement Directives. The importance of the defence market to the European economy is considerable. While the acquisition of supplies, services, and works is subject to the internal market, the recourse to a number of derogations, most notably Article 296 EC (Art 346 TFEU), has taken most armaments and related services outside the EU trade, competition, and procurement rules. This resulted in twenty-seven separate defence markets characterised by protectionism, inefficiencies, and often corruption, resulting in reduced levels of innovation and competitiveness, high prices and a lack of transparency. There are significant costs arising from not integrating the European defence markets.

The EU Defence and Security Procurement are areas of law and policy which rest at the borderline between core EU competence and core Member State sovereignty. This was due to the perceived lack of clarity of a number of defence and security exemptions in the EC Treaty, most notably the armaments exemption in Article 296 EC (Art 346 TFEU). The regime represents the most significant contribution of the Community (1st Pillar) legislator to the development of a European Defence and Security Policy, outside the Common Foreign and Security Policy. The Directive is also a major step towards the completion of the set of legislative instruments regulating public and utilities procurement in the EU, alongside the Public Sector Procurement Directive 2004/18/EC, the Utilities Procurement Directive 2004/17/EC.

Defence and security procurement frameworks under the premises of the EU Common Foreign and Security Policy form a significant part of the evolving industrial policy of the European Union. The European Defence Agency (EDA) was established in 2005, legally as part of the Common Foreign and Security Policy (CFSP) or second pillar of the EU and therefore institutionally as part of the Council. Within the context of this second pillar, the *sui generis* characteristics of Community law, such as supremacy, direct effect, and state liability and its democratic legislative process and judicial review do not apply. In 2006 the EDA introduced a nonbinding Code of Conduct for Armaments Procurement with its own contract portal for its participating Member States (now all EU Member States except Denmark). Moreover, EDA introduced nonbinding codes of conduct for supply management and offsets. It is maintained that these instruments represent a competing legal framework for the new Defence and Security Directive. However, political and economic interests also play a major role. Crucial is the division between Member States with and those without a significant defence industrial base. Furthermore, a number of Member States with the most developed defence industrial bases established the Organisation for Joint Armaments Procurement (OCCAR) and the Letter of Intent (LoI) forums. These were partly founded due to frustration with delays in the EU decision-making processes. Both forums have their own procurement rules for military equipment.

2   The Contracting Authority as a Concept of Public Sector Regulation

The remit and thrust of public sector regulation relies heavily on the connection between the private sector and contracting authorities as emanations of the state in their pursuit of public interest functions.

The Court has developed the test of *functionality,* interpreting the term *contracting authorities* in broad and functional terms[1] in order to bring under the remit of contracting authorities a range of undertakings connected with the pursuit of public interest. Contracting authorities under the Public Sector Directive embrace the state, regional or local authorities, bodies governed by public law, associations formed by one or several of such authorities or one or several of such bodies governed by public law.[2] The Utilities Directive recognises as contracting entities public undertakings, over which the contracting authorities may exercise directly or indirectly a dominant influence by virtue of their ownership of them, their financial participation therein, or the rules which govern them.[3] The Utilities Directive includes also as contracting entities undertakings which, although they are not contracting authorities or public undertakings themselves, operate on the basis of special or exclusive rights granted by a competent authority of a Member State through means of legislative, regulatory or administrative provisions.[4]

A comprehensive and clear definition of the term *contracting authorities,* a factor that determines the applicability of public procurement rules and brings together in a contractual interface the public and private sectors, has been attempted by European law. Contracting authorities encapsulate the purchasing behaviour of all entities, which have a close connection with the state. These entities, although not formally part of the state, disperse public funds in pursuit or on behalf of public interest. The Directives describe as contracting authorities the *state,* which covers central, regional, municipal and local government departments, as well as *bodies governed by public law.* Provision has been also made to cover entities, which receive more than 50 per cent subsidies by the state or other contracting authorities.

However, that connection might be weak to cover entities, which operate in the utilities sector (entities operating in the water, energy, transport and telecommunications and postal sectors), and have been privatised. A wide range of these entities is covered by the term *bodies governed by public law,* which is used by the Utilities Directives for the contracting entities operating in the relevant sectors. Interestingly, another category of contracting authorities under the Utilities Directives includes *public undertakings.* The term indicates any undertaking over which the state may exercise direct or indirect dominant influence by means of ownership, or by means of financial participation, or by means of laws and regulations, which govern the public undertaking's operation. Dominant influence can be exercised in the form of a majority holding of the undertaking's subscribed capital, in the form of majority controlling of the undertaking's issued shares, or, finally in the form of the right to appoint the majority of the undertaking's management board. Public undertakings cover utilities operators, which have been granted exclusive rights of exploitation of a service. Irrespective of their ownership, they are subject to the Utilities Directive inasmuch as the *exclusivity* of their operation precludes other entities from entering the relevant market under substantially the same competitive conditions. Privatised utilities could be, in principle, excluded from being the contracting authorities when a genuinely competitive regime[5] within the relevant market structure would rule out purchasing patterns based on noneconomic considerations.

THE PUBLIC CHARACTER OF CONTRACTING AUTHORITIES

Although the term *contracting authorities* appears rigorous and well defined, public interest functions are dispersed through a range of organisations which *stricto sensu* could not fall under the ambit of the term *contracting authorities,* since they are not formally part of the state, nor all criteria for the definition of bodies governed by public law are present. This is particularly the case of nongovernmental organisations (NGOs) which operate under the auspices of the central or local government and are responsible for public interest functions.[6] The Court addressed the *lex lacuna* through its landmark case *Beentjes.*[7] The Court diluted the rigorous definition of contracting authorities for the purposes of public procurement law, by introducing a *functional dimension* of the state and its organs. In particular, it considered that a *local land consolidation committee* with no legal personality, but with its functions and compositions specifically governed by legislation as part of the state. The Court interpreted the term *contracting authorities* in *functional terms* and considered the local land consolidation committee, which depended on the relevant public authorities for the appointment of its members, its operations were subject to their supervision and it had as its main task the financing and award of public works contracts, as falling within the notion of state, even though it was not part of the state administration in *formal terms.*[8] The Court held that the aim of the public procurement rules, as well as the attainment of freedom of establishment and freedom to provide services would be jeopardised, if the public procurement provisions were to be held inapplicable, solely because entities, which were set up by the state to carry out tasks entrusted to by legislation, were not formally part of its administrative organisation.

The Court in two cases applied a functionality test, when was requested to determine the nature of entities which could not meet the criteria of bodies governed by public law, but had a distinctive public interest remit. In *Teoranta*[9], a private company established according to national legislation to carry out business of forestry and related activities, was deemed as falling within the notion of the state. The company was set up by the state and was entrusted with specific tasks of public interest, such as managing national forests and woodland industries, as well as providing recreation, sporting, educational, scientific and cultural facilities. It was also under decisive administrative, financial and management control by the state, although the day-to-day operations were left entirely to its board. The Court accepted that since the state had at least indirect control over the *Teoranta*'s policies, in functional terms the latter was part of the state. In the *Vlaamese Raad*[10], the Flemish parliament of the Belgian federal system was considered part of the 'federal' state. The Court held that the definition of the state encompasses all bodies, which exercise legislative, executive and judicial powers, at both regional and federal levels. The Raad, as a legislative body of the Belgian state, although under no direct control by it, was held as falling within the definition of the state and thus being regarded as a contracting authority. The fact that the Belgian government did not, at the time, exercise any direct or indirect control relating to procurement policies over the Vlaamese Raad was considered immaterial on the grounds that a state cannot rely on its own legal system to justify noncompliance with EC law and particular Directives.[11]

The functional dimension of contracting authorities has exposed the Court's departure from the formality test, which has rigidly positioned an entity under state control on *stricto sensu* traditional public law grounds. Functionality, as an ingredient of assessing the relationship between an entity and the state demonstrates, in addition to the elements of management or financial control, the importance of constituent factors such as the intention and purpose of establishment of the entity in question. Functionality depicts a flexible approach in the applicability of the procurement Directives, in a way that the Court through its precedence established a pragmatic approach as to the nature of the demand side of the public procurement equation.

BODIES GOVERNED BY PUBLIC LAW

The category is subject to a set of cumulative criteria[12] in order to be classified as contracting authorities for the purposes of the Directives. In particular, *bodies governed by public law* i) must be established for the specific purpose of meeting needs in the general public interest not having an industrial or commercial character; ii) they must have legal personality; and iii) they must be financed, for the most part, by either the state, or regional or local authorities, or other bodies governed by public law; or subject to management supervision by these bodies, or having an administrative or supervisory board, more than half of whose members are appointed by the state, regional or local authorities or by other bodies governed by public law. There is a list of such bodies in Annex I of Directive 93/37 which is not an exhaustive one, in the sense that Member States are under an obligation to notify the Commission of any changes to that list. The term *bodies governed by public law* provided the opportunity to the Court to elaborate on each of the cumulative criteria and shed light on their constituent elements. The Court's jurisprudence has revealed the following thematic areas.

THE DEPENDENCY TEST

To assess the existence of the third criterion of bodies governed by public law, the Court assumed that there is a close dependency of these bodies on the State, in terms of corporate governance, management supervision and financing.[13] These dependency features are alternative, thus the existence of one satisfies the third criterion. The Court held in *OPAC*[14] that management supervision by the state or other contracting authorities entails not only administrative verification of legality or appropriate use of funds or exceptional control measures, but the conferring of significant influence over management policy, such as the narrowly circumscribed remit of activities, the supervision of compliance, as well as the overall administrative supervision. Of interest and high relevance is the Court's analysis and argumentation relating to the requirements of management supervision by the state and other public bodies, where it maintained that entities entrusted to provide social housing in France are deemed to be bodies governed by public law, thus covered by the public procurement Directives.

The Court (and the Advocate General) drew an analogy amongst the dependency features of bodies governed by public law on the state. Although the corporate governance and financing feature are quantitative (the state must appoint more than half of the members of the managerial or supervisory board or it must finance for the most part the entity in question), the exercise of management supervision is a qualitative one. The Court held that management supervision by the state denotes dependency ties similar to the financing or governance control of the entity concerned.

Receiving public funds from the state or a contracting authority is an indication that an entity could be a body governed by public law. However, this indication is not an absolute one. The Court, in the *University of Cambridge* case[15] was asked whether i) awards or grants paid by one or more contracting authorities for the support of research work; ii) consideration paid by one or more contracting authorities for the supply of services

comprising research work; iii) consideration paid by one or more contracting authorities for the supply of other services, such as consultancy or the
organisation of conferences; and iv) student grants paid by local education
authorities to universities in respect of tuition for named students constitute
public financing for the University.

The Court held that only specific payments made to an entity by the state
of other public authorities have the effect of creating or reinforcing a specific relationship or subordination and dependency. The funding of an entity
within a framework of general considerations indicates that the entity has
close dependency links with the state of other contracting authorities. Thus,
funding received in the form of grants or awards paid by the state or other
contracting authorities, as well as funding received in the form of student
grants for tuition fees for named students, constitutes public financing. The
rationale for such approach lies in the lack of any contractual consideration
between the entity receiving the funding and the state or other contracting
authorities, which provide it in the context of the entity's public interest
activities. The Court drew an analogy of public financing received by an
entity with the receipt of subsidies.[16] However, if there is a specific consideration for the state to finance an entity, such as a contractual nexus, the
Court suggested that the dependency ties are not sufficiently close to merit
the entity financed by the state meeting the third criterion of the term *bodies
governed by public law*. Such relationship is analogous to the dependency
that exists in normal commercial relations formed by reciprocal contracts,
which have been negotiated freely between the parties. Therefore, funding
received by Cambridge University for the supply of services for research
work, or consultancies, or conference organisation cannot be deemed as
public financing. The existence of a contract between the parties, apart from
the specific considerations for funding, indicates strongly supply substitutability, in the sense that the entity receiving the funding faces competition in
the relevant markets.

The Court stipulated that the proportion of public finances received by
an entity, as one of the alternative features of the third criterion of the term
bodies governed by public law, must exceed 50 per cent to enable it meeting that criterion. For assessment purposes of this feature, there must be an
annual evaluation of the (financial) status of an entity for the purposes of
being regarded as a contracting authority.

Dependency, in terms of overall control of an entity by the state or another
contracting authority presupposes a control similar to that which the state
of another contracting authority exercises over its own departments. The
'similarity' of control denotes lack of independence with regard to decision making. The Court in *Teckal*[17], concluded that a contract between a
contracting authority and an entity, which the former exercises a control
similar to that which it exercises over its own departments and at the same
time that entity carries out the essential part of its activities with the contracting authority, is not a public contract, irrespective of that entity being

a contracting authority or not. The similarity of control as a reflection of dependency reveals another facet of the thrust of contracting authorities: the nonapplicability of the public procurement rules for in-house relationships.

MANAGEMENT SUPERVISION

The close dependency of a body governed by public law on the state, regional or local authorities or other bodies governed by public law is recognized in case law of the Court.[18] More specifically, as regards the criterion of management supervision, the Court has held that that supervision must give rise to dependence on the public authorities equivalent to that which exists where one of the other alternative criteria is fulfilled, namely where the body in question is financed, for the most part, by the public authorities or where the latter appoint more than half of the members of its administrative, managerial or supervisory organs, enabling the public authorities to influence their decisions in relation to public contracts.[19]

The criterion of managerial supervision cannot be regarded as being satisfied in the case of mere review since, by definition, such supervision does not enable the public authorities to influence the decisions of the body in question in relation to public contracts. That criterion is, however, satisfied where the public authorities supervise not only the annual accounts of the body concerned but also its conduct from the point of view of proper accounting, regularity, economy, efficiency and expediency and where those public authorities are authorised to inspect the business premises and facilities of that body and to report the results of those inspections to a regional authority which holds, through another company, all the shares in the body in question.[20]

COMMERCIALITY AND NEEDS IN THE GENERAL INTEREST

Commerciality and its relationship with needs in the general interest is perhaps the most important theme that has emerged from the Court's jurisprudence in relation to the remit of bodies governed by public law as contracting authorities. In fact the theme sets to explore the interface between profit making and public interest, as features which underpin the activities of bodies governed by public law.

The criterion of specific establishment of an entity to meet needs in the general interest having noncommercial or industrial character has attracted the attention of the Court in some landmark cases.[21] The above criterion appears as the first of the three cumulative criteria for bodies governed by public law. The Court drew its experience from jurisprudence in the public undertakings field as well as case law relating to public order to define the term *needs in the general interest*.[22] The Court approached the above concept by a direct analogy of the concept 'general economic interest'.[23] The concept 'general interest' denotes the requirements of a community (local or national) in its entirety, which should not overlap with the specific or exclusive interest of a clearly determined person or group of persons.[24] However, the problematic concept of the *specificity* of the establishment of the body in question was approached by reference to the reasons and the objectives behind its establishment. Specificity of the purpose of an establishment does not mean exclusivity, in the sense that other types of activities can be carried out without escaping classification as a body governed by public law.[25]

On the other hand, the requirement of noncommercial or industrial character of needs in the general interest has raised some difficulties. The Court had recourse to case law and legal precedence relating to public undertakings, where the nature of industrial and commercial activities of private or public undertakings was defined.[26] The industrial or commercial character of an organisation depends much upon a number of criteria that reveal the thrust behind the organisation's participation in the relevant market. The state and its organs may act either by exercising public powers or by carrying economic activities of an industrial or commercial nature by offering goods and services on the market. The key issue is the organisation's intention to achieve profitability and pursue its objectives through a spectrum of commercially motivated decisions. The distinction between the range of activities which relate to public authority and those which, although carried out by public persons, fall within the private domain is drawn most clearly from case law and judicial precedence of the Court concerning the applicability of competition rules of the Treaty to the given activities.[27]

The Court in *BFI*[28] had the opportunity to clarify the element of noncommercial or industrial character. It considered that the relationship of the first criterion of bodies governed by public law is an integral one. The noncommercial or industrial character is a criterion intended to clarify the term *needs in the general interest*. In fact, it is regarded as a category of needs of general interest. The Court recognised that there might be needs of general interest, which have an industrial and commercial character and it is possible that private undertakings can meet needs of general interest, which do not have industrial and commercial character. The acid test for needs in the general interest not having an industrial or commercial character is that the state or other contracting authorities choose themselves to meet these needs or to have a decisive influence over their provision.

In the *Agora* case[29] the Court indicated that if an activity which meets general needs is pursued in a competitive environment, there is a strong indication that the entity, which pursues it is not a body governed by public law. The reason can be found in the relationship between competitiveness and commerciality. Market forces reveal the commercial or industrial character of an activity, irrespective the latter meeting the needs of general interest or not. However, market competitiveness as well as profitability cannot be absolute determining factors for the commerciality or the industrial nature of an activity, as they are not sufficient to exclude the possibility that a body governed by public law may choose to be guided by considerations other than economic ones. The absence of competition is not a condition necessarily to be taken into account in order to define a body governed by public law, although the existence of significant competition in the market place may be indicative of the absence of a need in the general interest, which does not carry commercial or industrial elements. The Court reached this conclusion by analysing the nature of the bodies governed by public law contained in Annex 1 of the Works Directive 93/37 and verifying that the intention of the state to establish such bodies has been to retain decisive influence over the provision of the needs in question.

THE DUAL CAPACITY OF CONTRACTING AUTHORITIES

The dual capacity of an entity as a public service provider and a commercial undertaking respectively, and the weighting of the relevant activity in relation to the proportion of its output, should be the decisive factor in determining whether an entity is a body governed by public law. This argument appeared for the first time before the Court in the *Strohal*[30] case. The Austrian government suggested that only if the activities in pursuit of the 'public services obligations' of an entity supersede its commercial thrust, the latter could be considered as a body covered by public law and a contracting authority. In support of its argument that the relevant entity (*Österreichische Staatsdruckerei*) is not a body governed by public law, the Austrian government maintained that the proportion of public interest activities represents no more than 15–20 per cent of its overall activities.[31]

In practice, the argument put forward implied a selective application of the public procurement Directives in the event of dual capacity entities. This sort of application is not entirely unjustified as, on a number of occasions, the public procurement Directives themselves utilise thresholds or proportions considerations in order to include or exclude certain contracts from their ambit. For example, these might include the relevant provisions stipulating the thresholds for the applicability of the public procurement rules as well as the provisions relating to the so-called mixed contracts, where the proportion of the value of the works or the supplies element in a public contract determines the applicability of the relevant Directive and finally the relevant provisions which regulate the award of works contracts which are subsidised *directly* by more than 50 per cent by the state.

The Court in *Strohal* established dualism, to the extent that it specifically implied that contracting authorities may pursue a dual range of activities; to procure goods, works and services destined for the public, as well as participate in commercial activities. They can pursue other activities in addition to those which meet needs of general interest not having an industrial and commercial character. The proportion between activities pursued by an entity, which on the one hand aim to meet needs of general interest not having an industrial or commercial character, and commercial activities on the other, is irrelevant for the characterisation of that entity as a body governed by public law. What is relevant is the intention of establishment of the entity in question, which reflects on the 'specificity' requirement. Also, specificity does not mean exclusivity of purpose. Specificity indicates the intention of establishment to meet general needs. Along theses lines, ownership or financing of an entity by a contracting authority does not guarantee the condition of establishment of that entity to meet needs of general interest not having industrial and commercial character.

THE CONNECTION OF CONTRACTING
AUTHORITIES WITH PRIVATE UNDERTAKINGS

There is considerable risk of circumventing the public procurement Directives, if contracting authorities award their public contracts via private undertakings under their control, which cannot be covered by the framework of the Directives. Under the domestic laws of the Member States, there is little to prevent contracting authorities from acquiring private undertakings in an attempt to participate in market activities. In fact, in many jurisdictions the socioeconomic climate is very much in favour towards public-private sector partnerships, in the form of joint ventures or in the form of private financing of public projects. A classic example of such an approach is the views of the UK government in relation to the involvement of the private sector in delivering public services through the *Private Finance Initiative (PFI)*, which attempts to create a framework between the public and private sectors working together in delivering public services.[32] The Court, prior to the *Stohal* case, did not have the opportunity to examine such corporate relationships and the effect that public procurement law has upon them. Even in *Strohal*, the Court did not rule directly on the subject, but instead it provided the necessary inferences for national courts, in order to ascertain whether such relations between public and private undertakings aim at avoiding the application of the public procurement Directives. Indeed, national courts, in litigation before them, must establish *in concreto* whether a contracting authority has established an undertaking in order to enter into contracts for the sole purpose of avoiding the requirements specified in public procurement law. Such conclusions must be beyond doubt based on the examination of the actual purpose for which the undertaking in questions has been established. The rule of thumb is the connection between the nature of a project and the aims and objectives of the undertaking which awards it. If the realisation of a project does not contribute to the aims and objectives of an undertaking, then it is assumed that the project in question is warded 'on behalf' of another undertaking, and if the latter beneficiary is a contracting authority under the framework of public procurement law, then the relevant Directives should apply. The Court followed the *Strohal* lines to *Teckal*[33], where the exercise of a similar control over the management of an entity by a contracting authority prevents the applicability of the Directives.

The dual capacity of contracting authorities is irrelevant to the applicability of public procurement rules. If an entity is a contracting authority, it must apply public procurement rules irrespective of the pursuit of general interest needs or the pursuit of commercial activities. Also, if a contracting authority assigns the rights and obligations of a public contract to an entity, which is not a contracting authority, that entity must follow public procurement rules. The contrary would be acceptable if the contract fell within the remit of the entity, which is not a contracting authority, and the contract was entered into on its behalf by a contracting authority.

Oymanns[34] brought under the conceptual premise of a 'body governed by public law' a statutory sickness fund which was indirectly financed by the state without any consideration in return, but it received mandatory contributions set by law from employers and private individual members and had no discretion in setting the levels or conditions of contributions. The justification rested on the principle that the statutory sickness fund was deemed to be financed, for the most part, by the state, as a result of the mandatory setting of the levels or conditions of contributions and had the sole objective to perform interests in the general needs such as social security functions, which do not have industrial nor commercial character. In similar vein, *Bayerischer Rundfunk*[35] considered the mandatory fee contributions of private individuals to a broadcasting fund, the level of which were set by law, as state financing of the relevant undertaking, thus bringing it into the category of 'body governed by public law'.

PRIVATE LAW ENTITIES AS CONTRACTING AUTHORITIES

An entity which is governed by private law but nevertheless meets all the requirements of bodies governed by public law is considered a contracting authority for the purposes of the public procurement Directives. In *Commission v. Spain*[36], the Commission argued that national law which excludes from the scope of the public procurement Directives private entities which may fulfil the requirements of contracting authorities is in default with public procurement *acquis*. The Commission argued that the scope *ratione personae* of the codified law does not coincide with that of Directives 93/36 and 93/37, insofar as the national law applies exclusively to bodies subject to a public law regime for the purposes of Spanish law, while the legal form of the body at issue falls outside the definition of 'body governed by public law' set out in the public procurement Directives. The Commission asserted that the concept 'body governed by public law' is a Community-wide concept of autonomous nature. The Commission maintained that, according to the Court's jurisprudence[37], a body governed by public law must be understood as a body which fulfils the three cumulative conditions and must be interpreted in functional terms.[38]

SEMIPUBLIC UNDERTAKINGS AS CONTRACTING AUTHORITIES

In *Staad Halle*[39], a question arose as to whether, where a contracting authority intends to conclude with a company governed by private law, legally distinct from the authority and in which it has a majority capital holding and exercises a certain control, a contract for pecuniary interest relating to public services, it is always obliged to apply the public award procedures laid down by that Directive. In other words, the question prompted the criteria and their references under which mere participation of a contracting authority, even in a minority form, in the shareholding of a private company with which it concludes a contract to be a ground for the applicability of the public procurement Directives. The Court held that where a contracting authority intends to conclude a contract for pecuniary interest with a company legally distinct from it, in whose capital it has a holding together with one or more private undertakings, the public award procedures laid down by that Directive must always be applied.

STATE COMMERCIAL COMPANIES AS CONTRACTING AUTHORITIES

Sociedad Estatal de Infraestruturas y Equipamientos Penitenciarios S.A (SIEPSA), a private company under the control of the Spanish government did not follow the provisions of the public procurement Directives in connection with the award of a contract for the *Centro Educativo Penitenciario Experimental de Segovia* (Experimental Educational Prison in Segovia). The question was whether such private companies under state control should be considered as contracting authorities.[40] The Court declared that state-controlled companies such as SIEPSA are bodies governed by public law and as a result contracting authorities as it is unlikely that they themselves should have to bear the financial risks related to their activities. If in fact, the state would take all necessary measure to protect the financial viability of such entities, such as measures to prevent compulsory liquidation.

PRIVATE COMPANIES AS CONTRACTING AUTHORITIES

Companies governed by private law established for the specific purpose of meeting needs in the general interest which do not have an industrial or commercial character, have legal personality, and are financed for the most part by public authorities or other entities governed by public law or are subject to supervision by the latter, or have an administrative, managerial or supervisory board more than half of whose members are appointed by public authorities or other entities governed by public law, are considered as contracting authorities.

The Court stated that, in order to be defined as a body governed by public law within the meaning of that provision, an entity must satisfy the three cumulative conditions set out therein, according to which it must be a body established for the specific purpose of meeting needs in the general interest, not having an industrial or commercial character, which has legal personality and is closely dependent on the state, regional or local authorities or other bodies governed by public law.[41] Moreover, the Court has repeatedly held that, in the light of the dual objective of opening up competition and transparency pursued by the directives on the coordination of the procedures for the award of public contracts, the term *contracting authority* must be interpreted in functional terms.[42] The Court has also stated that, in the light of that dual purpose, the term *body governed by public law* must be interpreted broadly.[43] The Court, for the purposes of settling the question whether various private law entities could be classified as bodies governed by public law, has proceeded in accordance with settled case law and merely ascertained whether those entities fulfilled the three cumulative conditions of bodies governed by public law considering that the method in which the entity concerned has been set up was irrelevant in that regard.[44]

It is apparent from the jurisprudence of the Court that an entity's private law status does not constitute a criterion for precluding it from being classified as a contracting authority. Furthermore, it should be pointed out that the effectiveness of the public procurement Directives would not be fully preserved if the application of those directives to an entity which fulfils the three aforementioned conditions could be excluded solely on the basis of the fact that, under the national law to which it is subject, its legal form and rules which govern it fall within the scope of private law.

The test of *dualism*[45], as developed by the Court refers to the ability of mixed-character undertakings to be regarded as contracting authorities, provided they pursue public interest functions of nonindustrial or commercial character. Consequently, *Commission v. Spain*[46] has recognised as contracting authorities private law entities and stipulated that an entity which is governed by private law but meets all the requirements of bodies governed by public law is considered to be a contracting authority. The entity's private law status does not constitute a criterion for precluding it from being considered as a contracting authority, and in particular as being incompatible with requirement of nonindustrial or commercial character of the general interest needs, since these factors must be assessed individually and separately from the legal status of an entity. An entity governed by private law as contracting authority is also compatible with the concept of public undertakings, in accordance with the Utilities Directive.

Adolf Truley and *Korhonen*[47] also regarded as contracting authorities private entities for industrial and commercial development, where in particular a limited company established, owned and managed by a regional authority meets a need in the general interest which has not a commercial or an industrial character, where it acquires services for the development of business and commercial activities on the territory of that regional authority. The Court maintained in *Universale-Bau*[48] that entities meeting needs of general interest retrospectively are contracting authorities.

Therefore, an entity which has not been established for the specific purpose of meeting needs in the general interest, not having an industrial or commercial character, but which has subsequently taken responsibility for such needs is considered as a body governed by public law, on condition that the assumption of responsibility for meeting those needs can be established objectively. *Stadt Halle*[49] regarded semipublic undertakings as contracting authorities, where in particular a company governed by private law and is legally distinct from a contracting authority, but in which the contracting authority has a majority capital holding and exercises a certain degree of control is considered as a contracting authority. The Court also considered a state-controlled commercial company as contracting authority when it is deemed unlikely that it will bear the financial risks related to its activities, as the state would take all necessary measure to protect its financial viability.[50]

ENTITIES MEETING NEEDS OF GENERAL INTEREST RETROSPECTIVELY

A question arose before the Court as to whether an entity which was not established for the specific purpose of meeting needs in the general interest, not having an industrial or commercial character, but which has subsequently taken responsibility for such needs, which it has subsequently been actually meeting, so as to be capable of being regarded as a body governed by public law within the meaning of that provision. In the dispute in the main proceedings, it emerged *Entsorgungsbetriebe Simmering GesmbH* (EBS) took over the operation of the main sewage treatment plant, under a contract made with the city of Vienna. It was not disputed that the company satisfies a need in the general interest not having an industrial or commercial character. However, its treatment as a body governed by public law depends on the answer to be given to the question whether the condition set out in the first indent of that provision precludes an entity from being regarded as a contracting authority where it was not established for the purposes of satisfying needs in the general interest having a character other than industrial or commercial, but has undertaken such tasks as a result of a subsequent change in its sphere of activities.[51] The Court concluded that a body which was not established to satisfy specific needs in the general interest not having an industrial or commercial character, but which has subsequently taken responsibility for such needs, which it has since actually satisfied, fulfils the condition required to be considered as body governed by public law.

PRIVATE ENTITIES FOR INDUSTRIAL AND COMMERCIAL DEVELOPMENT AS CONTRACTING AUTHORITIES

A question was referred to the Court as to whether a limited company established, owned and managed by a regional or local authority may be regarded as meeting a specific need in the general interest, not having an industrial or commercial character, where that company's activity consists in acquiring services with a view to the construction of premises intended for the exclusive use of private undertakings, and whether the assessment of whether that condition is satisfied would be different if the building project in question were intended to create favourable conditions on that local authority's territory for the exercise of business activities.[52] Taitotalo was a limited company whose capital was wholly owned by the town of Varkaus in Finland, and whose objects were to buy, sell and lease real property and shares in property companies, and to organise and supply property maintenance services and other related services needed for the management of those properties and shares. The company's board had three members, who were officials of the town of Varkaus, appointed by the general meeting of the company's shareholders, at which the town has 100 per cent of the voting rights.

The Court found that a limited company established, owned and managed by a regional or local authority meets a need in the general interest, where it acquires services with a view to promoting the development of industrial or commercial activities on the territory of that regional or local authority and as such should be regarded as contracting authority.

3   The Public Contract as a Concept of Public Sector Regulation

The existence of a public contract is a precondition to thrust of public sector regulation and in particular the application of the public procurement Directives[1], where the meaning of a public contract has been configured. The determining factor of its nature is not what and how is described as public contract in national laws, nor is the legal regime (public or private) that governs its terms and conditions, nor are the intentions of the parties. The crucial characteristics of a public contract, apart from the obvious written format requirement, are: i) a pecuniary interest consideration given by a contracting authority and ii) in return of a work, product or service which is of direct economic benefit to the contracting authority.

A functional application of the pecuniary interest consideration requirement by the Court revealed a variety of payment mechanisms such as direct or deferred payment by the contracting authority to the economic operator, commitment to lease-back an asset after its construction, asset swaps between the contracting authority and the economic operator or conferral to the economic operator of an exclusive right to collect third-party payments.

The pecuniary interest consideration requirement is also indissolubly linked with the ability of the contracting authority to specify the object of the public contract. Requirements specified by contracting authorities include measures which define the type of works or action on the part of contracting authorities which has decisive influence over the design of a project or the executions of works. The means of execution are irrelevant, in the sense that prime contracting or subcontracting could be utilised for the fulfilment of the contract's object with no effect on contractual obligations or liability issues arising from the public contract. Interestingly, the Court did not consider urban planning conditions as specifications by a contracting authority capable of attributing an immediate economic benefit, even if public interest is served by such conditions.

In *Köln Messe*[2] leasing and subleasing arrangements between the City of Cologne and *Grundstücksgesellschaft Köln Messe* for the construction and use for thirty years of four exhibition halls, ancillary buildings and relevant infrastructure were regarded as of pecuniary interest considerations.

Interestingly, planning gain contracts or contractual arrangements emanating from planning decisions of contracting authorities are covered by the public procurements Directives, irrespective of the identity of the entity responsible for their execution. The Court in *Ordine degli Architetti* has ruled[3] that the conditions attached to planning permission to develop and deliver certain infrastructure requirements specified by a contracting authority as a result of its granting planning to a landowner are capable of generating contractual obligations which are conducive to public contracts. However, the relationship between the contracting authority and the landowner is not a public contract, since the contacting authority does not have any choice over who was to be responsible for the execution of the planning gain requirements, as the only person responsible could be the landowner. That relation is regarded as a *mandate* emanating from the contracting authority and obliges the landowner to treat planning gain requirements as public contracts.

Commission v. France[4] touched upon agency or representation relations with the object of delegating project contracting between contracting authorities and entities district from them or their internal departments. Such relations are deemed public service contracts, provided a written agreement is concluded between the contracting authority and the agent or representative for pecuniary interest in return of agency or representation services, provided the agent or representative is responsible for signature, project authorisation or payments to third parties on behalf of the contracting authority and does not have sufficient autonomy in executive decisions to be considered as a beneficiary of the contract's objects.

Public contracts denote a demonstrable element of economic benefit or of risk directly attributable to the contracting authority. Features of direct economic benefit include ownership of asset by a contracting authority, a legal right over its use and future economic advantages enjoyed by the contracting authority or risks assumed by the contracting authority in relation to the materialisation of a project. In *Auroux*[5], a dispute arose relating to a leisure centre in the French town of Roanne, the design and execution of which was entrusted to a semipublic urban development company without the prior issue of a call for tenders. The project had some specific features inasmuch as only certain parts of the proposed leisure centre, once constructed, were intended for the town itself, while other parts were to be disposed of by the urban development company directly to third parties, although the town was to contribute towards their financing, take over those parts not disposed of at the end of the project, and bear the full risk of any losses incurred. The Court held that an agreement by which a contracting authority entrusts another contracting authority with the execution of a work constitutes a public works contract, regardless of whether or not it is anticipated that the first contracting authority is or will become the owner of all or part of that work. Ownership of an asset is crucial only in determining work concession contracts, for it is deemed necessary as the means to grant an exclusive exploitation right to the concessionaire.

The Court thus maintained in *Auroux* that, even if national laws oblige the conclusion of a contract with certain undertakings which are themselves contracting authorities and are bound to use the provisions of the public procurement Directives to the award of any following subcontractual arrangements directly related to the former contract, contracting authorities must regard the initial contract as a public contract and apply the procurement Directives to its award in order to preserve legal certainty and eliminate the potential avoidance of the application of public procurement rules by division of subcontracts into lots below the relevant thresholds. It follows that the contractual relation between two, *ipso facto,* contracting authorities is to be regarded as a prime public contact, which is capable in demonstrating a clear element of economic benefit or of risk attributable to the contracting authority, irrespective of the obligation imposed upon the second contracting authority to apply the public procurement rules for the award of the relevant subcontracts.

Auroux, although reflecting obvious similarities with *Commission v. Germany*[6] in the sense of public sector entities co-operating for the delivery of public projects, differs fundamentally in that the latter case introduced a genuine public-public partnership relation, where the contractual interface was not based upon pecuniary interest considerations nor any payment was materialised in return of the delivery of the contract's objects.

Auroux revealed that the legislative gap in procurement for public works contracts, in the sense that an analogous provision to Article 18 of the Public Sector Directive, which covers public service contracts awarded by a contracting authority to another contracting authority or an association of contracting authorities on the basis of an exclusive right based on law, regulation or administrative provision compatible with the Treaty, does not exist within the framework of the provisions relevant to public works contracts, can only be filled by the presence of the dependency test, i.e. the *Teckal* criteria.

Auroux left open the issue of double tendering, as the Court did not address the issue of consecutive procurement of prime public contracts and subsequent subcontracts.[7] The Court, however, ruled that in order to determine the value of a public contract, account must be taken of the total value of the works contract from the point of view of a potential tenderer, including not only the total amounts to be paid by the contracting authority but also all the revenue received from third parties. In cases of mixed public contracts, a quantitative evaluation reflecting contract values is applicable to the services/supplies divide, whereas a qualitative evaluation reflecting the object of contract is conducive to the works/services divide. The object of contract, which also reflects on the requirements and specification of contracting authorities, represents that decisive classification factor for the works/services divide.

The Court in *Helmut Müller*[8] held that the sale of assets or land by contracting authorities to economic operators or other contracting authorities are not deemed public contracts, as a public contract is based on a 'purchasing' capacity of contracting authorities and on the imperative of a contracting authority in being able to determine standards and specifications suitable to meet the conditions of immediate economic benefit. Thus, the sale of assets or land is not a public contract, unless a directly related public contract to that asset or land is imminent by the contracting authority or another contracting authority, in which case the land or asset sale and the consecutive public works should be viewed in their entirety as a public contract.

The Court in *Helmut Müller* reiterated that the concept of public works contracts does not require that the works which are the subject of the contract be materially or physically carried out for the contracting authority, provided that they are carried out for that authority's *immediate* economic benefit. The Court restricted the conditions which reflect the direct economic benefit to a contracting authority by inserting an element of functionality in the notion of public contracts, and rendered the ownership of assets irrelevant to the determination of direct economic benefit on the part of contracting authorities. In fact, the necessary conditions to satisfy an *immediate economic benefit* to contracting authorities reflect only on the legal right of a contracting authority over the use of an asset or on the future economic advantages enjoyed or risks assumed by the contracting authority in relation to the relevant asset.

Helmut Müller revealed that the immediate economic benefit from a concession contract to a contracting authority presupposes a significant assumption of operational or functional risks by the concessionaire and a different makeup of the pecuniary interest consideration, in that the concessionaire has the economic freedom to charge end-users or third parties for certain duration. The ability of an economic operator to obtain urban planning does not reflect operational risk and the unlimited duration of concessions could not be regarded as lawful.

CONTRACTS BELOW THE THRESHOLDS OF THE DIRECTIVES

The Court's settled case law[9] has made clear that contracts below the stipulated thresholds of the Directives are excluded from their applicability. *Vestergaard*[10] ruled that although such contracts are excluded from the scope of public procurement Directives, contracting authorities are nevertheless bound to comply with the fundamental principles of the Treaty.[11] *Medipac-Kazantzidis*[12], confirmed that contracts below the stipulated thresholds need to comply with the duty of transparency[13] as well as the principle of non-discrimination on grounds of nationality.[14] *Correos*[15] ruled that even in the absence of any discrimination on grounds of nationality, the principle of equal treatment is applicable to the award of public contracts below the stipulated thresholds.[16]

The principles of equal treatment and nondiscrimination on grounds of nationality imply, in particular, a duty of transparency which enables contracting authorities to verify that those principles are complied with. The duty of transparency which is imposed on contracting authorities consists in ensuring a sufficient degree of advertising to enable the relevant public contract to be opened up to competition and the impartiality of procurement procedures to be reviewed.[17] However, the application of the fundamental principles of the Treaty to contracts below the stipulated thresholds is based on the assumption that the contracts in question are of certain cross-border interest.[18]

The parameters which could determine if a contract is likely to be of certain cross-border interest and therefore attract economic operators from other Member States constitute of the contract's estimated value in conjunction with its technical complexity or the location of its execution. It is in principle for the contracting authority concerned to assess whether there may be cross-border interest in a contract whose estimated value is below the threshold laid down by the procurement Directives. However, such assessment should be subject to judicial review.

It is permissible, nevertheless, for national legislation to lay down objective criteria, at national or local level, stipulating certain cross-border interest for public contracts which fall below the thresholds of the public procurement Directives. Such criteria could include, *inter alia,* the quantum of the monetary value of a contract, or its strategic importance to economic operators, in conjunction with the place where the work is to be carried out. The projected profitability to an economic operator from a subdimensional contract may also be part of such criteria to determine certain cross-border interest for public contracts. Where the financial returns in the relevant contracts are very modest[19], the likelihood of a cross-border interest is considerably weakened. However, in certain cases, the geography and the particular location of the performance of a public contract could trigger cross-border interest, even for low-value contracts.

The Court held that exclusion of subdimensional public contracts of certain cross-border interest from the application of the fundamental rules and general principles of the Treaty could undermine the general principle of nondiscrimination, could give rise to collusive conduct and anticompetitive agreements between national or local undertakings and finally could impede the exercise of freedom of establishment and freedom to provide services.[20]

ANNEX II B SERVICES CONTRACTS

For Annex II B Services Contracts, which are also referred to as nonpriority public service contracts, the Community legislature assumed that contracts for such services are not, in the light of their specific nature, of cross-border interest such as to justify their award being subject to the conclusion of a tendering procedure in accordance with the public procurement Directives. For that reason, the Public Sector Directive merely imposes a requirement of publicity after the award of such service contracts.

An Post[21] touched on contracts concerning services which fall under Annex II B of the Public Sector Directive. The contracting authorities are bound only by the obligation to define the technical specifications by reference to national standards implementing European standards which must be given in the general contract documents and to send a notice of the results of the award to the Publications Office of the EU. The other procedural rules provided for by the Public Sector Directive, including those relating to the award procedures and award criteria are, by contrast, not applicable to those contracts.

However, the limited advertisement requirements contained in the Public Sector Directive for contracts relating to services within the ambit of Annex II B cannot justify the absence of any transparency, especially when the relevant contract is of certain cross-border interest. The Court held[22] that if a contract of certain cross-border interest is awarded to an undertaking located in the same Member State as the contracting authority without any call for competition, this action would amount to a difference in treatment to the detriment of undertakings which are located in other Member States and might be interested in that contract. Such a difference in treatment, by excluding all undertakings located in other Member States, amounts to indirect discrimination on grounds of nationality[23] and contravenes the purpose of the public procurement Directives to eliminate barriers to intra-Community trade in accordance to the fundamental principles of Community law, and in particular the right of establishment and the freedom to provide services.[24]

SERVICE CONCESSIONS AS PUBLIC CONTRACTS

Telaustria[25] recognised that concession services are contracts which are excluded from the scope of public procurement Directives by the fact that the consideration provided by the contracting authorities to the concessionaire consists in the latter obtaining the right to exploit for payment its own service. Notwithstanding such exclusion, contracting authorities concluding concession services are bound to comply with the fundamental rules of the Treaty, in general and, in particular, the principle of nondiscrimination on the ground of nationality and the duty of transparency. The latter is indented as verification of compliance with the relevant Treaty principles and consists in ensuring a degree of competitiveness in the award of such contracts, in conjunction with a review process of the award procedure.

Coname[26] held that the direct award by a municipality of a service concession does not comply with the transparency principle if, without necessarily implying an obligation to hold an invitation to tender, undertakings located in other Member States were precluded from having access to appropriate information with a view to expressing their interest in obtaining that service concession. The Court held that infringement of the duty of transparency triggers the potential infringement of the principles of free movement of services and the right of establishment.

In *Parking Brixen*[27], the Court reiterated that public authorities concluding services concessions are responsible to comply with the principle of nondiscrimination on grounds of nationality and the principle of equal treatment, which conceptually correspond to the principles of the right of establishment and the freedom to provide services.[28] The Court has suggested that the right of establishment and the freedom to provide services are specific expressions of the principle of equal treatment.[29] The prohibition on discrimination on grounds of nationality is also a specific expression of the general principle of equal treatment.[30] The Court stated that the principle of equal treatment in public procurement is intended to afford equality of opportunity to all tenderers, regardless of their nationality.[31] As a result, the principle of equal treatment is applicable to public service concessions even in the absence of discrimination on grounds of nationality. The principles of equal treatment and nondiscrimination on grounds of nationality imply, in particular, a duty of transparency which enables the concession-granting public authority to ensure that those principles are complied with and that a sufficient degree of competition for the award of the service concession is maintained. Finally, the transparency obligation ensures the imperative of reviewing the impartiality of procurement procedures.[32]

Recourse to Article 86(1) EC [Article 106(1) TFEU] does not alter the requirement of contracting authorities to comply with the principle of transparency for service concessions, as the granting of special or exclusive rights by Member States must not contravene the Treaty rules on equal treatment and the competition provisions.[33]

The essence of the definition of public service concessions under the public procurement Directives is that a service concession is a contract which meets the definition of a service contract except for the fact that the consideration for the provision of services consists either solely in the right to exploit the service or in that right together with payment. That corresponds to the Court's criterion of remuneration which comes not from the public authority concerned, but from sums paid by third parties. However, in addition, the Court has stressed that an essential feature of a public service concession is that the concession holder assumes the risk of operating the services in question.[34]

The Court has given some further guidance on what kind and degree of transfer of risk is required for a contract to be categorised as a service concession. In *Eurawasser*[35], it ruled that in relation to a contract for the supply of services, the fact that the supplier does not receive consideration directly from the contracting authority, but is entitled to collect payment under private law from third parties, is sufficient for that contract to be viewed as a service concession, where the service provider assumes all, or at least a significant share of the operating risk faced by the contracting authority, even if that risk appears limited.

The Court thus took the view that what matters is not that the operating risk should be significant in itself but that whatever risk is already assumed by the contracting authority should be transferred, either fully or to a significant extent, to the successful service provider. In *Eurawasser*, the Court expressly considered the fact that the limitation of the risk relevant to the contract derived from public regulations (common in the utilities sector) which were, on the one hand, beyond the control of the contracting authority and, on the other hand, such as to reduce the likelihood of any adverse effect on transparency or competition.

VERTICAL CONTRACTS

A functional approach to the concept of contracting authority under the public procurement Directives[36] might imply that the public procurement rules do not apply to a contracting authority which is a prospective supplier to another contracting authority. If a contracting authority, while trading as a supplier, subcontracts certain services to a third party, the selection of that subcontractor may well be based on noneconomic considerations, and it is also quite possible that, at some stage in the process, public funds will be used.[37] The fact that the matter of the subcontracting does not fall within the remits of the activities of the contracting authority[38] and might be also subject to competition[39] is immaterial.

Mannesmann Anlagenbau Austria[40]made no distinction between public contracts awarded by a contracting authority for the purposes of fulfilling its task of meeting needs in the general interest, and those which are unrelated to that task. It is immaterial that the activity in question may be unrelated to the body's task in the general interest, or may not involve any public funds. Where, under the terms of the public procurement Directives, a body ranks as a contracting authority, the Directives require the conduct of award procedures. Accordingly that rule applies even where the contracting authority itself is trading as a supplier on the market, and subcontracting certain parts of a contract to a third party. It is, after all, entirely possible that noneconomic considerations might be involved in the selection of a subcontractor, just as it is possible that public funds might be used in the course of the operation.

Contracting authorities are free to set up legally independent entities if they wish to offer services to third parties under normal market conditions. If such entities aim to make profit, bear the losses related to the exercise of their activities, and perform no public tasks, they are not to be classified as public bodies and hence not as contracting authorities for the purposes of the public procurement Directives. Their activities will therefore not be subject to the provisions of the public procurement Directives. A body which aims to make a profit and bears the losses associated with the exercise of its activity will not normally become involved in an award procedure on conditions which are not economically justified.[41]

It could be argued that the public procurement Directives do not require 'tenders within tenders'. The utilities Directive excludes contracts awarded

for the purposes of resale or hire to third parties from the scope of that
Directive by virtue of the fact that the purchase of the goods occurs in principle in a context of free competition, and the ensuing commercial discipline
prevents a contracting authority from favouring particular tenderers on noneconomic grounds. However, this provision cannot be applied by analogy
to supplies, works or services public procurement contracts, as the relevant
provisions stipulated in the public supplies, works and services Directives
respectively establish a dividing line between their regimes and the regime of
the utilities Directive[42] and do not extend the possibility of vertical procurement to contracting authorities in the public sector.[43]

SUBCONTRACTING

A provision in an invitation to tender which prohibits recourse to subcontracting for material parts of the contract is contrary to the public
procurement Directives.[44] On the contrary, all Directives envisage the possibility for a tenderer to subcontract a part of the contract to third parties,
as that provision states that the contracting authority may ask that tenderer
to indicate in its tender any share of the contract which it may intend to subcontract.[45] Furthermore, with regard to the qualitative selection criteria, all
public procurement Directives make express provision for the possibility of
providing evidence of the technical capacity of the service provider by means
of an indication of the technicians or technical bodies involved, whether or
not belonging directly to the undertaking of that service provider, and which
the latter will have available to it, or by indicating the proportion of the
contract which the service provider may intend to subcontract.

The Court ruled[46] that a tenderer cannot be eliminated from a procedure for the award of a public service contract solely on the ground that
that party proposes, in order to carry out the contract, to use resources
which are not its own but belong to one or more other entities. This means
that it is permissible for a service provider which does not itself fulfil the
minimum conditions required for participation in the procedure for the
award of a public service contract to rely, vis-à-vis the contracting authority, on the standing of third parties upon whose resources it proposes to
draw if it is awarded the contract. However, according to the Court, the
onus rests on a service provider which relies on the resources of entities or
undertakings with which it is directly or indirectly linked, with a view to
being admitted to participate in a tendering procedure, to establish that it
actually has available to it the resources of those entities or undertakings
which it does not itself own and which are necessary for the performance
of the contract.[47]

Nevertheless, the public procurement Directives do not preclude a prohibition or a restriction on the use of subcontracting for the performance
of essential parts of the contract precisely in the case where the contracting

authority has not been in a position to verify the technical and economic capacities of the subcontractors when examining the tenders.[48]

INTERADMINISTRATIVE AGREEMENTS AS PUBLIC CONTRACTS

In *Commission v. Spain*[49], national law excluded from its scope co-operation agreements concluded either between the general state administration and the Social Security, autonomous communities, local bodies, their autonomous bodies and any other public body, or between public bodies themselves. The Court held that exclusion of agreements between legally distinctive contracting authorities from the public procurement rules is incompatible with the public procurement rules and that interadministrative agreements are public contracts.

IN-HOUSE CONTRACTS

The test of *dependency*[50] applied by the Court in *Teckal*[51] reveals two distinctive features which provide for the establishment of in-house contracts. First, the similarity of control of an undertaking to that exercised by contracting authorities over their own departments and secondly, the operational connection of the undertaking's activities to the remit of the contracting authority exercising similar control over it.

SIMILARITY OF CONTROL

Teckal[52] inserted flexibility in determining the concept of contracting authorities and established the nonapplicability of the procurement rules to in-house relations. The first criterion of *Teckal* is present when *control similar to that which the contracting entity exercises over one of its own departments* is evident. The notion of control and the *similarity* requirement merit a comprehensive approach which should solely be based neither on company law features nor on the level of the contracting authority's shareholding. Normally, corporate control indicates decisive influence over management actions, operational and strategic decisions in a similar manner to the concept of majority shareholder control found in company laws of Member States. Nevertheless, any appraisal of the legal position of a majority shareholder in order to assert control must be taken in conjunction with the statutes governing the relevant entity over which the control is exercised and not by sole reference to national company law provisions, as often minority shareholdings provide for rights of decisive influence, such as specific oversight and blocking rights.

The notion of control for the purposes of in-house contracts, as developed by the Court, entails much more than the ingredients of 'dominant influence' as a company law notion, or as a public procurement notion which defines certain bodies as contracting authorities. In particular, control is extended beyond the 'dominant influence' notion found in Utilities Directive.[53] A public undertaking is any undertaking over which the contracting authorities may exercise directly or indirectly a dominant influence by virtue of their ownership of it, their financial participation therein, or the rules which govern it. Contracting authorities exercise dominant influence upon public undertakings when directly or indirectly, in relation to an undertaking, they hold the majority of the undertaking's subscribed capital, or control the majority of the votes attaching to shares issued by the undertaking, or can appoint more than half of the undertaking's administrative, management or supervisory body. For the purposes of in-house relations, the object of such control should not be confined to strategic market decisions or procurement decisions, but should embrace individual management and operational decisions as well. Corporate control is exercised by conclusive influence on both strategic objectives and significant decisions.

In *Parking Brixen*[54], the Court stated that the important point in relation to the control criterion is that there should be 'a potential power of decisive influence over both strategic objectives and significant decisions'. With respect to the means of control, the ability to possess rights to give instructions and rights to make appointments, as well as evidence of supervisory powers, reflect upon a guiding principle which is *de facto* conclusive of the power to influence corporate behaviour and is not emanating from legislative provisions alone.

In *Carbotermo*[55], it was maintained that joint-stock public companies exhibit similarity of control where a contracting authority holds, alone or together with other public authorities, all of the share capital in an entity. However, if the board of management of that entity is vested with the broadest possible powers and in the absence of any control or specific voting powers for restricting the board's freedom of action, the similarity of control is not present. If control exercised by a contracting authority over an entity could be viewed as consisting essentially of the majority shareholders' rights conferred by company law, such control cannot be deemed as similar to that exercised upon the contracting authority's own departments. Moreover, if control is exercised through an intermediary, such as a holding company, the intervention of such an intermediary may render the similarity of control requirement irrelevant or it may weaken any control exercised by the contracting authority over a joint-stock company merely because it holds shares in that company.

Nevertheless, if an entity is jointly controlled by several contracting authorities, the control criterion is satisfied provided the all contracting authorities exhibit control over the relevant entity which is similar to that over their own departments.[56] In such situations, as in the case of inter-municipal co-operative societies whose members are contracting authorities themselves, if joint control is exercised by the majority of controlling contracting authorities, the similarity of control criterion is met.[57]

Therefore, the concept of control must be understood in functional and not in formal terms. There is nothing to prevent it being applied to the relationship between a contracting authority and legal persons governed by private law, such as a limited liability company. The use of the term *departments* derives from the original reason for setting up autonomous bodies, which was to entrust particular departments with a function or the delivery of a specific public service. The control exercised over an entity or an undertaking by a public authority must be similar to that which the authority exercises over its own departments, but not identical in every respect and must be effective, but it is not essential that it be exercised individually.[58]

However, the existence of private capital participating in an entity which has corporate links with a contracting authority negates the similarity of control requirement. *Stadt Halle*[59] held that private sector participation cannot emulate the pursuit of public interest objectives entrusted to public sector entities. The relationship between a public authority which is a contracting authority and its own departments is governed by considerations and requirements proper to the pursuit of objectives in the public interest. Any private capital investment in an undertaking follows considerations appropriate to private interests and pursues objectives of a different kind.[60] The participation, even as a minority, of a private undertaking in the capital of a company in which the awarding public authority is also a participant excludes in any event the possibility of that public authority exercising over such a company a control similar to that which it exercises over its own departments.[61]

The category of semipublic entities or undertakings, which in their own right are regarded as contracting authorities, could not be viewed as entities upon which a contracting authority can exercise similar control to that over its own departments. The Court in *Mödling*[62] followed the *Stadt Halle* reasoning and interestingly held that if the award of an in-house public contract took place in accordance with the *Teckal* criteria, but within a very short period the controlling contracting authority transferred shares in the controlled entity to a private undertaking, this is tantamount to a device designed to conceal the award of public service contracts to semipublic companies and as a result it would prejudice the effectiveness and the principles of the public procurement Directives.

Parking Brixen prevents similarity of control in situations where there is visibility of imminent participation of private capital in a wholly owned public undertaking or entity. Interestingly, although *ANAV*[63] extends the *Teckal* criteria to companies limited by shares, it appears to link prospective privatisations as a ground for not meeting the *Teckal* exception. The Court held that if, for the duration of a contract, the capital of the controlled entity which has been awarded that contract based on the *Teckal* in-house criteria is open to private shareholders, the effect of such a situation would be the award of a public contract to a semipublic company without any call for competition, which would interfere with the objectives pursued by the procurement Directives and the principles of Community law.[64]

The combination of inferences found in *Parking Brixen* and *ANAV* should be viewed as defence mechanisms in order to prevent abuse of the *Teckal* exception, even when at the time of the award of an in-house public contract there is no private sector participation in the capital of the controlled entity. One could question that logic, as the Court reflected on situations where it invited national courts to pay consideration to future privatisation exercises or opening up wholly owned public undertakings' capital to private investors, dictated by either law or regulation or selected as policy choices by the contracting authority. Emphasis was drawn upon the concept of institutional public-private partnerships, where contracting authorities entrust the delivery of public services. Additionally, prospective privatisations could cause problems with the actual contractual arrangements, if *ANAV* is to apply to in-house relations, when a contract is well into its delivery.

Sea[65] appears to correct the potential problems deriving from *AVAV*. As a general rule, the existence of a private holding in the capital of the company to which a public contract is awarded must be determined at the time of that award.[66] Account should be taken in cases when national applicable legislation provides for the compulsory opening of that company whose entire capital it holds, in the short term, to other capital.[67]

However, when shares in the contracting entity which were previously wholly owned by the contracting authority, are transferred to a private undertaking shortly after the award of a contract to that undertaking, the in-house exemption is not possible[68] because the transfer is viewed as an artificial device to circumvent public procurement rules. Nevertheless, shares in a public company could be sold at any time to third parties. It would be inconsistent with the principle of legal certainty not to apply the in-house exemption on the mere possibility that the capital structure of a publicly controlled company might change in the future.

If a company's capital is wholly owned by the contracting authority, alone or together with other public authorities, when the contract in question is awarded to that company, the potential opening of the company's capital to private investors may not be taken into consideration unless there exists, at that time, a real prospect in the short term of such an opening. Therefore, when the capital of the contracting company is wholly public and in which there is no actual sign of any impending opening of that company's capital to private shareholders, the mere fact that private undertakings, at some point in time, may hold capital in that company could not support the conclusion that the condition relating to the control by the public authority over that company is not present. That conclusion is not contradictory to *Coname*[69] which indicated that the fact that a company is open to private capital prevents it from being regarded as a structure for the 'in-house' management of a public service on behalf of the municipalities which form part of it. In that case, a public service was awarded to a company in which not all, but most, of the capital was public, and so mixed, at the time of that award.

Sea made the situation clear when a contract were to be awarded, without being put out to competitive tender, to a public capital company, the fact that subsequently, but still during the period for which that contract was valid, private shareholders were permitted to hold capital in that company would constitute alteration of a fundamental condition of the contract. This scenario would not regard the contract as an in-house arrangement and it would require the full applicability of the public procurement Directives.

OPERATIONAL DEPENDENCY AND CONTRACTING AUTHORITIES

The *Teckal* second criterion specifies that an essential part of the controlled entity's activities must be carried out for the benefit of the controlling contracting authority or authorities. *Sea* held that the control exercised over that company by the shareholder authorities may be regarded as similar to that which they exercise over their own departments when that company's activity is limited to the territory of those authorities and is carried on essentially for their benefit. The Court maintained in *Parking Brixen* that the essential part of the controlled entities' activities cannot be carried out for the benefit of the controlling public authority, if the geographical area of whose activities has been extended to the entire country and abroad.

The 'essential part' criterion relates to a certain minimum proportion of the total activities performed by the controlled body. However, not only quantitative elements must be taken into account in determining the term *essential*. While it could be convenient to define the essential part criterion in line with a provision governing awards to undertakings affiliated with the contracting authority, namely the 80 per cent criterion, such approach has been rejected by the Court on grounds that a transposition of an exceptional provision from the Utilities Directive to the Public Sector Directive is of questionable *vires*. *Carbotermo*[70] revealed interesting insights on operational dependency. The Court declared that the 80 per cent rule of affiliated operational dependency cannot be imported into the public sector procurement for the reasons of that provision is being regarded as a restrictively interpreted exception applicable only to supply contracts, covering affiliated undertakings which are distinctively different than public sector procurement entities, being subject to a procedural notification regime which cannot be implemented in public sector procurement Directives and finally being explicitly ignored by the Community legislature during the 2004 reform of the public procurement Directives from incorporation into the Public Sector Directive 2004/18.

So, although an 'essential part' indicates a quantitative measure in relation to turnover or financial quantum of the volume of activities performed by the controlled entity, qualitative factors such as strategic services, organisational planning, market analysis, the profitability of the entity in pursuit of the activities for the controlling authority and also the market dynamics under which the controlled entity operates should be taken into account. *Carbotermo* also ruled that to determine whether an undertaking carries out the essential part of its activities with the controlling authority account must be taken of all the activities which that undertaking carries out on the basis of an award made by the contracting authority, regardless of who pays for those activities, and irrespective of being the contracting authority itself or the user of the services provided. The Court reiterated that the territory where the activities are carried out is highly relevant for determining the essential part feature of the *Teckal* exception. If the public authority which receives an essential part of an entity's activities controls that entity through another company, the control criterion is still present, provided that control is demonstrable at all levels of the contracting authority's corporate interface, being intermediate or indirect shareholding levels.

PUBLIC CO-OPERATION CONTRACTS

A public authority has the discretion of performing the public interest tasks conferred on it by using its own administrative, technical and other resources, without being obliged to call on outside entities not forming part of its own departments.[71] That possibility for public authorities to use their own resources to perform the public interest tasks conferred on them may be exercised in co-operation with other public authorities.[72] *Commission v. Germany*[73] provided a superb demonstration of flexibility in the hands of contracting authorities in relation to their freedom to organise and deliver public services. Co-operation between independent contracting authorities in the form of establishing an entity upon which no similar control is exercised to that over their own departments, resulting in the entrustment of a contract on behalf of the participant contracting authorities, can be deemed to meet the criteria for an in-house exception, provided the remit of such public co-operation exists in relation to a public task or service specified under Community law and there is no intention to circumvent public procurement rules and the contractual relation is not based on any pecuniary interest consideration nor any payments between the entity and the participant contracting authorities is materialised. The Court used an analogy with *Coditel Brabant*[74] where contractual relations between intermunicipal co-operative societies whose members are contracting authorities and a jointly controlled entity can be deemed in-house.

4 The Origins and Evolution of Public-Private Partnerships as a Global Phenomenon

The modern states across the world are obliged to provide a range of services to the public in the form of general infrastructure, health care, education, housing, transport, energy, defence, social security, policing.[1] Traditionally, the state either in its own capacity or through delegated monopolies and publicly controlled enterprises has engaged in market activities in order to serve public interest.[2]

The concept of the state encapsulates an entrepreneurial dimension to the extent that it deploys wealth as policy instrument (*dominium*).[3] However, although entering into transactions with a view to providing goods, services and works to the public, this type of action by the state does not resemble the commercial characteristics of entrepreneurship, inasmuch as the aim of the state's activities is not the maximisation of profits[4] but the observance of public interest.[5]

Such participation by the state in the relevant market takes place on behalf of the public and the society as a whole[6], and the whole process has been described as *corporatism*.[7] In fact, *corporatism* has been seen as a market phenomenon which has created a specific forum for the supply and demand sides. This forum is known as *public markets*.[8] Public markets, in contrast to private ones, are the forum where *public interest*[9] substitutes *profit maximisation*.[10] *Corporatism* has also revealed the dimension of the state as a service provider to the public and that notion has always been linked with the procurement and subsequent state-ownership of the relevant assets. As a process of public sector management, corporatism has primarily been delivered through competitive tendering in order to satisfy the needs for accountability and transparency. Alongside the above objectives, competitive tendering has also represented a procedural delivery system for corporatism which has aimed, at least in principle, at introducing a balanced equilibrium in the supply/demand public procurement equation.[11] Thus, the public and private sectors transact through an institutionalised structure which aims at replicating a regime of competition similar to that which exists in private markets.[12] Private markets are generally structured as a result of competitive pressures originating in the buyer/supplier interaction and their configuration can vary from monopoly/oligopoly to perfect competition, whereas public markets reveal a different picture, their structure being based upon a monopsony/oligopsony character.

Due to their different integral nature and structure, private and public markets require different control and regulation. Whereas the weaponry for the control of private markets is dominated by antitrust law and policy, public markets are market places where the structural and behavioural remedial tools of competition law have limited applicability, mainly due to the fact that antitrust often clashes with the monopolistic structures which exist in public markets. The control of private markets through antitrust law and policy reveal a set of rules of negative nature; contemporary antitrust is ill-disposed towards cartels and abuse of dominance, thus undertakings must restrict their activities to an acceptable range which is predetermined[13] by the competent authorities. On the other hand, public markets require a set of regulatory rules that have positive character and the sort of regulation envisaged aims at creating an appropriate environment which would facilitate *market access*.[14]

Irrespective of the different control and regulation private and public markets require, as a result of the difference in their integral nature and structure, the rationale behind the process of regulating public markets can be summarised as the attempt to establish an effectively competitive regime, similar to that envisaged for the operation of private markets.[15] The accomplishment of such objective could bring about two types of beneficial effects for the supply/demand equation and enhance the image of corporatism. On the one hand, competition in public markets could benefit the supply side of the equation (the industry), by means of optimal allocation of resources, rationalisation of production and supply, promotion of mergers and acquisitions and elimination of suboptimal firms and creation of genuinely competitive industries. On the other hand, corporatism operating through a genuinely competitive regime has been also deemed to yield substantial purchasing savings for the public sector.[16]

FROM CORPORATISM TO CONTRACTUALISED GOVERNANCE

Governments across the world have defended their choice to provide 'core' activities such as education, health care and correctional services on the grounds of the inability of markets to step in as a credible forum for the organisation and delivery of such activities in pursuit of public interest.[17] The routine and habit of seeing the state as the only credible organiser and deliverer of public services were eroded by questions over the lack of strategic vision of states to offer value-for-money solutions and by a growing belief that the state, due to universally experienced fiscal constraints, should adopt an enabling capacity in the delivery of public services.[18]

The enabling role of the state in delivering public services implies that the delivery of many services being transferred to the private sector, where the government continues to regulate and fund these services. The enabling relationship in public service delivery necessitates a surrender of at least partial control from the government to the private sector with two possible outcomes in relation to governance.[19] On the one hand, the private sector delivery could result in compromising pre-established public values; on the other hand, public values may be enhanced by the involvement of private actors and the participation of other stakeholders such as non-for-profit organisations in the delivery of public services.

A transition from the model of corporatism towards the model of contractualised governance emerged through the process of privatisation[20] which often runs in parallel with the phenomenon of contracting out.[21]

Privatisation reflects situations when the government sells assets or controlling interest in a service to the private sector.[22] This process often is augmented by regulation as an instrument to protect the public interest, as a result of asset transfer or relinquish of control. Privatisation is initiated as both an ideological stance of government organisation and also as a pragmatic response to current expectations in relation to standards of public service, contracted with falling revenue and fiscal constraints.[23]

A first departing step from corporatism towards government by contract appears to be the process of privatisation. Privatisation is a process whereby a reduction of the role of government or a sizable increase of the role of the private sector in the delivery of public services occurs. A view of privatisation as an exercise of reducing state responsibilities has found proponents within neoliberal economics, where the role of the government is reduced to maintaining a bare minimum of the welfare state. Conversely, privatisation has been seen as an instrument of effective governance where government intervention in delivering public services is channeled through market regulation and the private sector is seen as provider of investment and risk capital.[24]

Privatisation, as a process of transfer of public assets and operations to private hands, on grounds of market efficiency and competition, as well as responsiveness to customer demand and quality considerations is often accompanied by simultaneous regulation by the state, in the form of a legal framework within which privatised industries will pursue public interest functions. It is not entirely clear that the process of privatisation would reclaim public markets and transform them to private ones. One should never underestimate the fact that the control of operations related to public interest remains within the competence of the state in the form of the regulatory regime, thus maintaining strong public market characteristics. The extent to which the market freedom of a privatised entity could be curtailed by regulatory frameworks deserves a complex and thorough analysis, which exceeds by far the remit of this chapter. However, it could be maintained that through the privatisation process, the previously clear-cut distinction between public and private markets becomes blurred, as a new market place emerges.[25] This type of market embraces strong public law elements to the extent that it is regulated by the state with a view to observing public interest in the relevant operations. The economic freedom and the risks associated with such operations are also subject to regulation, a fact which implies that the above regulatory framework incorporates more than mere procedural rules. This market place reveals a transformation from traditional *corporatism* to a public management system where *governance is dispersed through contract* under terms and conditions determined by the state.

On the other hand, contracting out resembles the characteristics of outsourcing, is a quasi-privatised delivery of public services in that the government engages contractually with the private sector, although it retains control and accountability for the delivery of the relevant public service. Contracting out hybrids such as franchises and service or management licences focus on essential public services such as transport or facilities maintenance of public assets. The notion of *contracting out* represents a further departure from the premises of traditional corporatism. The notion of *contracting out* is an exercise which aims at achieving potential savings and efficiency gains for contracting authorities, when they *test the market* in an attempt to define whether the provision of works or the delivery of services from a commercial operator could be cheaper than that from the in-house team. Contracting out differs from privatisation to the extent that the former represents a transfer of undertaking only, whereas the latter denotes transfer of ownership. Contracting out depicts a price-discipline exercise by the state, against the principle of *insourcing*, where, the self-sufficient nature of corporatism resulted in budgetary inefficiencies and poor quality of deliverables to the public. Contracting out uses competitive tendering, which is the procedural mechanism for the delivery of corporatism as the Trojan horse in an attempt to maximise outsourcing in the delivery of public service.

Both the privatisation process and the contracting out phenomenon have prepared the ground for a more sophisticated form of contractualised governance, namely the public-private partnerships.[26] The partnership terminology implies, at least in theory, that government enters into a formal arrangement by creating an independent entity with a view to providing and delivering public services in partnership with the private sector where each partner contributes human and capital resources accordingly and shares the risks and benefits arising out of such arrangement.[1]

The choice among privatisation, contracting out and public-private partnerships solutions in delivering public services, in contrast to their direct delivery by the state, rests on the government's preferences regarding financing the provision of such public services and residual control in the delivery of such services respectively.[27] The phenomenon of contracting out is surrogate to direct delivery of public services due to the amount of residual control and accountability retained by the public sector. Contrarily, public-private partnerships tend to resemble the privatisation process[28], as control and often accountability migrates from the state towards new formats of governance.[29] Such migration of control and accountability from the government necessitates the design of a public policy which is conducive to new formats of governance.[30]

Contracting out is primarily viewed as a cost savings and service improvement exercise, whereas a partnership between public and private sectors includes the above attributes but also requires the private sector involvement to include private sector financing and the assumption of some degree of private ownership over assets relevant to the delivery of public services.[31]

Governments will have recourse to contracting out and partnerships to improve public service delivery by harnessing private sector expertise and efficiencies and by allocating risks and responsibilities between the public and private sector to the party best able to manage them.[32] The ultimate objective is an optimum equilibrium between private sector efficiency and societal welfare.[33]

Both the privatisation and contracting out processes resemble the *principle of outsourcing*[34] which is often utilised in restructuring exercises in the private sector. Outsourcing introduces elements of contractualisation in the production process, as subcontracting takes over from the in-house operation in the production chain. Government by contract, along the same lines, introduces the principle of outsourcing in the dispersement of public service, but the *contractualised governance*[35] appears far more stringent than private sector outsourcing by virtue of its regulation. Furthermore, apart from operational savings, outsourcing in the private sector would normally spread the risk factor amongst the operations in the production chain.[36] If the subcontractor could not deliver according to the expectations, the main operator could switch to an alternative with no major implications. Outsourcing, therefore, introduces an element of flexibility in the production process. It remains to be seen whether contractualised governance or government by contract conforms to the same parameters (savings, risk sharing, flexibility) as private sector outsourcing.

The integral characteristics of privately financed projects reveal the degree that the state and its organs are prepared to drift away from *traditional corporatism*[37] towards *contractualised governance*.[38] The degree of departure from traditional corporatism also reflects the state's perception vis-à-vis its responsibilities towards the public.[39] A shift towards contractualised governance would indicate the departure from the assumption that the state embraces both roles of asset owner and service deliverer.[40] It should also insinuate the shrinkage of the state and its organs and the need to define a range of core activities that are not to be contractualised.[41]

The United Nations has embraced the values and potential of public private partnerships, defining the concept as: 'Innovative methods used by the public sector to contract with the private sector, who bring their capital and their ability to deliver projects on time and to budget, while the public sector retains the responsibility to provide these services to the public in a way that benefits the public and delivers economic development and an improvement in the quality of life'.[42]

The UN devised a blueprint to close the gap between the poorest countries and industrialised nations in the UN Millennium Declaration, committing its members to a new global partnership and emphasising the potential of public-private partnerships in achieving the realisation of the United Nations Millennium Development Goals.[43]

One of the most sophisticated public-private partnerships initiatives has been developed in the United Kingdom[44] which delivers approximately about 24 per cent of public investment mostly in infrastructure.[45] Many continental European Union states, including Ireland, Sweden, Finland, Germany, Greece, Italy, the Netherlands, Portugal and Spain, have developed legal and policy frameworks to deliver public-private partnership projects, although their share in total public investment is between 5 and 15 per cent. Reflecting a need for infrastructure investment on a large scale, and weak fiscal positions, a number of countries in Central and Eastern Europe, including the Czech Republic, Hungary and Poland, have embarked on public-private partnerships.[46]

Other countries in the world with significant public-private partnership programs include Canada, Japan and Australia, in particular the state of Victoria.[47] Public-private partnerships in most of the above countries focus on road infrastructure projects, while the United States has considerable experience with leasing programs in the delivery of public services.[48] Mexico and Chile have pioneered the use of public-private partnerships to promote private sector participation in public investment projects in South America. In Mexico, public-private partnerships were first used in the 1980s to finance highways and, since the mid-1990s, a growing number of public investment projects in the energy sector. There are plans to extend the use of public-private partnerships to the provision of other public services. Chile has a well-established public-private partnership program that has been used for the development of transport, airports, prisons and irrigation. Brazil is planning significant use of public-private partnerships and there is also a regional approach to infrastructure development across the countries in South America. Public-private partnerships have also emerged in Asia, especially in India, Korea and Singapore, and there is strong interest in public-private partnerships in South Africa.[49]

In Canada over 157 public-private partnership projects covering fields such as communication, environment, government services, defence, justice and correction, recreation and culture, energy, education, real estate and transportation, Canada has an extensive and well-developed public-private partnership programme when compared with most countries of the EU. The Canadian Council for Public-Private Partnerships was established in 1993 as a member-sponsored organisation with representatives from both the public and the private sectors. As proponents of the concept of public-private partnerships, the Council conducts research, publishes findings, facilitates forums for discussion and sponsors an Annual Conference on topics related to public-private partnerships, both domestic and international. The Council influences the way public services are financed and delivered in Canada by providing information on public-private partnerships, sponsoring conferences and seminars on partnerships, conducting objective research on key issues that influence the effective use of partnerships, amongst others.[50] The United States has been using public-private partnerships for the delivery of public services long before most countries became aware of it. It has covered many areas such as transportation, energy, water/wastewater, technology, prisons, health, welfare, urban development, financial management, schools and many more. The U.S. Department of Transportation, Federal Highway Administration (FHWA) on Public Private Partnership provides resources, legislation, case studies, past, present and future developments on public-private partnerships.[51] The National Council for Public Private Partnerships (NCPPP) is a nonprofit organisation in the United States for public-private partnerships, and is dedicated to advocating and facilitating the formation of public-private partnerships at the federal, state and local levels, where appropriate and to raise the awareness of governments and businesses of the means by which their cooperation can cost effectively provide the public with quality goods, services and facilities. Membership of the Council includes organisation in both the public and private sectors, with interests in a wide range of areas appropriate for public-private partnerships.[52] Australia is yet another country that has an extensive public-private partnership programme, especially the State of Victoria. One of Australia's most substantial public-private partnership programmes is the Cooperative Research Centres (CRC) Program. It was launched in early 1990 and has been in operation for about twelve years.[53] Public Private Partnerships are vital to the development of social and economic infrastructure in Australia. The National Public Private Partnership (NPPP) Forum was established in 2004 by the Australian government. The forum provides information about projects that are being delivered, are in the process of being procured, or that governments have identified as potential candidates for Public Private Partnerships within Australia. The Forum brings together representatives from each of the Australian, state and territory governments and aims to facilitate greater consistency and co-operation across Australian regional jurisdictions in the provision of infrastructure through public-private partnerships.[54] Other institutional resources on public-private partnerships in Australia are Infrastructure Australia and Partnership Victoria. Infrastructure Australia was established in 2008. It is an independent statutory advisory council with twelve members drawn from industry and all levels of government, including five from the private sector. Partnership Victoria was introduced in 2000, and it provides the framework for government approach to the provision of public infrastructure and related ancillary services through public-private partnerships. Partnership Victoria aims to use the innovation, skills and abilities of the private sector in a way that is most likely to deliver value for money and improved services to the community. It is most useful for major and complex capital projects with opportunities for innovation and risk transfer. There are twenty-one Partnerships Victoria projects in existence worth approximately $10.5 billion in capital investment.[55] It also provides up-to-date information on past, present and future public-private partnership projects in the State of Victoria.

Public-Private Partnerships in Developing Countries

The delivery of infrastructure projects is viewed as essential for the economic growth of developing countries as it encourages economic growth and international competitiveness and also contributes towards the achievement of United Nations Millennium Development Goals (MDGs).[56] Almost all developing countries have undertaken a form of public-private partnerships in providing public services and infrastructure since the early 1990s. However, some countries and sectors have been much more prominent than others. Private investors in infrastructure have tended to favour developing and transition economies with relatively large and fast-growing markets which account for almost 90 per cent of total public-private partnership investment in the developing world.[57]

The primary reason that developing countries have recourse to public-private partnerships is to foster inward foreign investment. Private sector participation in infrastructure has high concentration in areas such as telecommunications, energy, transport, water and water sewage projects, privatisation, management and lease contracts, divestitures or concessions.[58] Based on the World Bank Private Participation in Infrastructure (PPI) Project database which covers public-private partnership projects in developing countries in four main infrastructure sectors: energy (electricity generation, transmission and distribution; and natural gas transmission and distribution); telecommunications (fixed or mobile local telephony, domestic long-distance telephony and international long-distance telephony); transport (airport runways and terminals; railway fixed assets, freight and intercity and local passenger service; toll roads, bridges, highways and tunnels; and seaport channel dredging and terminals); and water (potable water generation and distribution, as well as sewage collection and treatment), most private sector participation in the delivery of infrastructure in terms of number and value of projects has been concentrated in the Latin America and Caribbean regions, with 36 per cent and 44.4 per cent, respectively. The Middle East, North Africa, South Asia and Sub-Sahara Africa countries, although representing 50 per cent of the developing countries, have not benefited significantly from PPPs.[59]

THE CHARACTERISTICS OF PUBLIC–PRIVATE PARTNERSHIPS

Public-private partnerships have been utilised as a credible solution to bridge the infrastructure deficit of many states in both the developed and developing world. Public-private partnerships can provide a number of specific benefits to the public sector. In particular, they can offer value-for-money solutions, where the public-private partnership can attain lower costs, higher levels of service through innovation, and reduced risk for the public sector. One of the most significant attributes of public-private partnerships is the increased certainty of outcomes both in terms of on-time delivery of projects (the private partner is strongly motivated to complete the project as early as possible to control its costs and so that the payment stream can commence) and in terms of within-budget delivery of projects (the payment scheduled is fixed before construction commences, protecting the public from exposure to cost overruns).

Public-private partnerships possess some distinctive characteristics, when compared with traditional public-private contractual formats. These characteristics reveal a different ethos in public sector management. The pivotal characteristic is that the private sector partner is expected to play a strategic role in financing and delivering the infrastructure project or the public service by providing its input into the various phases such as the design, implementation, construction, completion, operation and maintenance stages of the project. As a result, the duration of the relations between public and private sectors must reflect the need for longevity, in order to allow affordability for repayment on the part of the public sector and also the ability of the private sector to recoup its investment profitably. Another characteristic that complements both the strategic role of the private sector and its long-term engagement in delivering infrastructure and public services is reflected in the distribution of risks between the public and private sectors, and in the expectation that the private sector will assume substantial risks. Risk assessment in public-private partnerships is a totally different exercise than the assessment of risk in traditional public contracts.[60]

A range of different risks feature in public-private partnerships: construction or project risk, which is related to design problems, building cost overruns, and project delays; financial risk, which is related to variability in interest rates, exchange rates and other factors affecting financing costs; performance risk, which is related to the availability of an asset and the continuity and quality of the relevant service provision; demand risk, which is related to the ongoing need for the relevant public services; and residual value risk, which is related to the future market price of an asset.[61] Finally, political risks cover a general term used to describe risks arising from external or internal factors that are determined or influenced by governments. External political risks, such as currency convertibility, war, sanctions and political instability may be avoided, mitigated, hedged or insured against and could be significantly mitigated by actions of the state within which the public-private partnership is structured. On the other hand, internal political risks, such as taxation, terrorism, inflation and industrial unrest are usually uninsurable and could affect the risk allocation within public-private partnerships. Their respective mitigation would potentially reflect on the perceptions of the parties to manage such risks.

Another essential dynamic of public-private partnerships is that the private sector provides the financing. Public-private partnership financing is specialised financing which is different from both public finance and corporate finance. The public-private partnership debt financing is regarded as off-balance sheet borrowing, which means that the borrowing does not affect the state's public sector borrowing requirements and any measurements or calculations of measures of its indebtedness. Public-private partnerships allow the public sector to access alternative sources of capital.

Public-private partnerships seek to transfer risk from the public sector to the private sector. Whilst the provision of private capital and the strategic involvement of the private sector partner in managing the delivery of public services could prove beneficial, significant risk transfer from the public to the private sector is necessary to derive a genuine value-for-money partnership. The impact of risk transfer on financing costs and the pricing of risk to ensure efficient risk transfer are crucial in understanding how risk is treated within public-private partnerships.

The cost of capital needed to finance a public-private partnership depends only on the characteristics of project-related risks and not on the source of finance. However, the source of financing can influence project risk depending on the maturity and sophistication of the risk-bearing markets. On the one hand, within advanced risk-bearing markets, it is irrelevant whether project risk is borne by the public sector or the private sector. On the other hand, when risk-bearing markets are less developed, project risk depends on how widely that risk is spread. Since the public sector can spread risk across taxpayers in general, the usual argument is that this gives the public sector an advantage over the private sector in terms of managing risk. Nevertheless, the private sector can spread risk across financial markets. The outcome is likely to be that project risk is lower in the private sector. The public sector's ability to forcibly spread risk across taxpayers, while financial markets have to be provided with an incentive to accept risk, may put the private sector at more of a disadvantage as far as large and risky projects are concerned. The scope for the private sector to spread risk will also be somewhat limited in countries with less developed financial markets.

This outcome might contravene the assumption that private sector borrowing generally costs more than government borrowing. However, this mainly reflects differences in default risk. The public sector's power to tax reduces the likelihood that it will default on its debt, and the private sector is therefore prepared to lend to the public sector at close to the risk-free interest rate to finance risky projects. The crucial issue is whether public-private partnerships result in efficiency gains that offset higher private sector borrowing costs.[62]

Risk transfer from the public sector to the private sector has a significant influence on whether a PPP is a more efficient and cost-effective alternative to public investment and publicly funded provision of services.[63] The public sector and the private sector typically adopt different approaches to pricing market risk. The public sector tends to use the social time preference rate (STPR) or some other risk-free rate to discount future cash flows when appraising projects.[64] The private sector in a public-private partnership project will include a risk premium in the discount rate it applies to future project earnings. Under the widely used capital asset pricing model (CAPM), the expected rate of return on an asset is defined as the risk-free rate of return plus a risk premium, the latter being the product of the market risk premium and a coefficient that measures the variance between the returns on that asset and market returns.

The Economic Environment as Platform for Public-Private Partnerships

Macro and micro conditions affect the development of public-private partnerships in both developed and developing countries. Macro conditions refer to those incentives which can be provided by a government to the private sector to engage in PPP arrangements. While government is motivated by efficiencies and savings in delivering public services through private participation, the private sector is motivated by profit-making, thus the profitability of a public-private partnership project is crucial to attracting private sector partners. Due to the high cost of infrastructure, generating revenues might take a long time, thereby increasing the commercial risk of such projects. Thus, incentives which ameliorate market conditions, such as demand for the services to be provided, the size of the market, low exchange rate risks can be provided for by the government to attract private investors.[65] Factors such as political stability, policy credibility and the existence of sound regulatory framework are necessary to lowering the apparent risk involved in investment in infrastructure and thus for attracting private capital, thereby, boosting macroeconomic variables such as GDP per capita, public investment, private investment and current expenditure commitments.[67] An efficient legal framework is another macroeconomic factor which provides for a significant and critical element of delivering PPPs. The transparency and accountability frameworks in a country are also critical determinants for long-term success of a public-private partnership.[66] On the micro level, there must be an interest and a commitment on the part of the different actors involved at different levels with different interests, to make the public-private partnership work. Each actor must bring to the partnership its skills, commitment, as well as financial capacity, organisational and management structure.

Governance and Regulation of Public-Private Partnerships

The existence of independent regulatory bodies enhances the efficiency of public-private partnerships in developing countries. Infrastructure investment in developing and emerging economies takes place in a very different environment from that of developed countries. This is as a result of the high level of 'institutional risks' in these countries due to their incomplete laws and regulations which are subject to change.[67] Public-private partnerships require a stable legal and regulatory framework to succeed. Where the laws and regulations guiding the ability to make investments and repay debts are subject to change, it creates uncertainty in the investment market. Uncertainty is not attractive to private investors.

There have been many international initiatives to encourage public-private partnerships in developing countries. One of such is the Commonwealth Initiative on public-private partnerships. This initiative seeks to promote public-private partnerships, mainly in infrastructure facilities in Commonwealth developing countries, in general, and postconflict ones in particular. The activities in this area are mainly aimed at bringing private investors to developing countries; raising awareness of member countries of opportunities for, and benefits of, public-private partnerships; enabling member countries to share experiences of public-private partnerships; and building the capacity of government institutions and officials on public-private partnership matters.[68] As a form of encouragement, public-private partnerships in developing and emerging market economies enjoy support by multilateral development agencies such as the World Bank through the Multilateral Investment Guarantee Agency (MIGA) and the International Bank for Reconstruction and Development (IBRD), and the International Finance Corporation (IFC). At the regional level, organisations like Inter-American Development Bank (IADB), European Bank for Reconstruction and Development (ERBD), European Investment Bank (EIB), and Asian Development Bank (ADB) also lend support to public-private partnership projects in their regions.[69]

THE EMERGENCE AND INFLUENCE OF THE PRIVATE FINANCE INITIATIVE UPON PUBLIC-PRIVATE PARTNERSHIPS

The United Kingdom has claimed the intellectual paternity of probably the most prolific program of contractualised governance.[70] It has developed the Public Finance Initiative (PFI), which has been in operation for twenty years and is currently responsible for about 24 per cent of public investment, with projects in most of the key infrastructure areas.[71] The PFI was introduced by the Conservative Government in the early 1990s and expanded rapidly under the Labour Government after 1997. Approximately 700 PFI projects with a capital value of £53 billion have been delivered in the UK, with at least half of the total value covering projects in education, health and defence.[72]

The Private Finance Initiative (PFI) represents a process of public sector management which envisages the utilisation of private finances in the delivery of public services and the provision of public infrastructure.[73] The Private Finance Initiative arrived in times when the role and the responsibilities of the state are being redefined and also has been seen as part of a process of slimming the state down to a bare minimum of fiscal responsibilities towards the public. The state then assumes a regulatory role in the market place where the private sector is elevated to a service deliverer. The principal benefit from such exercise could be that the public sector does not have to commit its own, often scarce, capital resources in delivering public services. Other reasons put forward for involving private finances in delivering public services include quality improvement, innovation, management efficiency and effectiveness, elements that are often underlying the private sector entrepreneurship. Consequently, the public sector would receive value-for-money in the delivery of services to the public, whereas it could also be maintained that through this process the state manages in a better way public finances, to the extent that capital resources could be utilised in priority areas.[74]

When the Private Finance Initiative was launched in 1992, it did not receive the envisaged response from either the public or the private sectors. The initial approach to privately financed projects by the public sector represented a disguised tendering for their financing, and as such it revealed a number of procedural and commercial inadequacies in the whole process. Policy makers incorrectly assumed that the mere private financing of projects could enhance their quality and value-for-money, as well as transform the often ill-fated traditional public procurement process into a supply chain system of advanced structure and entrepreneurial flair. The Private Finance Initiative was wrongfully conceived as a *panacea* for the limitations of the traditional public procurement process[75], which was blamed for inefficiencies and poor value-for-money. A number of reasons which have been put forward include *inter alia* poor specification design, wrong contractual risk allocation, poor control systems for contractual performance and bad planning and delivery processes. Criticism has been also directed towards the Private Finance Projects as expensive and inflexible, realising little risk transfer to the private sector and a way for government to evade public spending rules and fudge national accounts by excluding PFI expenditure liabilities.

In principle, privately financed projects destined for the public sector have been an option in the UK public procurement process since the 1980s, where the government, with great deal of caution, allowed the conclusion of a limited number of contracts. The government applied the so-called Ryrie Rules in the process of allowing private finances to be used in public projects, subject to two strict conditions. The first one concerned the cost-effective nature of the privately financed delivery in comparison with a publicly funded alternative.[76] To reach such a conclusion, contracting authorities should have established a public sector comparator, whereby the privately financed delivery model could be tested and compared against the traditional publicly funded one. The second condition for the government to give clearance for a privately finance project related to the compulsory substitution of publicly funded schemes with the privately funded ones. In other words, private finances were conceived as an exclusive alternative method in delivering public services and not as a complementary one.[77]

Meeting the two conditions of the rules was not an easy exercise for public authorities, particularly in attempting to establish the cost-effective nature of a privately financed project versus a publicly funded alternative and its value-for-money. Quite often the rationale behind such comparisons was founded upon unsound grounds. For example, in order to achieve a meaningful comparison, the two delivery models should be benchmarked against a set of *variable parameters* (e.g., technical merit, quality of deliverables, aesthetic reasons, maintenance facilities, warranties, and last but not least, overall price). This was not always the case, as the specifications of the project were firmly predetermined from the outset by the public authority in question and the pricing of a project evolved around them. Hence, the only *variable parameter* to compare the two delivery models unfolded around pricing. The procurement of privately financed projects was a disguised tendering for their financing, and as such it was bound to have very limited impact upon the procurement process. There was little chance that the private sector could beat the privileged position governments enjoy in the financial markets and raise the capital required to finance a service or an infrastructure project in more preferable terms. Furthermore, the private sector would normally require extra levels of capital return for the deferred payment facility that the public sector would use for repayments during the life of the contract. In the light of the above considerations, it is not a surprise that only a handful of privately financed projects were concluded, particularly complex projects of large scale and of multinational dimension.[78]

Against this background and the restraints on public expenditure, for example, prudence in Public Sector Borrowing Requirement (PSBR), EMU convergence criteria, the Private Finance Initiative was adopted as a key strategy for the 1997 Labour Government. In principle, public authorities in the United Kingdom were required to explore all potential ways of involving private finances in their public procurement process prior to committing their own funds.[79]

There are two broad categories under which privately financed projects can be classified. The first one covers the so-called financially free-standing ones, where it is expected that the private sector designs, builds, finances and then operates an asset. The recovery of its costs is guaranteed by direct charges on the users of the service which the particular asset provides. These projects are often described as *concession contracts*, where the successful contractor is granted an exclusive right over a period of time to exploit the asset that it has financed, designed and built. The state and its authorities may also contribute, in financial terms, to the repayments in order to render the project viable or the service charge to the end users acceptable. The second category of privately financed projects embraces projects which have as their object the provision of services by the private sector to the public, in conjunction with and subject to the relevant investment in assets that are necessary to deliver the required service to the public. In such cases, the private sector provider is reimbursed by a series of future payments by the contracting authority, payments which depend upon the successful delivery of those services in accordance with certain specified quality standards.

Privately financed projects have two constituent elements which are prerequisites for their completion: i) a genuine allocation of contractual risk and ii) value-for-money for the public sector. The first element represents the integral balance of contractual relationships. Under traditional public procurement transactions, a widespread assumption indicates that contractual relationships are based upon a disproportionate risk allocation amongst the parties.[80] Although in traditional public procurement systems, the demand side appears the dominant part in the equation, when it comes to risk allocation, the roles appear reversed.[81] Risk allocation is a much misunderstood concept in contractual relationships in general, but particularly in public purchasing transactions it has never been properly addressed.[82] Risk allocation is the result of negotiations between the parties and is normally expected to reflect the pricing element of contractual arrangements between them. Thus, risk and pricing operate in an analogous relation within a contract. The more risk a party resumes, the higher the price to be paid by the other party, and vice versa.[83]

In traditional public procurement transactions the demand side inevitably undertakes too much risk, as a result of its practices.[84] The award of publicly funded contracts takes place predominately by reference to *the lowest price,* which constitutes one of the two permissible award criteria under the procurement rules (the other being the criterion of *the most economically advantageous offer*). When contracting authorities award their contracts by reference to pricing, this would normally reflect the amount of risk they are prepared to resume.[85]

There is not any golden rule as to what represents an acceptable risk transfer in a contract, the latter being private or public, for risk allocation primarily reflects the parties' perception of a transaction with reference to their own criteria. These criteria are often influenced by a range of parameters such as speculation, fear, certainty, as well as by a number of qualitative attributes of the parties, for example, sound forecast and planning, market intelligence.

On the other hand, value-for-money as the second constituent element of a privately financed project should reflect a benchmarked comparison between public and privately financed models of service delivery. The comparison should not only take into account factors such as quality or technical merit, but mainly aspects of sound supply chain management reflecting efficiency gains, in the sense that the conclusion of a privately financed project would resemble to a large extent a contractual arrangement between private parties. Value-for-money as an element in a PFI deal is a precursor of best purchasing practice by contracting authorities and also reflects the underlying competitive elements which are necessary in order to meet the accountability and transparency standards and principles.[86]

The Intellectual Origins of the Private Finance Initiative

The origins of the Private Finance Initiative could be traced in the attempts to moderate the widespread dissatisfaction from traditional public procurement methods. The nexus of contractual relations between public authorities and the private sector has been often criticised for not giving the best value-for-money.[87] The criticism has been primarily directed towards three elements of the process: i) adversarial contractual relations as a result of compulsory competitive tendering, ii) inefficient risk allocation and iii) poor contractual performances resulting in delayed and overbudgeted completions.[88]

Competitive tendering in public procurement has been reproached for creating a confrontational environment[89], where the antagonising relations which emanate from the tendering and contract award processes are often reflected in the performance stage of the contract. Public procurement procedures which are based upon a win-to-win process have been deemed to deprive significant elements one can expect in the delivery of public services. For example, competitive tendering has been dissociated with innovation and quality. Also, as a result of inefficiently written specifications upon which the tender should be constructed, the deliverables often differ dramatically from contractual expectations.

On the other hand, risk allocation is probably the most crucial element in contractual relations that affects pricing as well as the overall contractual framework. Risk represents the level of financial exposure of a party prior to, after the conclusion of a contract or during its performance. In traditional public procurement, the risk allocation tends to favour the supply side, which mainly assumes the risks related to the tendering process. During the performance stage of the contract and up to its completion, the demand side could, usually, shift a considerable amount of risk by requesting from the supply side performance or defects bonds or other means of financial guarantees.[90]

Finally, traditional procurement methods have often revealed a picture of poor contracts management as a result of inefficient control systems operated by public authorities. Poor contracts management have resulted in abysmally out-of-control contractual performances with all the financial consequences attributed to the delayed completions of the projects.

Competitive tendering, amongst other things, has been deemed responsible for cyclical demand structures in public purchasing, a situation where the supply side (the industry) responds to the demand side (public authorities) through cycles of institutionalised bureaucracy (tender submission, selection, evaluation and contract award processes). The demand side has institutionalised the procurement process, by imposing a disciplinarian compartmentalisation of the relevant processes (advertisement, expression of interest, selection, qualification, tender and contract award).

The institutionalisation of the procurement process intends to facilitate the main objectives of the European public procurement rules: the establishment of the principles of transparency and competitiveness in the award of public contracts and the achievement of savings for the public sector. The bureaucratic system which supports traditional public procurement uses the effects of transparency as leverage for value-for-money results. The fact that more suppliers are aware of a forthcoming public contract and the fact that interesting suppliers are aware that their rivals are informed about it indicates two distinctive parameters which are relevant to savings and value-for-money. The first parameter focusses on value-for-money for the demand side and reveals the possibility for contracting authorities to compare prices and quality. The second parameter has an effect on the supply side of the equation (the suppliers) which amongst other things cannot longer rely on lack of price comparisons when serving the public sector. Openness in public procurement, by definition, results in price competition and the benefits for contracting authorities appear achievable. The institutionalised nature of the public of the procurement process also reflects the relative balance of powers in the demand/supply equation.

However, the traditional public procurement process often suffers from unnecessarily repetitive functions (in particular the advertisement, selection and qualification processes) which can be cost-ineffective and pose a considerable financial burden on the demand side. In addition, the institutionalised process of public procurement may pose a question over long-term savings and value-for-money considerations. Price competition, as a result of the awareness of forthcoming public contracts, represents a rather static effect in the value-for-money process. The fact that more and more interested suppliers are aware and do submit tenders, in the long run, appears rather as a burden. If transparency and the resulting price competitiveness are based on a *win-to-win* process, the potential benefits for contracting authorities could easily be counterbalanced by the administrative costs in tender evaluation and replies to unsuccessful tenders. Furthermore, the risk management factor is much higher in a win-to-win purchasing scenario. Price competitiveness represents also some threats for contracting authorities, to the extent that quality of deliverables as well as the delivery process itself could be jeopardised, if contracting authorities deal with different and unknown contractors. It could thus be argued here that price competitiveness, as a trade effect potentially beneficial for the demand side of the public purchasing equation, has a static character. It seems that it does not take into account medium- or long-term purchasing patterns, as well as counter effects of competition. Two elements deserve further analysis here.

The first raises questions over the aggregate loss of the economy through transparent competitive purchasing patterns. For example, if a large number of interested suppliers submit their offer to a particular contracting authority, two types of costs should be examined. Firstly, the cost which is attributed to the response and tendering stage of the procurement process. Human and capital resources are directed by the suppliers towards the preparation of documents and the submission of the offers. If one of these suppliers wins the contract, the remaining would have suffered an unrecoverable loss. If that aggregate loss exceeds the benefit/saving accomplished by the contracting authority by following transparent and competitive purchasing patterns, value for money has not been achieved. Secondly, along the same lines, the evaluation and selection process during tendering represents a considerable administrative cost for the contracting authorities. If the principle of transparency complements the principle of equal treatment, contracting authorities should give the same attention to all interested suppliers that have submitted a response. Downsizing the list through evaluation and assessment based on stipulated criteria is by no means an inexpensive exercise. Human and capital resources have to be directed by contracting authorities towards meeting that cost. If the latter exceeds the potential savings achieved through the competitive tendering route, then value for money is unaccomplished.

The second element that deserves attention relates to the definition of price competitiveness in public purchasing as well as its interrelation with antitrust law and policy. A question which arises in price competitive tendering patterns is *what would be the lowest offer contracting authorities can accept*. If the maximisation of savings is the only achievable objective in the public procurement process, the transparent/competitive pattern cannot guarantee and evaluate safeguards in relation to underpriced offers. If the supply side responds to the perpetuated competitive purchasing pattern by lowering prices, contracting authorities could face a dilemma: where to stop. It should be mentioned here that the European rules provide for an automatic disqualification of an 'abnormally low offer'. The term has not been interpreted in detail by the judiciary at European and domestic levels and serves rather as a 'lower bottom limit'.[91] Also, when an offer appears low, contracting authorities may request clarifications from the tenderer in question. Contracting authorities face a dilemma in evaluating and assessing low offers other than abnormal ones. It is difficult for them to identify dumping or predatory pricing disguised behind a low offer for a public contract. In addition, even if there is an indication of anticompetitive price fixing, the European public procurement rules do not provide for any kind of procedure. The suspension of the award procedures (or even the suspension of the conclusion of the contract itself) would be unlikely without a thorough and exhaustive investigation by the competent antitrust authorities.

Against this background, the Private Finance Initiative was originally construed as the process that could bring the public and private sectors closer and break the mistrust which has surrounded traditional public procurement. The Private Finance Initiative should not be conceived as a capital facility to the state and its organs in the process of delivering public services. It should not been seen as a borrowing exercise by the public sector, as the latter can acquire capital in much more preferential terms than any private person. The Private Finance Initiate should be rather conceived as a process of involving the private sector in the delivery of public services. As such, the Private Finance Initiative attempts to introduce a contractual element in the delivery of public services, to the extent that private sector, as a contractual party undertakes the responsibility to provide not only an asset but to deliver its associated functions to the public. Therefore, the Private Finance Initiative has contributed in changing the traditionally acquisitorial nature of public sector contracts by inserting a service delivery element.

One of the most important attractions of the Private Finance Initiative has been the ability of public authorities to classify the relevant transactions as exempted from the Public Sector Borrowing Requirement (PSBR), thus bypassing centrally controlled budgetary allocations and cash limits in the public sector spending. In such a way, the Private Finance Initiative represented a viable solution to cash-stranded public authorities, which could, independently, proceed and strike deals that otherwise would not have been materialised.[92] Furthermore, the public spending relating to the repayments of the privately financed transactions would not appear as public debt. By taking privately financed transactions out of the PSBR balance sheet, the government may implicitly have attempted to liberalise public purchasing from budgetary constraints and public spending capping. It could be also argued that such an attempt could indicate the beginning of the end to the institutionalised decision-making process and control of public procurement imposed under the European (and domestic) public procurement regime.[93]

The paramount implication of not classifying privately financed projects as public debt could be that such purchasing would not fall under the annual comprehensive spending review of the government. In fact, noninclusion of PFI deals in the PSBR could transform the structure of public markets[94] by reversing the roles and the relative importance of the demand and supply sides. Indeed, it was originally suggested[95] that the private sector should initiate demand by exploring the overall potential and delivery options and then introducing the plan to the relevant public authority. Such scenario could also mean dismantling of public markets and the elevation of private markets[96] as the forum for the pursuit of public interest.[97]

The Function of the Private Finance Initiative

A Private Finance Initiative project could be based on a standardised contractual format. Typical areas cover roads, bridges, hospitals, schools, prisons, police stations, government departments, social housing, waste projects and IT projects. Usually, after competitive tendering, a consortium comprising private sector partners is appointed as the preferred partner to contract with the public sector through a special purpose vehicle (SPV). The contractual interface covers a long-term service contract often in the range of twenty-five to thirty years and provides for output specifications with clear requirements whereas the payment mechanism is often comprising a unitary charge for services once these services are available.

A different format of Private Finance Initiative projects covers joint ventures in areas such as low-carbon technologies, defence equipment, water management and regeneration. Under such joint ventures, the government, in conjunction with a number of private sector parties, makes a contribution to a commercial venture, shares aspects of control and aims to share risks and returns on an agreed basis.

Another format of Private Finance Initiative projects covers strategic infrastructure partnerships such as Local Education Partnerships in Schools (LEPs) and Local Improvement Finance Trusts in primary care (LIFT). Such strategic interface is deemed suitable for procuring a stream of projects as a bundle of projects which otherwise would not be suitable to attract private finance. Special, often exclusive rights are conferred to the private sector to address infrastructure-related issues over a period of time.

A different format of Private Finance Initiative is public-private joint venture based on local asset, often referred to as Local Asset Backed Vehicle (LABV). In such arrangements, the public sector contributed land and property and the private sector brings in financial and other resources. The development of the asset is expected to yield returns to cover costs and fund development. The partners share the increase or bear any decrease in value of the land and property, usually on an equal basis. Local Asset Backed Vehicles as a PFI model are suitable where there is a visible pipeline of projects. Often the public sector shares more of the risks and rewards than in other privately financed arrangements as it has greater influence and leverage over projects due to the fact that it can shape the outcome of certain policies such as planning and environmental ones.

Concessions appear as a favourable private finance initiative mode in a way where the private sector is granted with exclusive rights to build, operate and maintain a ring-fenced asset over a long period of time. The private sector recovers its investment through future charges for services once the project is in operation and often bears high risks associated to future demand for the use of the asset upon which it has exclusive rights. The public sector has no or little involvement in contract management.

Finally, one of the most sophisticated modes of private finance in public service delivery is the integrator model. Under such model, the engagement of the private sector is channeled through private equity which is held by a special purpose vehicle (SPV) which specialises in integrating different partners rather than subcontracting with partners who are also its shareholders. The public sector procures a project delivery organisation, the integrator, to manage the delivery of a project through preprocurement preparation, procurement and construction and operation. Under such model, there is scope for project risks to be better managed because the integrator only profits from the project development work, not from subcontracts. The integrator model has a positive impact on interface risks because it reduces the integration of design, build and operations, as these are carried out by businesses with no interest in the project company.

Private finance projects are contractual arrangements between the public and private sectors, which use at least some funding raised through the private sector, to deliver public authorities' objectives. The costs, including the finance costs, are eventually paid by the public authority through annual payments, or by the users through charges. In this context, public authorities are public sector bodies that commission the project. In doing this, public authorities manage the tendering, governance and contractual relationships for the public sector.[98] The most common method of financing PFI projects is project finance. All the financing for the project is tied to the project, normally in a special company set up for the purpose. There is meant to be no cross subsidy to and from other projects; the intention is that if the project fails, the finance cannot be paid back. Consequently, the cost of the private finance reflects the project's risks of failing or not having enough money to pay back its borrowings. PFI projects typically use around 90 per cent debt finance and 10 per cent equity funding. The debt finance is in the form of bank loans or, prior to the credit crunch, bond finance.

The equity finance is provided by contractors or financial institutions, and comprises of a mixture of shares and loans which take second precedence to the payment of the debt finance. There are basically two types of PFI equity transactions. On the one hand, SPV shareholders sell equity in individual projects or in a group of projects. On the other hand, the sale of secondary market infrastructure funds that have a portfolio of PFI equity stakes in SPVs. In both cases the partial or full ownership of equity in the SPV transfers to a new owner. Four trends are evident in the secondary market: portfolio building by some construction companies; recycling and profit-taking by other construction companies; the growth of joint ventures between PFI construction companies and banks, infrastructure funds and pension funds; and the growth of secondary market infrastructure funds.

PFI supporters maintain that private capital at risk has brought much-needed rigour and efficiency to building and maintenance of public infrastructure and delivered more than would have been possible without them. There are a number of reasons which justify the appropriateness of PFI and the value for money to the public sector. These include the transfer of key project risks such as construction delay and cost overruns to the private sector away from the public sector and taxpayers; the fact that assets are maintained to a government-specified standard over a contractually agreed period, reducing the unfortunate 'boom and bust' maintenance spending patterns otherwise evident in much of the government-managed infrastructure estate; the focus of procurers on the whole-life cost and performance of infrastructure rather than making short-term decisions based on short-term budgets; the focus of the public sector to specify in detail what services it requires and understand what it can afford at the outset; the fact that the long-term nature of PFI contracts allows the private sector to procure efficiently and to invest to deliver services economically, including staff training, life-cycle maintenance regimes, asset plans and planned rather than reactive maintenance; and finally the use of a standardised risk framework has focussed the competition and developed a detailed contractual structure which apportions risk to several subcontractors and financiers, so that risk transfer is allocated to subcontractors who are incentivised to perform or bear the consequences of failure. At the outset financiers perform detailed due diligence on assets, costs and contracts using technical advisors to ensure the project will be delivered on time and to budget.

5 The Development of Public-Private Partnerships in the EU

Public-private partnerships denote a sophisticated interface between public authorities and private sector undertakings, which aims at delivering infrastructure projects[1], as well as public services.[2] According to the EU institutions, the term *public-private partnership* refers to 'forms of cooperation between public authorities and the world of business which aim to ensure the funding, construction, renovation, management or maintenance of an infrastructure or the provision of a service'.[3] At European level and as part of the Initiative for Growth, the Council has approved a series of measures designed to increase investment in the infrastructure of the trans-European transport networks and also in the areas of research, innovation and development[4], as well as the delivery of services of general interest.[5]

The term *public-private partnership* is not defined at European Union level. Public-private partnerships denote a contractual format between public authorities and private sector undertakings.[6] Such relations aim at delivering infrastructure projects, as well as many other schemes in areas covering transport, public health, education, public safety, and waste management and water distribution and have the following characteristics[7]: the relatively long duration of the relationship; the funding source for the project; the strategic role of the private sector in the sense that it is expected to provide input into different stages of the project such as design, completion, implementation and funding and finally the distribution of risks between the public and private sectors and the expectation that the private sector will assume substantial risk.[8]

Public authorities in the Member States often have recourse to public-private partnership arrangements to facilitate mainly infrastructure projects.[9] Budget constraints confronting national governments and the widespread assumption that private sector know-how will benefit the delivery of public services appear as the main policy drivers[10] for selecting a public-private partnership route.[11] Also, the accounting treatment of public-private partnership contracts benefits national governments as the assets involved in a public-private partnership should be classified as nongovernment assets[12], and therefore recorded off-balance sheet for public accountancy purposes[13], subject to two conditions: i) that the private partner bears the construction risk, and ii) that the private partner bears at least one of either availability or demand risk.[14] However, it is necessary to assess whether a public-private partnership option offers real value added[15] compared with the conclusion of traditional public contracts.[16]

The principal benefit from involving the private sector in the delivery of public services has been attributed to the fact that the public sector does not have to commit its own capital resources in funding the delivery of public services, whereas other benefits include quality improvement, innovation, management efficiency and effectiveness, elements that are often underlying private-sector entrepreneurship.[17] Consequently, the public sector receives value-for-money in the delivery of public services, while it can also be maintained that through this process the state manages in a better, more strategic way the public finances. Value-for-money denotes a concept which is associated with the economy, the effectiveness and the efficiency of a public service, product or process, that is, a comparison of the input costs against the value of the outputs and a qualitative and quantitative judgment of the manner in which the resources involved have been utilised and managed.[18]

The erosion of confidence in the role of the public sector as organiser and asset holder in the sphere of public services has led to attempts to moderate the widespread dissatisfaction from traditional public procurement methods in delivering public services and infrastructure projects.[19] The outcome revealed that the nexus of contractual relations between public authorities and the private sector were not providing genuine value-for-money outcomes.[20] The criticism has been primarily directed towards: (i) adversarial contractual relations as a result of competitive tendering, (ii) inappropriate risk allocation and (iii) poor contractual performances resulting in delayed and overbudget completions.[21]

Competitive tendering as a procedure to deliver public services has been reproached for creating a confrontational environment, where the antagonising relations, which emanate from the tendering processes, are often adversely reflected in the performance stage of the contract. In addition, competitive tendering has been dissociated with innovation and quality. Also, as a result of inefficiently written specifications upon which the tenders have been constructed, the deliverables or the outcomes often differ dramatically from contractual expectations and stipulations.[22]

On the other hand, risk allocation is probably the most crucial element in contractual relations between public and private sectors that affects pricing as well as the overall contractual framework. Risk represents the level of financial exposure of a party prior to, after the conclusion of, or during its performance of a contract. In a traditional public contract, risk is apportioned in accordance with the expected modalities, features or perceptions of the public and private sectors; contractual elements of risk, which are associated with the design or construction of a project, maintenance and operational matters, are usually passed to the private sector. On the other hand, risks related to the required investment, financing and currency transactions, planning issues, residualisation, obsolescence, political and legal aspects, industrial relations and usage volumes remain with the public sector.

In traditional public procurement, the risk allocation tends to favor the supply side (the private sector), which mainly assumes the risks related to the tendering process, and includes project risks. During the performance stage of the contract and up to its completion, the public sector would, usually, place an amount of risk to the private sector by requiring performance bonds or other means of financial guarantees. Risk allocation is the result of negotiations between the parties and is normally expected to reflect the pricing element of contractual arrangements between them. Thus, risk allocation and overall pricing for a traditional public contract operate in an analogous relation within a contract. The more risk a party assumes, the higher the price to be paid by the other party, and vice versa.

An acceptable transfer of risk in a contract between the public and private sectors is difficult to establish. Risk allocation primarily reflects the parties' perception of a transaction with reference to their own criteria. These criteria are often influenced by a range of parameters such as speculation, fear and certainty, as well as by a number of qualitative attributes of the parties, such as forecast and planning, as well as market intelligence. In traditional public contracts the public sector inevitably accepts excessive risks as a result of its procurement practices. Where the award of publicly funded contracts is predominately based upon *the lowest price,* which constitutes one of the two permissible award criteria under the procurement rules (the other being the criterion of *the most economically advantageous offer*), this would normally reflect the amount of risk the relevant public sector contracting authorities are prepared to accept. Two criteria laid down in the public procurement Directives provide the conditions under which contracting authorities award public contracts: the lowest price or the most economically advantageous offer. The first criterion indicates that, subject to the qualitative criteria and financial and economic standing, contracting authorities do not rely on any other factor than the price quoted to complete the contract. The most economically advantageous offer includes a series of factors chosen by the contracting authority, including price, delivery or completion date, running costs, cost-effectiveness, profitability, technical merit, product or work quality, aesthetic and functional characteristics, after-sales service and technical assistance, commitments with regard to spare parts and components and maintenance costs, and security of supplies.[23]

Finally, traditional procurement methods have often revealed a picture of poor contracts management as a result of inefficient control systems operated by public authorities. Poor contracts management systems have often resulted in out-of-control contractual performances with all the adverse financial consequences attributed to the delayed completions of the projects. The traditional public procurement process often suffers from unnecessarily repetitive functions, which do not offer long-term savings and value-for-money-considerations—particularly the advertisement, selection and qualification processes—and could pose a considerable financial burden on the public sector.

As part of the Initiative for Growth, the European Council approved a series of measures designed to increase investment[24] in the infrastructure of the trans-European transport networks and also in the areas of research, innovation and development[25], as well as the delivery of services of general interest.[26] European law does not lay down any special rules covering the award or the contractual interface of public-private partnerships. Nevertheless, such arrangements must be examined in the light of the rules and principles resulting from the European Treaties, particularly as regards the principles of freedom of establishment and freedom to provide services[27], which encompass in particular the principles of transparency, equality of treatment, proportionality and mutual recognition[28] and the public procurement Directives.[29] The Commission has already taken initiatives under public procurement law to deal with the award of public-private partnerships[30], in which it defined, on the basis of the rules and principles derived from the Treaty and applicable secondary legislation, the outlines of the concept of concession in European law and the obligations incumbent on the public authorities when selecting the economic operators to whom the concessions are granted.

One of the most advanced[31] public-private partnerships programmes has been developed in the United Kingdom[32] and is responsible for about 24 per cent of public investment, with projects in most of the key infrastructure areas.[33] Many continental European Union states, including Ireland, Sweden, Finland, Germany, Greece, Italy, the Netherlands, Portugal and Spain, have developed legal and policy frameworks to deliver public-private partnership projects, although their share in total public investment is between 5 and 15 per cent. Reflecting a need for infrastructure investment on a large scale, and weak fiscal positions, a number of countries in Central and Eastern Europe, including the Czech Republic, Hungary and Poland, have embarked on public-private partnerships.

A range of projects have been delivered through public-private partnership arrangements in EU Member States and have allowed for the buildup of an effective body of expertise in public-private partnerships which points towards the effectiveness of the public-private partnerships as an instrument in delivering public services and infrastructure. The projects covered include wastewater treatment works, public use motorways, toll roads, power plants, telecommunications infrastructure, tunnels school buildings, airport facilities, toll bridges, government offices, prisons, light rail systems, railways, parking stations, subways, museum buildings, harbours, pipelines, road upgrading and maintenance, health services and waste management.[34] According to the European Investment Bank (EIB) Economic and Financial Report 2010/04, more than 1,300 public-private partnership contracts have been signed in the EU from 1990 to 2009, representing a capital value of more than 250 billion euro. This includes approximately 369 new projects with a value of almost 70 billion euro having reached financial close in 2007–2009.[35]

THE LEGAL FORMATS OF PUBLIC–PRIVATE PARTNERSHIPS

The EU Green Paper on Public Private Partnerships[36] distinguishes three major formats of public-private partnerships: the concession, the contractual public-private partnership, and finally, the institutional public-private partnership, often described as the 'joint-venture model'.

The Notion of Public Concessions

A concession is a public contract where the consideration of the private sector for the provision of services consists either solely in the right to exploit the service or in this right together with some form of payment by the public sector. The notion of a concession is based on the fact that no contractual payment remuneration is paid by the granting public entity to the concessionaire. The latter must therefore simply be given the right to economically exploit the concession, although this right may be accompanied by a requirement to pay some consideration to the grantor, depending on elements of risk allocation agreed between the parties.

There are three main distinctive features in public concessions. First, the beneficiaries of the service provided must be third parties (usually the public or end-users of a public service) rather than the awarding public entity itself. Second, the subject of the service upon which the concession is based must concern a matter that is in the public interest. Finally, the concessionaire must assume the economic risk related to the performance of the relevant service.[37] A public concession is a revenue generating public-private partnership which involves an infrastructure or a service, the use of which necessitates the payment of fees borne directly by end-users, and any operation or function emanating from the sale, rent or exploitation of public land or buildings.[38]

It is maintained that the absence of consideration passing from the granting entity to the concessionaire constitutes the essence of a public concession.[39] The above characteristic represents a fundamental feature of a concession whose importance is not limited to projects that are concerned with infrastructure or the delivery of public works projects, but also extends to projects concerning the delivery of public services. This feature finds justification in the fact that the concessionaire itself must bear the principal, or at least the substantive, economic risk attaching to the performance of the service involved. If the argument is satisfied that the economic burden or risk has effectively been passed to the concessionaire by the grantor of the concession, then there must be a very strong presumption that the arrangement concluded between them amounts to a concession rather than a contract.

The single most important indication of whether economic risk is to be borne by the concessionaire will emerge from examining the nature of the exploitation in which the supposed concession requires it to engage.[40] Thus, where, for example the public authorities effectively guarantee to indem-nify the concessionaire against future losses, or where there is no effective exploitation by the concessionaire of the service whose performance is ceded, the arrangement at issue could not amount to a concession.[41]

In a concession, the beneficiary of the service must be a third party uncon-nected with the contractual relationship and the concessionaire effectively must obtain at least a significant proportion of its remuneration, not from the granting entity, but from the exploitation of the service. Therefore, a case-by-case approach has been adopted to answer the question of whether a contract amounts to a concession or a service contract. Such a fact-specific inquiry necessarily takes account of all indicative factors, the most impor-tant of which is whether the supposed concession amounts to a conferral of a right to exploit a particular service as well as the simultaneous transfer of a significant proportion of the risk associated with that transfer to the concessionaire. The likelihood that the concessionaire will be able benefi-cially to exploit the concession would not suffice to ascertain that there is no economic risk. Such assessment would need to satisfy the probability of economic loss on the part of the concessionaire.[42]

The current economic state of concession for the EU Member States which have made use of such method in delivering public services is the following:

In France, concession contracts worth around 80 billion euro. Over 10,000 concession-type contracts deliver services in water and sanitation, waste management, gas and electricity infrastructure management, motor-ways, sport facilities and heating networks. In France, concessions account for 2.1 per cent of GDP. In Italy concession contracts with a total value of 8.4 billion euro (out of which 536 million euro corresponded to service concessions) account for 2.1 per cent of GDP and deliver services mainly in the municipal, water, sanitation and energy sectors. In the UK, the value of concession amounts to over 60 billion euro and represent 3 per cent of GDP, delivering public services public transport, roads and bridges, waste management, wastewater management, marine services and care homes. In Denmark, concessions worth 3 billion euro, which is equivalent to 0.1 per cent of GDP delivering services in water and energy supply, schools, sport and leisure sectors. In Spain, the total capital value of concessions is estimated at 8 billion euro, which is equivalent to 0.9 per cent of GDP. Concessions are most prevalent in the road sector, in water distribution and wastewater management as well as in sanitation sectors. In the Czech Republic, conces-sions have a capital value of 1.1 billion euro, equivalent to 1.1 per cent of GDP and deliver services in health, transport and public buildings, waste/ drinking water and waste sectors. In Greece, prior to the current environ-ment, concessions with a capital value of 5.7 billion euro represented the equivalent to 2.5 per cent of GDP, delivering services in the construction and maintenance of hospitals, government buildings, schools, prisons and universities. In Portugal, concession representing a value of 32.5 billion euro is equivalent to 20 per cent of GDP delivering services in water distribution and wastewater, waste, energy and heating services, transport, port and airport services, health services, road and motorway maintenance.[43]

The Significance of Concessions for the Internal Market

Concession contracts are different from public contracts, which are traditionally used by public authorities to procure supplies, works or services. In the case of public contracts, an economic operator is awarded a fixed payment for completing the required work or service. Concessions, on the other hand, are contractual arrangements between a public authority and an economic operator (the concession holder) where the latter receives substantial remuneration by being permitted to exploit the work or service. Hence, concessions involving private partners are a particular form of public-private partnerships. Although public-private partnerships have never been defined in EU law, they are usually referred to as relationships of cooperation between a public authority and a private partner, where the latter bears risks that are traditionally borne by the public sector and often contribute to financing the project. Many public-private partnerships are based upon a contractual structure, but the majority of public-private partnerships in the EU take the form of concessions.

The award of public contracts and work concessions is subject to EU rules.[44] The same rules do not apply to different categories of concessions and public contracts. Unlike public contracts, which are exhaustively regulated in Public Procurement legislation, and works concessions, which are partially covered by the Public Procurement Directives, the award of service concessions is only subject to the general principles of the EU Treaty. This has resulted in irregularities and economic inefficiencies, and has a negative impact on the achievement of value for public money. In order to apply the Treaty principles more effectively and efficiently, secondary legislation was developed containing specific rules on award procedures.[45]

The European legislature decided to differentiate between *public contracts*, conceived of as the procurement of works, goods or services against payment, and *concession contracts*, where works or services are provided to contracting authorities or to users in consideration for the right to exploit a facility.[46] With regard to the latter, it should be pointed out that the award of *works concessions* under the Classic Directive is currently subject to a limited number of provisions only.[47] In particular, it is compulsory to publish a concession notice in the Official Journal and to respect a minimal period for the submission of applications. Moreover, there are rules on the obligations of concession holders. Bidders also enjoy judicial protection and review procedures provided by the Remedies Directive 2007/66.[48] Their award is supplemented by the general Treaty principles. On the other hand, the award of works concessions under the Utilities Directive is only subject to the general principles of the TFEU.[49] Similarly, *service concessions* are currently subject only to the general principles of the TFEU.

In practice, the distinction between works concessions and service concessions may prove to be difficult to determine. Concession contracts underpin an important share of economic activity in the EU. They are particularly significant in economic sectors that are of great importance to both citizens and economic operators, such as network industries and services of general economic interest. They are important vehicles in the long-term structural development of infrastructures and strategic services, as they help to harness private sector expertise, achieve efficiency and deliver innovation. Moreover, their role is also likely to become more prominent in years to come in the face of increasing constraints on public finances. Indeed, by transferring the main operating risks to a private partner and alleviating the public authorities of this burden, concessions make it possible, in certain cases, to carry out much needed public works and services while keeping the corresponding commitments out of the government balance sheet. There is further potential for concessions in many projects supported by the European Union funds, where the use of public-private partnerships in co-funded projects is currently low.[50]

A decision by Member States and contracting authorities to resort to a concession should be assessed on a case-by-case basis and its costs and benefits should always carefully and comprehensively be compared with those of alternative solutions. The fact that Member States use different definitions for concessions and the current lack of transparency on their award makes systematic and precise measurement of their economic and social importance difficult. Comparable data across the Internal Market are generally lacking or remain inconsistent, particularly in Member States where concessions are not sufficiently regulated. Network industries providing services of general economic interest were estimated to account for 7 per cent of the EU fifteen Member States total value added. In the new Member States of the latest accession in 2007, this proportion was higher, ranging from 9.8 per cent in Hungary to 14.3 per cent in the Slovak Republic. The significance of concessions for employment is also highly demonstrable as approximately 10.5 million people are employed in EU network industries corresponding to 5.4 per cent of the total workforce. For public services in the EU, the European Commission estimates the number of persons employed by concessions delivering services of general interest to be over 64 million. The number of enterprises providing SGI is estimated to be more than 500,000. Concessions in the EU have also significant implications for investment, as providers of electricity, gas, water, transport, post and telecommunications and research contribute to 6.4 per cent of the total investment in the EU, which is estimated to be approximately 150 billion euro.[51]

With regard to public-private partnerships and concessions in several Member States where concessions are subject to specific rules, concessions are mostly used in water distribution and treatment, road and rail transport, ports and airports services, motorway maintenance and management, waste management, energy or heating services, leisure facilities and car parks. Concessions in these sectors imply significant amounts of capital investment. According to the European Investment Bank (EIB), more than 1,300 public-private partnership contracts were signed in the EU from 1990 to 2009, representing a capital value of more than 250 billion euro. The EIB itself, which is Europe's foremost funder of public-private partnership projects, has a portfolio of 120 projects representing an investment of around 25 billion euro. Funding of new projects was in excess of 3.5 billion euro in 2008 and in 2009–2010 was worth 2 billion euro despite the current adverse economic conditions.[52]

Concessions in the Utilities Sectors

The utilities sectors cover important activities such as water, ports, airports, energy and heating. These sectors are characterised by a significant number of concessions, but even works concessions are at present excluded from the scope of application of the Utilities Procurement Directive[53], thus allowing for direct awards between the Member States and the selected concessionaires or awards based on exclusive rights. In the utilities sector, the grant of exclusive rights for the operation of a network is part of specific legislative measures aimed at liberalising such sectors. An exclusive right granted in compliance with EU law makes it unnecessary and redundant to follow a competitive procedure for the award of a concession of network management services to the holder of an exclusive right since no other competitor would be in a position to apply for such contract. Moreover, the transparency resulting from a mandatory publication of the act granting the exclusive right should permit all interested parties to fully evaluate the compliance of such right with EU law or sectoral legislation.

The Utilities Procurement Directive[54] provides for its inapplicability in cases of public contracts awarded pursuant to international rules[55], or secret contracts and contracts requiring special security measures or contracts related with the protection of Member States' essential interests.[56] Interestingly, the Public Sector Directive also does not cover public contracts of which their object is to provide or exploit public telecommunications networks[57]; contracts for the acquisition or rental of land; contracts related to broadcasting services; contracts related with financial securities, capital-raising activities and central bank services; employment contracts; and research and development contracts which do not benefit the relevant contacting authority.[58] The Utilities Directive does not apply to contracts awarded in a third country[59]; contracts awarded by contracting entities engaged in the provision or operation of fixed networks for the purchase of water and for the supply of energy or of fuels for the production of energy[60]; contracts subject to special arrangements for the exploitation and exploration of oil, gas, coal or other solid fuels by virtue of European law[61]; contracts and framework agreements awarded by central purchasing bodies[62]; contracts of which their object activity is directly exposed to competition on markets to which access is not restricted[63] and contracts related to works and service concessions[64] which are awarded by contracting entities carrying out one or more of the activities covered by the Utilities Directive and in particular activities including gas, heat and electricity, water, transport services, postal services, exploration for oil, gas or other solid fuels, extraction of oil, gas or other solid fuels and provision of ports and airports where those concessions are awarded for carrying out those activities.

Concessions in Transport

European institutions preempted the significance of concessions which have to be granted to transport operators through obligations that have to be fulfilled in order to provide the required services to the public. Such obligations which are inherent in public services in the transport sectors can be imposed by Member States upon transport undertakings (public or private), as a transport operator would not assume such services or ventures to the same extent and under the same conditions, if it were considering its own commercial interests. The notion of public service obligations (PSO) is thus embraced by the format of a concession between the state and the transport operator which provided for exclusive rights over a period of time to perform and commercially exploit certain tasks on condition of adhering to and observing predetermined conditions in the public service obligations.

Four characteristics emerge from the examination of public service obligations in transport and reflect on the relevant concessions upon which they are based: their exceptional nature, their restrictive application, their compensatory reimbursement and the need to create a competitive environment for their function.

The exceptional nature of public service obligations is reflected on their separation from other similar services provided by transport undertakings, on the grounds that they are not commercially viable and their reimbursement for their provision has traditionally reflected a *stricto sensu* commercial assessment of a venture which embraces such obligations.

Their restrictive character is depicted in the requirement imposed upon Member States to terminate all obligations which are connected to a public service in transport, unless the maintenance of existing public service obligations or the imposition of new ones is confined to cases where they are essential to the provision of adequate transport services, and the compensation for such services must be uniform and predetermined in common procedures for passenger rates and terms and conditions. This requirement reflects on the anxiety of European institutions that state aid could be disguised as reimbursements for public service obligations, and consequently distort competition.

The compensatory reimbursement for the provision of public service obligations is demonstrated through the concept of *the public service contract*, a significant development in relation to the concept of public services in transport. The concept of public service contracts covers contractual relations between the competent authorities of a Member State and transport under-takings (public or private) with a view to providing the public with adequate transport services. A public service contract may cover: i) transport services satisfying fixed standards of continuity, regularity, capacity and quality; ii) additional transport services; iii) transport services at specified rates and sub-ject to specified conditions, in particular for certain categories of passenger or on certain routes; iv) adaptation of services to actual requirements.[65] The con-tractualisation of the obligation to provide transport services inserts elements of competition in the selection process. This is reflected in the Commission's vision to utilise public service contracts as a platform for the provision of essential public services.[66] Finally, the introduction of the concept of public service contracts takes the notion of public service obligations to a different level and reveals their fourth characteristic, which is the need for a competi-tive environment for selecting undertakings to provide such obligations.

For air transport services, public service obligations[67] can only be con-ferred to operators by reference to a specific procedure, which links their compensation with a selection process based on a public tender.[68]

Pursuant to Regulation 1008/2008, a Member State may impose a public service obligation (PSO) with respect to scheduled air services between two airports in the Union, in particular when one of them serves an outlying or developing region.[69] To this end, the Regulation lays out a very detailed procedure for setting up these PSOs and for compulsory tendering. The sig-nificance of this process is such as to allow Member States to determine the value for a public service by taking into account both the users' interests and costs incurred by the relevant operator. The criteria for calculating the com-pensation involve only factors relevant to the operating deficit incurred on a specific route, including a reasonable remuneration for capital employed.[70] The implementation of public service obligation must be transparent and the selected transport operators are expected to account annually for the relevant costs, including fixed costs and revenues attributed to the relevant routes. Thus, a public service contract to perform public service obligations is awarded to the operator which requires the lowest financial compensation.[71]

The compensation in the form of a public service contract awarded through the tendering process stipulated in Regulation 2408/92 reveals a neutral commercial operation between the relevant Member State and the selected air carrier. The neutrality of such transaction is based on the reimbursement limited solely to losses sustained because of the operation of a specific route and does not bring about any special benefit for the air carrier[72], which has been selected according to uniform, transparent and objective criteria. Compensation of costs incurred by a carrier which has not been selected according to the specific rules or which is not calculated on the basis of the lowest-cost criterion will be assessed under the general state aid rules. Compensation will be considered state aid if it diverts significant volumes of traffic or allows carriers to cross-subsidise routes on which they compete with other Community air carriers.[73]

In the field of maritime transport, the treatment of public service contracts follows similar patterns with the parameters set for such arrangements in the air transport sector. The award of such contracts reflects on the principle of nondiscrimination between Community-registered shipping undertakings and is limited to requirements concerning the relevant ports to be served, regularity, continuity and frequency of service, capacity to provide the service, rates to be charged and manning of vessels. Certain criteria must be present to enable a public service contract in maritime transport to avoid the clutches of state aid regulation: i) the presence of public tenders to ensure transparency and competition, ii) adequate publicity and information to be given to all interested parties regarding requirements concerning the level and frequency of the service, capacity, prices and standards; iii) award of the public service contract to the bidder submitted the lowest financial compensation requirements for the provision of the relevant service.

The Commission's practice in assessing the compensation for public service contracts encapsulating public service obligations is consistent with its practice relevant to air transport. The Commission considers that reimbursement of operating losses incurred as a direct result of fulfilling public service obligations must be calculated on the basis of the deficit incurred by the operator in providing the service and it should be accounted for separately for each such service so to eliminate the possibility of overcompensation or cross-subsidy.

Compensation for public service obligations could be available to all Community shipping undertakings. Existing public service contracts may remain in force up to the expiry date of the relevant contract. Restrictions of access to the route to a single operator may only be granted if, when the public service contract is awarded according to the above-mentioned procedure, there is no competitor providing, or having a demonstrated intention to provide, scheduled services on the route.

A special regime in public service contracts in the maritime transport sector allows for Member States to conclude such contracts as a condition for the provision of *cabotage* services, on shipping undertakings carrying regular services to, from and between islands. Public service obligations may also be imposed for scheduled services to ports serving peripheral regions of the Community or routes considered vital for the economic development of that region, in cases where the operation of market forces would not ensure a sufficient service level. The duration of such public service contracts is limited to a period of five years, to avoid monopolistic market structures.

The concept of public service contracts, which encapsulates the reasoning and remit for the operation of public service obligations, reflects on an intricate facet of their pursuit of regional and social policy aims, which in turn attempts to bring the concept of public service obligations under the notion of services of general economic interest. As a surrogate category of the latter, public service obligations reveal a 'commissioning' role in the relation between Member States and undertakings (being public or private) entrusted with their delivery. Such commissioning role has the intention to exonerate of the relevant services from the remit of the general state aid rules.

The compensatory nature of the reimbursement, on the other hand, reflects on two main elements: the deficit-based calculation method for their value and, as a result, the noncommercial nature of the markets within which such services are delivered. It is assumed that a service regarding public obligations has minimal commercial value. Market forces cannot provide for the needs of the public, as a number of factors deter entry into the relevant market (profitability, set-up costs, risk, volume and levels of demand, intramode competition). Thus the markets within which public service obligations are dispersed are *sui generis*. The most important repercussion of the above statement is the nonapplicability of tools used to compare the value of a relevant service such as the private investor principle. The lack of a reliable comparator, the noncommercial nature of public service obligations and the calculation method for their reimbursement might pose problems in determining an objective and uniformly acceptable value for their delivery. It appears that there are difficult elements surrounding demand structure, infrastructure investment and costs, scale economies and revenue levels. However, the market-oriented character of their award, as depicted in the tendering process, intends to establish a transparent and objective framework for their delivery.

The inland public passenger transport sector is considered sufficiently distinctive to other transport modalities so it is subject to a more precise and specific set of rules[74] which include the possibility of awarding contracts to 'internal operators'.[75] For this reason, and in order not to interfere with the objectives of EU transport policy, and to maintain the stability of the legal framework, service concessions currently subject to the Transport Regulation should be excluded from the scope of the future EU legislation on concessions on the basis that this sector already provides for transparency and a fair degree of legal certainty.

Concessions in Priority and Nonpriority Services

Nonpriority services (e.g. port services, catering, health, education and social services) are at present only partially covered by the Public Procurement Directives. The intention of the legislator was that certain specific service contracts, which were considered not to have much potential for cross-border trade, should be excluded from the full application of the rules of the Directives, for a transitional period. The predecessor to 2004/18 EC Directive, Directive had adopted a two-tier approach in classifying services procured by contracting authorities. This classification was based on a 'priority' and a 'nonpriority' list of services, according to the relative value of such services in intracommunity trade. Priority services included Maintenance and repair services; Land transport services (except for rail transport services), including armoured car services and courier services, except transport of mail; Air transport services of passengers and freight, except transport of mail; Transport of mail by land and by air; Telecommunications services (except voice telephony, telex, radiotelephony, paging and satellite services); Financial services including (a) Insurance services, (b) Banking and investment services (except contracts for financial services in connection with the issue, sale, purchase or transfer of securities or other financial instruments, and central bank services); Computer and related services; Research and development services; Accounting, auditing and bookkeeping services; Market research and public opinion polling services; Management consultant services (except arbitration and conciliation services) and related services; Architectural services, engineering services and integrated engineering services, urban planning and landscape architectural services, related scientific and technical consulting services, technical testing and analysis services; Advertising services; Building-cleaning services on a fee or contract basis; Publishing and printing services on a fee or contract basis; Sewage and refuse disposal services; Sanitation and similar services.

On the other hand, nonpriority services included: Hotel and restaurant services, Rail transport services, Water transport services, Supporting and auxiliary transport services, Legal services, Personnel placement and supply services, Investigation and security services, Education and vocational education services, Health and social services, Recreational, cultural and sporting services. The division was not permanent and the European Commission had under constant review the situation, by assessing the performance of 'nonpriority' services sectors. The two-tier approach, in practical terms, means that the award of priority services contracts are subject to the rigorous regime of the public procurement Directives (advertisement, selection of tenderers, award procedures, award criteria), whereas the award of nonpriority services contracts must follow the basic rules of nondiscrimination and publicity of the results of the award.

Nevertheless, services such as social, health and education continue to have a limited cross-border dimension, due to the strong impact of different national cultural traditions. Furthermore, concessions are less prevalent in the above sectors. It must also be said that the full coverage of these services by the complete framework is politically very sensitive. It is therefore appropriate to establish a specific regime for the award of these services. This regime should include the obligation to publish by contracting authorities at the beginning of the budgetary year, a prior information notice. Such a notice would ensure adequate transparency, without prejudice to national systems of purchase of this kind of services. Such a legal framework should also encompass a requirement to publish a concession award notice.

Direct Awards and Concessions

In many EU Member States concession markets remain predominantly national, with a limited presence of companies originating in other EU Member States. Entry barriers stem from divergent national legal regimes for the award of concessions, as well as from inappropriate or even unlawful practices of the national awarding authorities. Identified divergence of legal regimes in Member States reveals several potential problems, including issues with the definition of concession, whereby economic operators have to contend with a complex pattern of setups considered to be concessions in different Member States (e.g. administrative authorisations or licences) and contracts qualifying as concessions under EU law but not considered as such by national legislators. In addition, divergent publication standards where, as a result of different national frameworks, concessions of the same type and importance are being published at different levels in different Member States and even within the same Member State.[76]

Barriers emanating from a divergence of national regimes are made worse by the often unlawful practices of contracting authorities, which stem from the lack of clarity of EU rules. One of the fundamental problems in this regard is the direct award of a concession contract with a cross-border interest. Direct awards originate from inadequate application of the principle of transparency, either by national lawmakers or by contracting authorities.[77] This situation concerns, in particular, Member States that do not regulate the award of concessions, but it also often concerns Member States where the award is governed by national rules.

Direct awards have particularly negative consequences for the proper functioning of the internal market. This applies to concession contracts, which are often extended or renewed without any competition or transparency. Concessions are also granted as licences or authorisations (usually encompassing exclusive rights) in breach of the Treaty principles. This means that a concession contract is wrongly qualified as a unilateral act and may be granted without a competitive procedure. Despite this, the Court has made it clear that granting a licence encompassing an exclusive right must comply with the principles of equal treatment and transparency.[78] It also acknowledged the existence of a wide derogation from these principles, excluding from this transparency obligation licences granted to either public operators subject to direct state supervision or private operators subject to strict control by the public authorities.

Finally, the lack of clear rules also leads to the unlawful use of nonobjective selection and award criteria in concessions for public services.[79] This is the case when objectives unrelated to the subject matter of the contract are included in the evaluation of the best offer. For instance, contracting authorities may want to take into account tenderers' social commitments not related to the subject matter of the contract or relations of trust with one of the bidders. Nonobjective and discriminatory criteria undermine the fairness of the award. The same can be said about discretion in setting selection criteria, which may lead to some certain companies being disadvantaged. This problem concerns Small and Medium Enterprises (SMEs) in particular, which appear to be reduced largely to the role of subcontractors.[80]

The above problems primarily concern service concessions and works concessions in the utilities sector, as the existing provisions on works concessions in the Classic Directive cover the issues of publication. An additional problematic area is the lack of judicial review for concessions, which is normally afforded for public contracts. Pursuant to Article 47 of the Charter of Fundamental Rights of the EU, anyone whose rights and freedoms guaranteed by the law of the Union are violated has the right to an effective remedy.[81] However, this right is not fully ensured to tenderers participating in procedures for the award of concessions. The Remedies Directive does not cover concessions falling outside the scope of the Public Sector Directive.[82] Hence, tenderers do not benefit from an adequate system guaranteeing effective enforcement of EU Treaty principles. Although some Member States (such as France, Portugal and Romania) extended the application of the Remedies Directive to service concessions, a number of others (Germany, UK, Sweden and Netherlands) have not done so.[83]

Legal certainty is essential to any economic activity and is particularly important in the context of long-term, high-value contracts such as most concessions. However, the grant of concessions is currently impaired, on the one hand by the lack of a clear and adequate definition of these contracts in EU law and, on the other hand, by the imprecise character of the obligations arising from the Treaty principles. These problems are often not resolved by national regimes for awarding concessions. Uncertainty with regard to the definition of concession appears already at the stage of qualification of a given arrangement as falling within the scope of the rules on public purchases. The distinction between public contracts and concessions on the one hand and other types of agreements or unilateral acts (such as licences and authorisation schemes) on the other hand, is unclear and stakeholders (e.g. in the ports sector) reported that it is often difficult to know which legal regime applies to a given scheme.[84] Furthermore, the lack of clarity stretches to certain activities carried out in the form of public-public cooperation.

The current definition of concessions makes it difficult to distinguish between concessions and public contracts. The Commission has provided some clarity in this respect in its Interpretative Communication, explaining that the risk inherent in the exploitation of the work or service that the concessionaire has to bear is the essential feature of a concession[85] and the Court has offered valuable insights on fundamental elements, such as the level and types of risk.[86] There is also some uncertainty regarding the distinction between works concessions and service concessions. Indeed, most works concessions also involve, to a certain extent, the provision of services. And, as it is not always easy to ascertain what the main purpose of the contract is, certain works concessions might be awarded as service concessions, thus unduly avoiding the application of the secondary rules.[87]

Moreover, Member States' definitions of concession do not remove the aforementioned uncertainty at EU level. Some of them are as unclear as the current definition in the Directive. Moreover, it is unclear whether those national definitions that provide additional clarification do in fact comply with EU law.

The legal uncertainty regarding the definition of concessions is compounded by doubts regarding the content and application of the obligations of transparency and nondiscrimination arising under the Treaty, which guide the award of concessions. Although the Court confirmed in *Telaustria* that contracting authorities that award concessions are bound to comply with the fundamental rules of the Treaty, it did not sufficiently explain the content of those rules.[88] Thus it remains difficult to judge the adequacy of measures aimed at ensuring compliance with the principles of equal treatment, nondiscrimination and transparency. A problem of uncertainty as to the applicable rules has also been identified in case of a contract modification. Many stakeholders have identified this issue as an important one. Although the case law of the Court applicable to modifications of public contracts also applies to concessions, the level of certainty provided by these judgements does not seem to be adequate.

The Contractual Public-Private Partnership

The contractual model of public-private partnerships reflects on a relation between public and private sectors, which is based solely on contractual links. It is unlikely that there would be any element of exclusive asset exploitation or end-user payments levied by the private sector partner.[89] However, mechanisms of profit sharing, efficiency gain sharing, as well as risk allocation between the public and private partners distinguish contractual public-private partnerships from traditional public contracts for works or services. The contractual model of public-private partnerships assumes that the private sector partner will provide the financing for completing the project and the public sector partner will pay back by way of 'service or unitary charges' which reflect payments based on usage volumes or demand (i.e. payments in lieu of fees or tolls for public lighting, hospitals, schools or roads with shadow tolls). A variety of types of contractual public-private partnerships have been developed in many jurisdictions in the EU.[90]

The Institutional Public-Private Partnership

The institutional model of public-private partnerships involves the establishment of a separate legal entity held jointly by the public partner and the private partner. The joint entity has the task of ensuring the raising of finance and the delivery of a public service or an infrastructure project for the benefit of the public. The direct interface between the public partner and the private partner in a forum with a distinctive legal personality allows the public partner, through its presence in the body of shareholders and in the decision-making bodies of the joint entity, to retain a relatively high degree of control over the development and delivery of the project.[91] The joint entity could also allow the public partner to develop its own experience of running and improving the public service in question, while having recourse to the support of a private partner.[92] An institutional public-private partnership can be established either by creating an entity controlled by the public and private sector partners, or by the private sector taking control of an existing public undertaking or by the participation of a private partner in an existing publicly owned company which has obtained public contracts or concessions.[93]

THE OPERATIONAL TYPES OF PUBLIC-PRIVATE PARTNERSHIPS

Three major operational types of public-private partnerships exist.

First, the private sector designs, builds, owns, develops, operates and manages an asset with no obligation to transfer ownership to the public sector. Public-private partnerships with such modalities include formats such as:

- Design-Build-Finance-Operate (DBFO), where the private sector partner designs, builds, finances and operates a public asset covering all aspects of management and maintenance with an option to sell at the end of the contractual period. Design-Build-Finance-Operate (DBFO) Public Private Partnerships include the delivery of hospitals where ownership of the facility stock is retained by the private sector.
- Build-Own-Operate (BOO), where the private sector partner finances, builds, owns and operates a facility or service for a stipulated period. Public sector control is exercised through the original contract or through a regulatory authority. After a specified period, there could be the possibility that ownership is transferred back to the public sector. Build-Own-Operate (BOO) Public Private Partnerships include the delivery of prisons, where regulatory regimes regarding standards operate alongside the retention of ownership of the assets by the private sector.
- Build-Develop-Operate (BDO), where the private sector finances, builds, develops commercially and operates for a stipulated period an asset or a facility. Build-Develop-Operate (BDO) Public Private Partnerships include the delivery of commercial developments such as exhibition centres and recreational facilities where ownership of the facility stock is retained by the private sector.
- Design-Construct-Manage-Finance (DCMF), where the private sector finances the design and construction of a facility or infrastructure and subsequently manages it for a stipulated period. Design-Construct-Manage-Finance (DCMF) Public Private Partnerships include the finance and delivery of schools and university accommodation projects.

Secondly, the private sector buys or leases an existing asset from the public sector, renovates, modernises, and/or expands it and then operates the asset, again with no obligation to transfer ownership back to the public sector. Public-private partnerships with such modalities include formats such as:

- Buy-Build-Operate (BBO), where the public sector transfers a public asset to the private or quasi-public sector partner to operate and maintain for a specified period of time. Public sector control is exercised at the time of transfer. Buy-Build-Operate (BBO) Public Private Partnerships include housing and regeneration development contracts between local and municipal authorities and the private sector.
- Lease-Develop-Operate (LDO), where the public sector leases a public asset to the private or quasi-public sector partner to operate and maintain for a specified period of time. Public sector control is exercised at the initiation of lease. Lease-Develop-Operate (LDO) Public Private Partnerships include housing and regeneration development projects and the delivery of commercial developments such as exhibition centres and recreational facilities where the lease-holding of the facility stock is retained by the private sector.
- Operate under Licence (OL): The private sector partner receives a licence or rights to operate a public service, usually for a specified term. This is often used in IT projects. The options available for delivery of public services range from direct provision by a ministry or government department to outright privatisation, where the public sector transfers all responsibilities, risks and rewards for service delivery to the private sector. Within this spectrum, public-private partnerships can be categorised based on the extent of public and private sector involvement and the degree of risk allocation. Operate under Licence (OL) Public Private Partnerships include the delivery of IT-related projects in the health, transport and defence sectors, where the private sector engages through licences with the public sector to deliver a project.

Thirdly, the private sector designs and builds an asset, operates it and then transfers it to the public sector when the operating contract ends, or at some other specified time. The private partner may subsequently rent or lease the asset from the public sector. Public-private partnerships with such modalities include formats such as:

- Build-Operate-Transfer (BOT), where the private sector designs, finances and constructs a new facility under a long-term contract, and operates the facility during the term of the contract after which ownership is transferred back to the public sector if not already transferred upon completion of the facility. Build-Operate-Transfer (BOT) Public Private Partnerships include the delivery of infrastructure projects in transport such as motorways and bridges.
- Build-Own-Operate-Transfer (BOOT), where a private entity receives a franchise or a concession to finance, design, build and operate a facility (and to charge user fees) for a specified period, after which ownership is transferred back to the public sector. Build-Own-Operate-Transfer (BOOT) Public Private Partnerships include the delivery of government

buildings and accommodation projects, with the option or obligation to transfer ownership of an asset at the end of the partnership's life span.

• Build-Lease-Operate-Transfer (BLOT), where a private entity receives a franchise to finance, design, build and operate a leased facility (and to charge user fees) for the lease period, against payment of a rent. Build-Lease-Operate-Transfer (BLOT) Public Private Partnerships include the delivery of transport infrastructure projects such as airports and ports.

THE FINANCING OF PUBLIC–PRIVATE PARTNERSHIPS

A public-private partnership financing can take one of the following forms: (i) *a stand-alone project*, where the funding raised is for only one specific project; (ii) *a Special Purpose Vehicle* as the borrower, where an independent legal vehicle (SPV) is created to raise the funds required for the project; (iii) a high ratio of debt to equity through either gearing or leverage, where the newly created project company usually has the minimum equity required to issue debt for a reasonable cost, with equity generally averaging between 10 to 30 per cent of the total capital required for infrastructure projects; (iv) *private lending* based on project specific cash flow and not a corporate balance sheet, where the project company borrows funds from lenders. The lenders look to the projected future revenue stream generated by the project and the project company's assets to repay all loans; and (v) *various financial guarantees*, where the guarantees are provided by the private sector partners, often limited to their equity contributions.[94] The state usually does not provide financial guarantees to lenders. As a result of the private sector guarantees, the lender receives its payment from the income generated from the project or directly from the public sector.

The private sector can raise funds for investment in public-private partnerships through a variety of ways. First, where services are destined for the public as end-users, the private sector can access private financing in the money markets using the projected income stream from the public paying for the public services (i.e. toll revenue) as collateral. However, where the public sector is the main recipient or purchaser of the relevant services from the public-private partnership, payments related to the demand for services or service payments by the public sector under operating contracts, which are based on continuity of service supply, can be used (i.e. shadow tolls paid by the public sector). The public sector may also make a direct contribution to project costs. This can take the form of equity (where there is profit sharing), a loan or a subsidy (where social returns exceed private returns). The public sector can also guarantee private sector borrowing.

Second, public-private partnership financing can be provided via special purpose vehicles (SPVs) comprising consortia of banks and other financial institutions, which are set up to combine and coordinate the use of their capital and expertise, as well as share any relevant risks. Accountancy treatment of the SPVs consolidated accounts is aligned with the party that controls the SPV.[95] If the private sector partner controls the SPV, its debt is recorded off-balance sheet for public sector borrowing considerations. If an SPV is controlled by the public sector, it should be consolidated with public sector borrowing, and its operations should be reflected in the fiscal accounts. A private partner–controlled SPV could be used to move debt from the public sector balance sheet through the direct involvement of public financial institutions, an explicit government guarantee of borrowing by an SPV or a presumption that the public sector stands behind it. However, if risk stays with the public sector, even if the SPV is controlled by the private sector partner, the SPV consolidation should be recorded in the public sector accounts.[96]

Third, a public-private partnership can be financed by securitisation of claims on future project revenues. In a typical public-private partnership securitisation operation, the public sector would sell a financial asset—its claim on future project revenue—to an SPV. The SPV would then sell securities backed by this asset to private investors and use the proceeds to pay the public sector, which in turn would use them to finance the public-private partnership. Interest and amortisation would be paid by the SPV to investors from the public sector's share of project revenue. Since investors' claim is against the SPV, government involvement in the public-private partnership appears limited. However, the public sector is in effect financing the public-private partnership, although recording sale proceeds received from the SPV as revenue masks this fact. Securitisation operations have often raised questions as to their appropriate accounting treatment. If assets or real estate are sold to an SPV below market price for the latter to use as collateral in issuing bonds on its own account to pay the public sector, the bonds should be treated as debt and the sale of the real estate should be recorded on budget because the risks and rewards related to ownership have not been transferred to the SPV.[97]

Risk and Public-Private Partnerships

The European Union has provided guidance on the risk transfer and the treatment of risk in public-private partnerships. Eurostat has issued a Decision which holds that a private partner will be assumed to bear the balance of public-private partnership risk if it bears most of the construction risk, and either most of the availability risk (which is also referred to as performance risk) or most of the demand risk.[98] The Eurostat Decision covers long-term contracts in areas where the private partner builds an asset and delivers services mainly to the public sector. Eurostat recommends that assets involved in public-private partnerships should be classified as nongovernment assets, and therefore recorded off-balance sheet for government if: (i) the private partner bears the construction risk, and (ii) the private partner bears one of either availability or demand risk.

Construction risk covers events such as late delivery, low standards, additional costs, technical deficiency and external negative effects. If the public sector makes payments to the private partner irrespective of the state of the asset, this indicates that the public sector bears most of the construction risk. Availability risk relates to the ability of the private partner to deliver the agreed volume and quality of service. Public sector payments to the private partners that are independent of service delivery indicate that the public sector bears most of the delivery risk. Demand risk covers the impact of the business cycle, market trends, competition and technological progress on the continued need for the service. Public sector payments to the private partner that are independent of demand indicate that the public sector bears most of the demand risk. Changes in demand due to changes in government policy are excluded.

Assessing Risk Transfer in Public-Private Partnerships

Public-private partnerships possess some distinctive characteristics, when compared with traditional public-private contractual formats. These characteristics reveal a different ethos in public sector management. The pivotal characteristic is that the private sector partner is expected to play a strategic role in financing and delivering the infrastructure project or the public service by providing its input into the various phases such as the design, implementation, construction, completion, operation and maintenance stages of the project. As a result, the duration of the relations between public and private sectors must reflect the need for longevity, in order to allow affordability for repayment on the part of the public sector and also the ability of the private sector to recoup its investment profitably. Another characteristic that complements both the strategic role of the private sector and its long-term engagement in delivering infrastructure and public services reflects on the distribution of risks between the public and private sectors and on the expectation that the private sector will assume substantial risks. Risk assessment in public-private partnerships is a totally different exercise than the assessment of risk in traditional public contracts.[99]

A range of different risks[100] features in public-private partnerships: *construction or project risk,* which is related to design problems, building cost overruns and project delays; *financial risk,* which is related to variability in interest rates, exchange rates and other factors affecting financing costs; *performance risk,* which is related to the availability of an asset and the continuity and quality of the relevant service provision; *demand risk,* which is related to the ongoing need for the relevant public services; and *residual value risk,* which is related to the future market price of an asset. Finally, political risks cover a general term used to describe risks arising from external or internal factors that are determined or influenced by governments. External political risks, such as currency convertibility, war, sanctions, political instability may be avoided, mitigated, hedged or insured against and could be significantly mitigated by actions of the state within which the public-private partnership is structured. On the other hand, internal political risks, such as taxation, terrorism, inflation and industrial unrest are usually uninsurable and could affect the risk allocation within public-private partnerships. Their respective mitigation would potentially reflect on the perceptions of the parties to manage such risks.

Another essential dynamic of public-private partnerships is that the private sector provides the financing. Public-private partnership financing is specialised financing which is different from both public finance and corporate finance. The public-private partnership debt financing is regarded as off-balance sheet borrowing, which means that the borrowing does not affect the state's public sector borrowing requirements and any measurements or calculations of measures of its indebtedness. Public-private partnerships allow the public sector to access alternative sources of capital.

Public-private partnerships seek to transfer risk from the public sector to the private sector. Whilst the provision of private capital and the strategic involvement of the private sector partner in managing the delivery of public services could prove beneficial, significant risk transfer from the public to the private sector is necessary to derive a genuine value-for-money partnership. The impact of risk transfer on financing costs and the pricing of risk to ensure efficient risk transfer are crucial in understanding how risk is treated within public-private partnerships.

The cost of capital needed to finance a public-private partnership depends only on the characteristics of project related risks and not on the source of finance. However, the source of financing can influence project risk depending on the maturity and sophistication of the risk bearing markets. On the one hand, within advanced risk-bearing markets, it is irrelevant whether project risk is borne by the public sector or the private sector. On the other hand, when risk-bearing markets are less developed, project risk depends on how widely that risk is spread. Since the public sector can spread risk across taxpayers in general, the usual argument is that this gives the public sector an advantage over the private sector in terms of managing risk. Nevertheless, the private sector can spread risk across financial markets. The outcome is likely to be that project risk is lower in the private sector. The public sector's ability to forcibly spread risk across taxpayers, while financial markets have to be provided with an incentive to accept risk, may put the private sector at more of a disadvantage as far as large and risky projects are concerned. The scope for the private sector to spread risk will also be somewhat limited in countries with less developed financial markets.

This outcome might contravene the assumption that private sector borrowing generally costs more than government borrowing. However, this mainly reflects differences in *default risk*. The public sector's power to tax reduces the likelihood that it will default on its debt, and the private sector is therefore prepared to lend to the public sector at close to the risk-free interest rate to finance risky projects. The crucial issue is whether public-private partnerships result in efficiency gains that offset higher private sector borrowing costs.[101]

Risk transfer from the public sector to the private sector has a significant influence on whether a public-private partnership is a more efficient and cost-effective alternative to public investment and publicly funded provision of services. The public sector and the private sector typically adopt different approaches to pricing market risk. The public sector tends to use the social time preference rate (STPR) or some other risk-free rate to discount future cash flows when appraising projects. The private sector in a public-private partnership project will include a risk premium in the discount rate it applies to future project earnings, where under the widely used capital asset pricing model (CAPM), the expected rate of return on an asset is defined as the risk-free rate of return plus a risk premium, the latter being the product of the market risk premium and a coefficient which measures the variance between the returns on that asset and market returns.

Some criteria have been devised to assess the degree of risk transfer involved in public-private partnerships. Where public-private partnership contracts do not provide a basis on which to distinguish between the risks associated with ownership and operation, the extent of risk transfer can be assessed by reference to the overall risk characteristics of a public-private partnership, where the specific aim for separable contracts (a distinction between asset ownership and delivery of public service elements) and non-separable contracts, is to determine whether the public sector or the private operator has an asset in a public-private partnership.[102]

For nonseparable contracts, the baseline for the assessment rests on the balance of demand risk and residual value risk borne by the public sector and the private operator.[103] Demand risk, which is an operating risk, and is the dominant consideration, is borne by the public sector if service payments to a private operator are independent of future need for the service. Residual value risk, which is an ownership risk, is borne by the public sector if a public-private partnership asset is transferred to the public sector for less than its true residual value. Residual value risk is borne by the public sector because the private operator reflects the difference between the expected residual value of the asset and the price at which the asset will be transferred to the public sector in the price it charges the public sector for services, or the revenue the public sector receives from a project. If the asset ends up being worth more or less than the amount reflected in the service payment or government revenue, any resulting gain benefits the public sector and any loss is borne by the public sector. Reference can also be made to various qualitative indicators, including government guarantees of private sector liabilities, and the extent of government influence over asset design and operation. The final conclusion is a judgement based on all relevant factors.[104]

6 The Procurement of Public-Private Partnerships

Considerable emphasis has been placed on observing the principles of transparency and accountability, competitiveness and value for money during the procurement process of public-private partnerships.[1]

The principles of transparency and accountability reveal the skeleton of public procurement regulation. They have direct influence on two fronts: i) the behavioral patterns of the state, public bodies and contracting authorities and ii) the emergence and structure of a *sui generis* market place which should have a certain level of competitiveness. The regulation of public procurement, through the principles of transparency and accountability provides for a pedestal of the legal, economic and policy interface between public and private sectors. The principles of transparency and accountability emanating from public procurement regulation also have a transferable nature within public administrations of Member States. Although generic at first sight, their application unfolds desirable effects in the spheres of law and policy, effects which have long-lasting influences.

THE DILEMMA OF SELECTING A PRIVATE PARTNER

The selection of a private partner in a public-private partnership to undertake the financing, organisation and delivery of public interest tasks while functioning as part of a mixed entity—the public-private partnership—can therefore not be based exclusively on the quality of its capital contribution or its experience, but should also take account of the characteristics of its offer in terms of the specific services to be provided. The conditions governing the creation of the entity must be clearly laid down when issuing the call for competition for the tasks that one wishes to entrust to the private partner. Also, these conditions must not discriminate against or constitute an unjustified barrier to the freedom to provide services or to freedom of establishment, or be disproportionate to the desired objective.

In this context, the transaction involving the creation of such an entity does not generally present a problem in terms of the applicable Community law when it constitutes a means of executing the task entrusted under a contract to a private partner. However, the conditions governing the creation of the entity must be clearly laid down when issuing the call for competition for those tasks that one wishes to entrust to the private partner. Also, these conditions must not discriminate against or constitute an unjustified barrier to the freedom to provide services or the freedom of establishment, or be disproportionate to the desired objective.

In many jurisdictions, legislation allows the mixed entities, in which the participation by the public sector involves the contracting body, to participate in a procedure for the award of a public contract or concession even when these entities are only in the course of being incorporated.[2] In this situation, the entity will be definitively incorporated only after the contract has actually been awarded to it. In many states a practice has developed that tends to confuse the phase of incorporating the entity and the phase of allocating the tasks.[3] Thus the purpose of the procedure launched by the contracting authority is to create a mixed entity to which certain tasks are entrusted.

Such a solution does not provide satisfactory results nor does it comply with EU law. In the first case, there is a risk that the effective competition will be distorted by the privileged position enjoyed by the company being incorporated and, consequently, by the private partner participating in this company. In the second case, the specific procedure for selecting the private partner also poses many problems. The contracting authorities encounter certain difficulties in defining the subject matter of the contract or concession in a sufficiently clear and precise manner, as they are obliged to do. This in turn raises problems not only with regard to the principles of transparency and equality of treatment, but even risks prejudicing the general interest objectives that the public authority wishes to attain. It is also evident that the lifetime of the created entity does not generally coincide with the duration of the contract or concession awarded, and this appears to encourage the extension of the task entrusted to this entity without true competition at the time of this renewal. In addition, it should be noted that the joint creation of such entities must respect the principle of nondiscrimination with respect to nationality in general, and the free circulation of capital in particular. Thus, for example, the public authorities cannot normally make their position as shareholder in such an entity contingent on excessive privileges that do not derive from a normal application of company law.[4]

On the other hand, the creation of an institutional public-private partnership may also lead to a change in the body of shareholders of a public entity. When public authorities grant an economic operator a definite influence in a business under a transaction involving a capital transfer, and when this transaction has the effect of entrusting to this operator tasks falling within the scope of the law on public contracts which had been previously exercised, directly or indirectly, by the public authorities, the provisions on freedom of establishment require compliance with the principles of transparency and equality of treatment in order to ensure that every potential operator has equal access to performing those activities that had been reserved.[5]

On the other hand, the creation of an institutional public private partnership may also lead to a change in the body of shareholders of a public entity. When public authorities grant an economic operator a definite influence in a business under a transaction involving a capital transfer, and when this transaction has the effect of entrusting to this operator tasks falling within the scope of the law on public contracts which had been previously exercised, directly or indirectly, by the public authorities, the provisions on freedom of establishment require compliance with the principles of transparency and equality of treatment, in order to ensure that every potential operator has equal access to performing those activities which had been reserved.

The Public Procurement regime[6] which governs the award of public contracts in the supplies, works and services sectors, as well as in utilities offers a workable framework upon which public-private partnerships may be procured and concluded by Member States and their contracting authorities.

SELECTION AND QUALIFICATION

The public procurement Directives relating to the qualitative selection and qualification criteria refer to the technical ability and knowledge of tenderers, where proof may be furnished by evidence of educational or professional qualifications, previous experience in performing public contracts and statements on the contractor's expertise.[7] The references, which the tenderers may be required to produce, must be specified in the notice or invitation to tender. The rules relating to technical capacity and eligibility of tenderers represent an exhaustive list and are capable of producing direct effect.[8] The *Transporoute* legacy paved the way for the Court to elaborate on forms of selection and qualification, such as registration in lists of recognised contractors. Such lists exist in Member States and tenderers may use their registration in them as an alternative means of proving their technical suitability, also before contracting authorities of other Member States. *CEI—Bellini* followed the same line[9], although it conferred discretion to contracting authorities to request further evidence of technical capacity, other than the mere certificate of registration in official lists of approved contractors, on the grounds that such lists might not be referring to uniform classifications.

Ballast Nedam I[10] took qualitative selection and qualification criteria a step further. The Court ruled that a holding company which does not itself carry out works may not be precluded from registration on an official list of approved contractors, and consequently, from participating in tendering procedures, if it shows that it actually has available to it the resources of its subsidiaries necessary to carry out the contracts, unless the references of those subsidiaries do not themselves satisfy the qualitative selection criteria specified in the Directives. *Ballast Nedam II*[11] conferred an obligation to the authorities of Member States, which are responsible for the compilation of lists of approved contractors to take into account evidence of the technical capacity of companies belonging to the same group, when assessing the parent company's technical capacity for inclusion into the list, provided the holding company establishes that it has available to it the resources of the companies belonging to the group that are necessary to carry out public contracts. *Holst Italia*[12], by analogy applied the *Ballast* principle to undertakings that belong to the same group structure but do not have the status of a holding company and the requisite availability of the technical expertise of its subsidiaries. The Court held that with regard to the qualitative criteria relevant to the economic, financial and technical standing, a tenderer may rely on the standing of other entities, regardless of the legal nature of the links which it has with them, provided that it is able to show that it actually has at its disposal the resources of those entities which are necessary for performance of a public contract.

However, for the purposes of assessing the financial and economic standing of contractors, an exception to the exhaustive (and directly applicable) nature of technical capacity and qualification rules has been made. Evidence of financial and economic standing may be provided by means of references including: i) appropriate statements from bankers; ii) the presentation of the firm's balance sheets or extracts from the balance sheets where these are published under company law provisions; and iii) a statement of the firm's annual turnover and the turnover on construction works for the three previous financial years. The nonexhaustive character of the list of references in relation to the contractors' economic and financial standing was recognised by the Court in the *CEI-Bellini* case[13], where the value of the works which may be carried out at any one time may constitute a proof of the contractors' economic and financial standing. The contracting authorities are allowed to fix such a limit, as the provisions of the public procurement Directives do not aim at delimiting the powers of Member States, but at determining the references or evidence which may be furnished in order to establish the contractors' financial and economic standing. Of interest is the recent case *ARGE*[14], where even the receipt of aid or subsidies incompatible with the Treaty by an entity may be a reason for disqualification from the selection process, as an obligation to repay an illegal aid would threaten the financial stability of the tenderer in question.

The Court also maintained[15] that the examination of a contractor's suitability based on its technical capacity and qualifications and its financial and economic standing may take place simultaneously with the award procedures of a contract.[16] However, the two procedures (the suitability evaluation and bid evaluation) are totally distinct processes, which shall not be confused.[17] In *Lianakis*, the specific issue in question was the fusion of selection and award criteria, an issue already clarified by the Court. The Court has maintained[18] that the examination of a contractor's suitability based on its technical capacity and qualifications and its financial and economic standing may take place simultaneously with the award procedures of a contract.[19] However, the two procedures (the suitability evaluation and bid evaluation) are totally distinct processes, which shall not be confused.[20]

In *Lianakis* the contracting authority specified the bidder's experience on projects in the last three years, as well as the bidder's manpower and equipment and the bidder's ability to complete project by deadline as award criteria. The Court reiterated that award criteria cannot be 'essentially linked to the tenderer's ability to perform the contract in question', pointing that the criteria used by the contracting authorities were in fact selection criteria in order to establish suitability of interested tenderers, and they must relate to financial standing and technical capability of interested tenderers. The Court concluded that the public procurement Directives prohibit selection criteria from being used as award criteria and reminded contracting authorities the selection and award processes are two independent and separate process in a public procurement and that a fusion of selection and award criteria is infringing public procurement rules. In *Commission v. Greece*[21], a railway utility advertised a contract for engineering services whereby non-Greek engineers were excluded since they submitted qualifications different from those required for the relevant contract. The Court ruled that the utility had confused selection and award criteria and applied the *Lianakis* ruling *verbatim*.

References as a Selection Criterion

A question arose[22] as to whether the public procurement rules preclude contracting authorities from utilising references relating to the products offered by tenderers to other customers as an award criterion, even in cases where the award of the contract is made to the most economically advantageous offer. The Court held that any references obtained by a contracting authority in relation to products or services offered by tenderers to other customers should not be used as an award criterion, as they are irrelevant to the economic or qualitative evaluation of the tenders. Such references may only serve as a criterion for establishing suitability of tenderers for carrying out the contract, a process which must be distinct from the award procedures.[23]

Location of Contractors as Selection Criterion

The location of contractors can only play a role in the selection and qualification stage[24] and not in the award stage of public contracts. The principle of nondiscrimination which underpins the public procurement rules precludes a favourable assessment of a tenderer's offer on the grounds of its physical proximity to the premises of the contracting authority in order to facilitate product inspections. The Court maintained that such a criterion cannot constitute an award criterion. It forwarded two reasons. First, any physical inspection requirements for products or services or any site visits required by contracting authorities fall under specific provisions of the public procurement Directives[25] regarding technical capacity and suitability of tenderers, and as such can only be used as selection criteria. Secondly, the proximity of contractors' premises to the premises of the contracting authority cannot be a factor in deciding the award criteria, even if the award is made to the most economically advantageous offer, since it cannot identify qualitative or economic factors. Lower transport or delivery costs, as a result of the proximity of tenderers to the contracting authority or the *locus* of the contract itself, could only influence the evaluation of their technical capacity and suitability.

Market Testing and Selection of Undertakings

Participation in the preparatory stages of a public contract should not preclude an undertaking from submitting a tender for that public contract, where that undertaking has not been given an opportunity to prove that his previous involvement with the preparation of the contract has not distorted competition amongst the tenderers.[26] According to the Court[27], public procurement law precludes a particular tender being eliminated as a matter of course and on the basis of a criterion which is applied automatically. The exclusion of an undertaking, particularly in the case of participation in preparatory works, must be preceded by a full and differentiated examination of the kind of preparatory works concerned, in particular as regards access to the contract specifications. Exclusion is possible only if the undertaking has obtained, through its preparatory activity, specific information relating to the contract which gives it a competitive advantage. The principle of nondiscrimination[28] which underlies the public procurement regime is applicable to all tenderers, including those who have participated in the preparatory stage of the contract. The latter should be excluded from participating in a public contract only if it appears clearly and specifically that by such participation alone they have gained an advantage which distorts competition as the ultimate objective of the regime is the promotion of effective competition in public markets.[29]

The principle of nondiscrimination requires that comparable situations must not be treated differently and that different situations must not be treated in the same way unless such treatment is objectively justified.[30] The Court recognised that an undertaking who has been instructed to carry out research, experiments, studies or development in connection with a public contract may have an advantage over other tenderers. However, on the grounds of the principle of proportionality and in pursuit of the objectivity doctrine enshrined in the public procurement *acquis*, all tenderers must have equality of opportunity when formulating their tenders[31], including tenderers that have carried out certain preparatory work. The Court expanded its conclusions to cover even public undertakings which have previously assisted other contracting authorities in the preparation of specifications related to public contracts, as well as private undertakings which are connected with undertakings that have assisted in the preparation of tender documents or contract specifications.

Reliance of Tenderers on Other Sources, Subcontracting and Substitution of Consortia Members

The Court reiterated[32] that a tenderer or a candidate which, with a view to being admitted to participate in tendering procedures, intends to rely on the resources of entities or undertakings with which it is directly or indirectly linked, must demonstrate the availability of those resources which are necessary for the performance of the contract.[33] A provision in an invitation to tender which prohibits recourse to subcontracting for material parts of the contract is contrary to the public procurement Directives.[34] Nevertheless, the public procurement Directives do not preclude a prohibition or a restriction on the use of subcontracting for the performance of essential parts of the contract in the case where the contracting authority has not been in a position to verify the technical and economic capacities of the subcontractors when examining the tenders.[35]

Makedoniko Metro[36] posed the question of disqualifying a successful consortium which had been awarded a public contract on the grounds of changing its composition by means of substitution amongst its members.[37] The incomplete harmonisation of laws with respect to consortia participation in public procurement and the existence of only selective rules on their legal status[38] provide for discretion on the part of Member States as to the legal consequences of changes in the composition of a consortium. However, the Court positioned the fundamental principles of transparency and competition[39] which underpin public procurement law, as parameters of the Member States' freedom to implement aspects which have not been expressly provided for in the relevant Directives. The principle of transparency equates to the principle of equal treatment and represents a verification of the principle of nondiscrimination, as a means of compliance.[40] The Court suggested that even in the case where the principle of transparency cannot be observed within the public procurement Directives, its surrogate principle of equality, which is recognised as a general principle of European law, should prevail.[41]

Proportionality and Exclusion Grounds for Tenderers

Contracting authorities may apply measures which result in exclusion of private sector undertakings from participating in tendering procedures on grounds of equal treatment and transparency, only if these measures are proportionate. In *Michaniki*[42] the Court ruled that Greek law prohibiting all media companies from bidding for public contracts was unlawful, as it contravenes with the principle of freedom to provide services. Also, *Assitur*[43] ruled that Italian law prohibiting affiliates from the same group from submitting separate bids in a tendering procedure contravenes the public procurement Directives and finally *Serrantoni*[44] maintained that a ban on a consortium participating in the same tender as members of that consortium was against the spirit and letter of the procurement Directives and the underlying Community law principle on freedom to provide services.

AWARD PROCEDURES

Negotiated Procedures without Prior Publicity

The rules governing negotiated procedures without prior publication are defined restrictively in the public procurement Directives.[45] The Court has reiterated their exceptional character[46] and the exhaustive nature of the grounds of their application.[47]

Use of Negotiated Procedure for Technical Reasons or Exclusive Rights

The definition of the condition that the works may 'only be carried out by a particular contractor' should be interpreted restrictively, as it constitutes derogation and should apply only where there exist exceptional circumstances.[48] The Court rejected[49] the existence of exclusive rights on the grounds of contractual relations between the contracting authority and the undertakings concerned and regarded the abuse of this provision as contrary to the right of establishment and freedom to provide services. Interestingly, the Court elucidated that exclusive rights might include contractual arrangements such as know-how and intellectual property rights.[50] Contracting authorities cannot justify the use of negotiated procedures without prior publicity by simply invoking technical constraints in nonspecific terms.[51] Instead they must explain in detail why, in the circumstances of the case, technical reasons made it absolutely necessary for the contract to be awarded to a particular contractor. The burden of proof of the existence of exceptional circumstances lies on the contracting authority seeking to rely on them.[52]

The Court maintained that a contracting authority may take account of criteria relating to environmental protection at the various stages of a procedure for the award of public contracts.[53] Therefore, it is not impossible that a technical reason relating to the protection of the environment, such as the thermal treatment of waste and the proximity of the disposal plant, may be taken into account in an assessment of whether the contract at issue may be awarded to an undertaking without prior publicity.[54] However, contracting authorities must furnish evidence which objectively justify the use of negotiated procedures without prior publicity on environmental grounds.[55] Furthermore, the procedure used where there is a technical reason of that kind must comply with the fundamental principles of Community law, in particular the principle of nondiscrimination, the right of establishment and the freedom to provide services.[56]

Extreme Urgency as a Reason for Negotiated Procedure

The Court maintained the need for a justification test based on the proportionality principle, as well as the existence of a causal link between the alleged urgency and the unforeseen events.[57] The causality of conditions justifying extreme urgency is based on a strict burden of proof test[58] and an irrefutable factual link between unforeseeable event and the extreme urgency.[59] The Court maintained that where the causality link is not present, accelerated restricted procedures should be used.[60] The wording of the relevant provisions of the public procurement Directives ('strictly necessary', 'extreme urgency', 'events unforeseen') attaches strict conditions to any reliance on the procedure and must be construed narrowly.[61] The circumstances invoked to justify extreme urgency must not in any event be attributable to the contracting authorities.[62] Thus, organisational issues and internal considerations on the part of the contacting authority cannot justify any urgency requirements.

Repetition of Similar Works within Three Years

This procedure may only be adopted during the three years following the conclusion of the original contract and subject to notice which should be given in the original invitation to tender. The Court, based on the principle of legal certainty, held[63] that in the light of a comparison[64] of the language versions of that provision, the expression 'conclusion of the original contract' must be understood as meaning the time when the original contract was entered into and not as referring to the completion of the works to which the contract relates.

THE COMPETITIVE DIALOGUE AS THE PROCUREMENT PROCEDURE FOR DELIVERING PUBLIC-PRIVATE PARTNERSHIPS

The competitive dialogue is the most publicised change brought about by the new EU public procurement regime[65] and has been regarded as a benchmark of a process in procuring public-private partnerships worldwide. Its inception is attributed to three reasons: i) the inability of open or restricted procedures to facilitate the award of complex public contracts, including concessions and public-private partnerships, ii) the exceptional nature of negotiated procedures without prior advertisement[66] and iii) the restrictive interpretation[67] of the grounds for using negotiated procedures with prior advertisement.

In cases of particularly complex contracts, contracting authorities may provide that where the use of the open or restricted procedure will not allow the award of the contract, the use of the competitive dialogue procedure is the appropriate award procedure.[68] The competitive dialogue is a procedure in which any economic operator may request to participate and whereby the contracting authority conducts a dialogue with the candidates admitted to that procedure, with the aim of developing one or more suitable alternatives capable of meeting its requirements, and on the basis of which the candidates chosen are invited to tender.[69] However, the competitive dialogue must be used exceptionally in cases of particularly complex contracts, where the use of the open or restricted procedures will not allow the award of the contract, and the use of negotiated procedures cannot be justified. A public contract is considered to be particularly complex where the contracting authorities are not able to define in an objective manner the technical specifications which are required to pursue the project, or they are not able to specify the legal or financial make-up of a project.

A public contract is considered to be particularly complex where the contracting authorities are not able to define objectively the technical means of the contract.[70] In particular, to formulate the technical specifications required for the performance of the contract, contracting authorities must take into account any mandatory national technical rules, to the extent that they are compatible with Community law.[71] In addition, the technical specifications must be formulated by sufficiently precise parameters having reference to the performance or functional requirements, including environmental characteristics, of the works, supplies or services. The requirement of sufficient precision in the formulation of the technical specifications must be present in order to allow tenderers to determine the subject matter of the contract and also to allow contracting authorities to award the contract. In such cases, where the technical specifications cannot be formulated with sufficient precision so they are capable of satisfying their needs or objectives of the contracting authority, the contract is deemed to be particularly complex.[72]

A public contract is also considered particularly complex in cases where contracting authorities cannot determine the performance or functional requirements of a project in conformity with the technical standards defined in Annex VI of the Directive and, in order of preference, national standards transposing European standards, European technical approvals, common technical specifications, international standards or any equivalent standard.[73] In such cases, the inability to comply with the required technical standards precludes the contracting authority from determining the technical specifications necessary for the performance of the contract and as a consequence, the needs and objectives of the contracting authority cannot be met.[74] Therefore, the public contract is deemed to be particularly complex.

Finally, when contracting authorities cannot objectively specify the legal or the financial make-up of a project, the contract is deemed to be particularly complex. The competitive dialogue procedure is complex, time-consuming and expensive on both public and private sectors, as it has three main phases and many options within these phases.

Firstly, the advertisement phase obliges contracting authorities to publish a contract notice or a descriptive document outlining their needs and basic specifications of the project. After that phase and before launching a competitive dialogue for the award of a contract, contracting authorities may, using a technical dialogue, seek or accept advice which may be used in the preparation of the specifications, provided that such advice does not have the effect of precluding competition.

Secondly, a selection phase reduces the candidates to be invited to the competitive dialogue according to the procedure for verification of the suitability and choice of participants and award of contracts, criteria for qualitative selection, and suitability to pursue a professional activity.[75] The minimum number of candidates should be three but it could be lower if there is sufficient evidence of competitiveness in the process or the limited number of initial respondents to the contract notice precludes the invitation of at least three candidates.

Thirdly, the competitive dialogue is opened by the commencement of the award phase. Contracting authorities must open a dialogue with the candidates selected in accordance with, the aim of which is to identify the means best suited to satisfying their needs. They may discuss all aspects of the contract with the chosen candidates, ensuring equality of treatment among all tenderers. In particular, they must not provide information in a discriminatory manner which may give some tenderers an advantage over others. Contracting authorities may not reveal to the other participants' solutions proposed or other confidential information communicated by a candidate participating in the dialogue without prior agreement granted from that candidate.

Contracting authorities may provide for the competitive dialogue to take place in successive stages in order to reduce the number of solutions to be discussed with the candidates. They may continue the dialogue until they can identify the solution or solutions which are capable of meeting their needs. Having declared that the dialogue is concluded and having informed the participants, contracting authorities must ask them to submit their final tenders on the basis of the solution or solutions presented and specified during the dialogue.

After this phase is over (closure of the competitive dialogue), there are four stages until the contract award. Firstly, contracting authorities must ask all remaining candidates to submit their final tenders. Secondly, these tenders need to be finalised prior to their evaluation. Thirdly, the selection of the winning tenderer must take place in accordance with the criteria stipulated in the contract notice and fourthly the winning tenderer must provide further clarification and his commitment to undertake the project.

The tenders must contain all the elements required and considered necessary for the performance of the project. They may be clarified, specified and fine-tuned at the request of the contracting authority. However, any additional information must not involve any changes to the basic features of the tender or the call for tender, nor allow for variations which are likely to distort competition or have a discriminatory effect. In the author's view, there is a great deal of uncertainty over the meaning of clarification, additional provision of tender specification and the extent of fine-tuning, to the degree of compromising the competitiveness and integrity of the procedure.

Contracting authorities must assess the tenders received on the basis of the award criteria laid down in the contract notice or the descriptive document and must choose the most economically advantageous tender. At the request of the contracting authority, the tenderer identified as having submitted the most economically advantageous tender may be asked to clarify aspects of the tender or confirm commitments contained in the tender provided this does not have the effect of modifying substantial aspects of the tender or of the call for tender and does not risk distorting competition or discriminating against other candidates.

THE COMPETITIVE DIALOGUE IN PRACTICE

The Conduct of the Competitive Dialogue

When contracting authorities wish to use the competitive dialogue as an award procedure, they must publish a notice for the contract setting out their needs and requirements.[76] The notice must define in clear and objective manner the needs and requirements to be achieved through the contract. Alternatively, a descriptive document may be use to stipulate the contracting authority's need and requirements. Contracting authorities may specify prices or payments to the participants in the dialogue.[77]

The preliminary phase of the competitive dialogue is to select a number of candidates with which contracting authorities may commence a dialogue with the aim to identify the means best suited to meet the needs and requirements. The selection process should take place in accordance with the usual selection provisions found in Articles 44 to 52 of the Directive, covering *inter alia* the personal situation of the candidates, their suitability to pursue a professional activity, their economic and financial standing and their technical and professional ability. The Directive does not specify the minimum number of candidates to be invited to participate in the competitive dialogue. However, the number of candidates should be adequate in order to provide sufficient competition and to identify enough solutions from which the solution which meets the needs and requirements of the contracting authority will emerge.

The Opening of the Competitive Dialogue

The most important requirement in this phase is the equal treatment of candidates by the contracting authority.[78] They may discuss all aspects of the contract with the chosen candidates. However, they must not provide information in a discriminatory manner which may give some candidates an advantage over others.

The opening of the competitive dialogue commences when contracting authorities simultaneously and in writing invite the selected candidates to take part in the dialogue.[79] The invitation to the candidates must include either a copy of the specifications or of the descriptive document and any supporting documents or a reference in order to access by electronic means the specifications and any supporting documents.[80] Where an entity other than the contracting authority responsible for the award procedure has the specifications, the descriptive document or any supporting documents, the invitation must state the address from which those documents may be requested and, if appropriate, the deadline for requesting such documents, and the sum payable for obtaining them and any payment procedures.

The invitation to participate in the dialogue must contain also[81] a reference to the contract notice published; the date and the address set for the start of consultation and the language or languages used; a reference to any additional documents to be submitted, either in support or supplementing of verifiable declarations by the participants that they meet minimum capacity levels required for the contract, levels which must be related to and be proportionate to the subject matter of the contract and previously indicated in the contract notice; the relative weighting of criteria for the award of the contract or, where appropriate, the descending order of importance for such criteria, if they are not given in the contract notice, the specifications or the descriptive document.

The deadline for the receipt of the tenders, the address to which the tenders must be sent and the language or languages in which the tenders must be drawn up must not appear in the invitation to participate in the dialogue but instead in the invitation to submit a tender.

In principle, contracting authorities may not reveal to the other participants solutions proposed or other confidential information communicated by a candidate participating in the dialogue without that candidate's prior agreement.[82] The dialogue should be continued until the contracting authority can identify the solution or solutions, if necessary after comparing them, which are capable of meeting its needs.[83]

The dialogue with the selected candidates can take place in a single stage or in successive stages.[84] The reason for the successive stages in the competitive dialogue is to reduce the number of solutions to be discussed by the contracting authority and the candidates. When contracting authorities wish to have recourse to successive stages during the competitive dialogue, their intention must be mentioned in the contract notice or the descriptive document. In order to reduce the solutions on offer during the competitive dialogue, contracting authorities must apply the award criteria in the contract notice or the descriptive document. Contracting authorities must ensure that the elimination of solutions proposed by candidates does not jeopardise a genuine competition, which is necessary for the final tendering stage of the competitive dialogue.[85]

The Closure of the Competitive Dialogue

When a particular solution or a number of solutions have been identified, the contracting authority must declare that the dialogue is concluded.[86] It must communicate its decision to all candidates that have participated and at the same time ask them to submit their final tenders on the basis of the solution or solutions presented and specified during the dialogue. The minimum number of candidates which could be invited to submit tenders is three.

The Submission of Final Tenders

The tenders submitted by the invited candidates must contain all the elements required and necessary for the performance of the project, as identified in the solution or the solutions during the dialogue between the contracting authorities and the candidates.[87]

These tenders may be clarified, specified and fine-tuned at the request of the contracting authority. However, such clarification, specification, fine-tuning or additional information may not involve changes to the basic features of the tender or the call for tender, variations in which are likely to distort competition or have a discriminatory effect.

For the assessment of the tenders, contracting authorities must apply the criteria specified in the contract notice or the descriptive document.[88] After the assessment exercise of the tenders, the contracting authority must identify the candidate that submitted the most economically advantageous tender in accordance with Article 53 of the Directive.

The Award of the Contract under the Competitive Dialogue

Contracting authorities may award the contract straightforward or seek clarifications of any aspects of the tender or commitments contained which were contained in the tender.[89] A public contract awarded under the procedures of the competitive dialogue must be based solely on the most economically advantageous tender as the award criterion. The candidate which submitted the most economically advantageous tender, at the request of the contracting authority, may be asked to clarify aspects of the tender or confirm commitments contained in the tender provided this does not have the effect of modifying substantial aspects of the tender or of the call for tender and does not risk distorting competition or causing discrimination.

AWARD CRITERIA

Two criteria laid down in the public procurement Directives provide the conditions under which contracting authorities award public contracts: the lowest price or the most economically advantageous offer.[90]

The first criterion indicates that, subject to the qualitative criteria and financial and economic standing, contracting authorities do not rely on any other factor than the price quoted to complete the contract. The tenderer who submits the cheapest offer must be awarded the contract. It should be mentioned that the Directives provide for an automatic disqualification of an 'obviously abnormally low offer'. The term has not been interpreted in detail by the Court and serves rather as an indication of a 'lower bottom limit'.[91] The Court, however, pronounced that contracting authorities are required to examine the details of the tender before deciding the award of the contract. The contracting authorities are under duty to seek from the tenderer an explanation for the price submitted or to inform him that his tender appears to be abnormally low and to allow a reasonable time within which to submit further details, before making any decision as to the award of the contract.

On the other hand, the meaning of the most economically advantageous offer includes a series of factors chosen by the contracting authority, including price, delivery or completion date, running costs, cost-effectiveness, profitability, technical merit, product or work quality, aesthetic and functional characteristics, after-sales service and technical assistance, commitments with regard to spare parts and components and maintenance costs, security of supplies. The above list is not exhaustive and the factors listed therein serve as a guideline for contracting authorities in the weighted evaluation process of the contract award. The Court reiterated the flexible and wide interpretation of the relevant award criterion[92] and had no difficulty in declaring that contracting authorities may use the most economically advantageous offer as award criterion by choosing the factors which they want to apply in evaluating tenders[93], provided these factors are mentioned, in hierarchical order or descending sequence in the invitation to tender or the contract documents[94], so tenderers and interested parties can clearly ascertain the relative weight of factors other than price for the evaluation process. However, factors, which have no strict relevance in determining the most economically advantageous offer by reference to objective criteria do involve an element of arbitrary choice and therefore should be considered as incompatible with the Directives.[95]

Social Considerations as Award Criteria

The most economically advantageous offer as an award criterion has provided the Court for the opportunity to balance the economic considerations of public procurement with policy choices. Although in numerous instances the Court has maintained the importance of the economic approach[96] to the regulation of public sector contracts, it has also recognised the relative discretion of contracting authorities to utilise noneconomic considerations as award criteria. In *Beentjes*[97], the Court ruled that social policy considerations and in particular measures aiming at the combating of long-term unemployment could only be part of the award criteria of public contracts, especially in cases where the most economically advantageous offer is selected.

In *Nord-pas-de-Calais*, the Court considered whether a condition linked to a local project to combat unemployment could be considered as an award criterion of the relevant contract. The Court held that the most economically advantageous offer does not preclude all possibility for the contracting authorities to use as a criterion a condition linked to the campaign against unemployment provided that that condition is consistent with all the fundamental principles of EU law.[98] The Court therefore accepted the employment considerations as an award criterion, part of the most economically advantageous offer, provided it is consistent with the fundamental principle of nondiscrimination and it is advertised in the contract notice.

Environmental Considerations as Award Criteria

In *Concordia*[99], the Court was asked *inter alia* whether environmental considerations such as low emissions and noise levels of vehicles could be included amongst the factors of the most economically advantageous criterion, in order to promote certain types of vehicles that meet or exceed certain emission and noise levels. The Court followed the *Beentjes* principle, and established that contracting authorities are free to determine the factors under which the most economically advantageous offer is to be assessed and that environmental considerations could be part of the award criteria, provided they do not discriminate over alternative offers, as well as they have been clearly publicised in the tender or contract documents. However, the inclusion of such factors in the award criteria should not prevent alternative offers that satisfy the contract specifications being taken into consideration by contracting authorities. Clearly the Court wanted to exclude any possibility of environmental considerations being part of selection criteria or disguised as technical specifications, capable of discriminating against tenderers that could not meet them. Criteria relating to the environment, in order to be permissible as additional criteria under the most economically advantageous offer, must satisfy a number of conditions, namely they must be objective, universally applicable, strictly relevant to the contract in question, and clearly contribute an economic advantage to the contracting authority.[100]

Variants

According to the public procurement Directives[101], where the criterion for the award of the contract is that of the most economically advantageous tender, contracting authorities may take account of variants which are submitted by a tenderer and meet the minimum specifications required by the contracting authorities. Contracting authorities must state in the contract documents the minimum specifications to be respected by the variants and any specific requirements for their presentation and they must indicate in the tender notice if variants are not permitted. Contracting authorities may not reject the submission of a variant on the sole grounds that it has been drawn up with technical specifications defined by reference to national standards transposing European standards, to European technical approvals or to common technical specifications referred to in the public procurement Directives.[102]

Where the contracting authority has not excluded the submission of variants, it is under an obligation to set out in the contract documents the minimum specifications with which those variants must comply. Consequently, a reference made in the contract documents to a provision of national legislation cannot satisfy the requirements of transparency and equal treatment of tenderers wishing to forward a variant bid.[103] Tenderers may be deemed to be informed in the same way of the minimum specifications with which their variants must comply in order to be considered by the contracting authority only where those specifications are set out in the contract documents. This involves an obligation of transparency designed to ensure compliance with the principle of equal treatment of tenderers, which must be complied with in any procurement procedure governed by the Directive.[104]

A question arose as to whether a contracting authority can reject an alternative tender which differs from a tender conforming to the contract specifications in that it proposes different technical specifications, without specifying the comparative parameters to be used to assess the equivalence of all tenders.[105] The Court asserted that that consideration of variants is subject to fulfillment of the requirement that the minimum specifications with which those variants must comply be set out in the contract documents and that a mere reference in those documents to a provision of national legislation is insufficient to satisfy that requirement. Variants may not be taken into consideration where the contracting authority has failed to comply with the requirements with respect to the statement of the minimum specifications, even if they have not been declared inadmissible in the tender notice. The Court held that award criteria based on the most economically advantageous offer can apply only to variants which have been properly taken into consideration by a contracting authority.

The obligation to set out the minimum specifications required by a contracting authority in order to take variants into consideration is not satisfied where the contract documents merely refer to a provision of national legislation requiring an alternative tender to ensure the performance of work which is qualitatively equivalent to that for which tenders are invited, without further specifying the comparative parameters on the basis of which such equivalence is to be assessed.[106]

Criteria Related to the Subject Matter of the Contract

Although in numerous instances the Court has maintained the importance of the economic approach[107] to the regulation of public procurement, it has also recognised the relative discretion of contracting authorities to utilise noneconomic considerations as award criteria. Under the most economically advantageous offer award criterion, environmental[108] and socioeconomic considerations[109] are allowed to play a part in the evaluation process and determine the award of public contracts, provided that they are linked to the subject matter of the contract, do not confer an unrestricted freedom of choice on the authority[110], are expressly mentioned in the contract documents or the tender notice[111], and comply with all the fundamental principles of Community law, in particular the principle of nondiscrimination.[112] Often, questions are asked as to the possibility of a contracting authority to lay down criteria that pursue advantages which cannot be objectively assigned a direct economic value, such as advantages related to the protection of the environment or the promotion of employment policies. The Court held that each of the award criteria used by contracting authorities to identify the most economically advantageous tender must not necessarily be of a purely economic nature.[113]

The Court maintained that a criterion relating to the reliability of supplies is a legitimate factor in determining the most economically advantageous offer for a contracting authority.[114] However, the capacity of tenderers to perform the terms and conditions of the contract cannot be legitimately linked with the subject matter of the contract, unless the contracting authority provides for an objectively determined verification. Therefore, the link of noneconomic criteria to the subject mater of the contract presupposes the existence of procedural requirements which permit the authentication of the accuracy of the information contained in the tenders and confirm that the criteria serve the objective pursued.

Criteria relevant to the procurement of energy from renewable sources[115] as well as ecological criteria including the requirement for reduction of emissions or noise levels could comprise features of the most economically advantageous offer, as factors which are not purely economic may influence the value of a tender from the point of view of the contracting authority. When contracting authorities decide to award a contract to the tenderer who submits the most economically advantageous tender, they may take criteria relating to the preservation of the environment into consideration, provided that they are linked to the subject matter of the contract, do not confer an unrestricted freedom of choice on the authority, are expressly mentioned in the contract documents or the tender notice, and comply with all the fundamental principle of nondiscrimination.

Publicity of Weighting of Criteria

The Court held that publicity requirements under the public procurement rules are extended to the weighting of the selection criteria for the award of public contracts[116], although the public procurement Directives contain no specific provision relating to the prior advertisement concerning the criteria for selecting the candidates who will be invited to tender in the context of award procedures.[117] The Court reiterated that the criteria and conditions which govern public contracts must be given sufficient publicity by contracting authorities[118], on the grounds of the principle of nondis-crimination, which implies an obligation of transparency in order to enable verification that the former has been complied with.[119]

THE PROCUREMENT OF CONCESSIONS

Legislative Reforms on Concessions

The Commission announced its intention to introduce a legislative frame-work on concessions.[120] The Europe 2020 strategy highlights the importance of public-private partnerships for accelerating growth and boosting inno-vation. In addition, the Single Market Act announced the adoption of a legislative initiative on concessions in 2011 in order to promote public-private partnerships and to help deliver better value for money for users of services and for contracting authorities, while improving market access for EU undertakings by ensuring transparency, equal treatment and a level playing field across the EU. The Commission considered that a legislative proposal in the field of concessions as one of the key measures that will facilitate the setting up of public-private partnerships, and as such it will render it as a means of stimulating economic recovery in the context of the current economic crisis across the EU. Public-private partnerships are also important for accomplishing structural reforms and could play an increas-ing role in accompanying EU policies in the context of the EU multi-annual financial frameworks.

The main reasons for adoption of a set of rules on concessions which is separate from the framework of the substantive public procurement Direc-tives are reflecting the differences of the objectives pursued as well as the very nature of the envisaged rules on concessions. The purposed new direc-tive on concessions envisages a comprehensive, clear and unambiguous set of provisions in an economic area of the Member States which so far has been characterised by a continuous uncertainty and erroneous inter-pretation, often leaving room for unlawful practices. Secondly, concession contracts display a number of distinct characteristics as compared to pub-lic contracts. These include the exposure of the contractor to the economic risk of providing the services, much longer contractual duration in com-parison to traditional public contracts, greater structural complexity and higher contract value. The most distinctive feature of service concessions reveals a plethora of national rules determining the status of concessions in Member States.

Furthermore, the specific character and the focussed legislative thrust of the proposed rules for the award of service concessions allows for the cre-ation of a joint framework covering concessions in both the public sector and the utilities sector, preserving the specificities of the utilities when absolutely necessary. By contrast, more general and developed rules covering service concessions both under public sector and utilities procurement would have presented striking differences between both sectors, which would not have allowed for such a simplification.

The lack of homogeneity in the legal treatment of concessions by the Member States fundamentally affects the efficient functioning of the EU Internal Market. Most of the EU Member States have not uniformly interpreted, nor sufficiently clarified nor implemented the relevant Treaty principles for the correct attribution of concessions contracts. The ensuing lack of legal certainty and foreclosure of markets is unlikely to be removed without intervention at the appropriate centralised level. Even if Member States were to take legislative action to establish a legal framework based on the Treaty principles of transparency and equal treatment at national level, at least two problems would remain unresolved; first, the risk of legal uncertainty related to interpretations of those principles by national rules, and secondly the risk of wide disparities among legislations in different Member States, resulting from the lack of precision of applicable EU standards.

In order to eliminate disparities among national regimes and ensure homogenous application of the Treaty principles across Member States, the Commission considers necessary that these principles must be given concrete expression and translated into EU secondary legislation in order to achieve a workable Internal Market on concessions, which ensures the function of a competitive market based upon equal opportunities for all EU economic operators.

EU centralised intervention is therefore the most appropriate way to overcome existing barriers to the EU-wide concession market and to ensure convergence and a level playing field in the EU, ultimately guaranteeing the free movement of goods and services across the EU Member States. The regulation of the award of service concessions is envisaged to mirror the case for works concessions (with the exception of the utilities sector), which are currently subject to provisions of EU secondary legislation, as well as the award of traditional public contracts, which are fully covered by the public procurement Directives. The award of works concessions is presently subject to a limited number of secondary law provisions, while service concessions are covered only by the general principles of the TFEU. This loophole gives rise to serious distortions of the Internal Market, in particular limiting access by European businesses, especially small and medium-sized enterprises, to the economic opportunities offered by concession contracts. The lack of legal certainty also results in inefficiencies.

EU secondary rules in the field of public procurement have shown to improve efficiency and specify the obligations derived from the application of the fundamental freedoms, of which the most important are the free movement of goods and services and the right of establishment. The most appropriate legal instrument to regulate service concessions in the EU is Directives. According to 14 TFEU, the European Union adopts the measures for the approximation of the provisions laid down by law, regulation or administrative action in Member States which have as their object the establishment and functioning of the Internal Market. Moreover, whenever the EU legislates in the field of the right of establishment and free movement of services, it must ground its action in the provisions of Article 53(1) and 62 TFEU. The aforementioned provisions restrict the choice of the European lawmaker to directives as the only possible legal instrument to coordinate national legislations facilitating the establishment of economic operators and their access to the services market.

The proposed Directive on concessions is expected to guarantee transparency, fairness and legal certainty in the award of concession contracts, and thereby contribute to improved investment opportunities and ultimately to more and better quality of works and services. It will apply to concessions awarded after its entry into force. This provision is in line with rulings by the Court of Justice on modifying contracts, without prejudice to the temporary arrangements that may prove strictly necessary to ensure the continuity of the provision of the service pending the award of a new concession.

There are certain principles enshrined in the proposed Directive which are expected to bring about a significant increase of legal certainty and ensure a better access to the concessions markets for all European undertakings. The main objective of the Directive is to provide for clarity on the legal framework applicable to the award of concessions, but also to clearly delineate the scope of application of this framework. The specific obligations in the field of concessions will increase legal certainty, on one hand by providing contracting authorities and contracting entities with clear rules incorporating the Treaty principles governing the award of concessions, and on the other hand by providing economic operators with legal guarantees with regard to the award procedure.

The present proposal for a Directive on the award of concession contracts provides for a more precise definition of concession contracts with reference to the notion of operational risk. It makes clear what types of risk are to be considered operational and how to define significant risk. It also provides references as to the maximum duration of concessions. The proposal extends the majority of the obligations which currently apply to the award of public works concessions to all services concessions. It also lays down a number of concrete and more precise requirements, applicable at different stages of the award process on the basis of the Treaty principles, as interpreted in the case law of the Court of Justice of the European Union. Moreover, it extends the application of secondary law to the award of concession contracts in the utilities sector, which is currently exempt from such legislation.

The proposed Directive touches upon the issue of public-public cooperation. Currently, there is considerable legal uncertainty as to how far cooperation between public authorities should be covered by public procurement rules. The relevant case law of the Court of Justice of the European Union is interpreted differently between Member States and even between contracting authorities. Hence the proposal clarifies the cases in which contracts concluded between contracting authorities are not subject to the application of concession award rules. Such clarification is reflecting upon the jurisprudence and the principles set out by the Court.

The modification of concessions during their term has become an increasingly relevant and problematic issue for practitioners. A specific provision on modifying concessions incorporates the basic solutions developed in the case law and provides a pragmatic solution for dealing with unforeseen circumstances requiring a concession to be modified during its term.

The proposal provides for a fundamental improvement of economic operators' access to the concessions markets. The provisions are primarily designed to increase the transparency and fairness of award procedures by restricting the arbitrariness of contracting authorities and contracting entities' decisions on such issues as prior and postpublication, procedural safeguard, selection and award criteria and the deadlines imposed on tenderers. Furthermore, they provide for a better access to justice in order to prevent or to address violations of those provisions.

In order to ensure transparency and equal treatment to all economic operators, the proposal provides for compulsory publication of concession contracts with a value equal to or greater than 5 million euro. This threshold, which already applies to works concessions, has now been extended to services concessions taking into account the public consultations and studies carried out by the Commission in preparing this proposal. It is aimed at keeping any additional administrative burden and costs proportionate to the value of the contract and at focussing on contracts with a clear cross-border interest. The threshold applies to the value of such contracts calculated following a methodology spelled out in the contract. In the case of services, this value reflects the estimated overall value of all services to be provided by the concessionaire during the whole term of the concession. The new rules also define the minimum scope of information to be given to potential tenderers.

The proposal also sets a minimum deadline for the submission of interest in any concession award procedure, amounting to fifty-two days, as this is currently the case for public works concessions. It has been decided to provide for concessions a longer deadline than in case of public contracts, given that concession contracts are usually more complex.

The proposed Directive provides for obligations relating to the selection criteria to be applied by the contracting authorities or contracting entities when awarding concessions. These rules are less restrictive than similar provisions currently applicable to public contracts. However, they restrict the selection criteria to those related to the economic, financial and technical capacity of the bidder and limit the scope of the acceptable exclusion criteria. The rules maintain an obligation to apply objective criteria linked to the subject matter of the concession, ensuring compliance with the principles of transparency, nondiscrimination and equal treatment, guaranteeing that tenders are assessed in conditions of effective competition allowing an overall economic advantage for the contracting authority or the contracting entity to be determined. These criteria should prevent arbitrary decisions by contracting authorities and contracting entities and must be published in advance and listed in descending order of importance. Member States or contracting authorities or contracting entities may also provide for or apply the 'most economically advantageous tender' criterion for the award of concessions.

Unlike the public procurement Directives, the proposed rules do not contain a predetermined range of award procedures. This solution allows contracting authorities and contracting entities to follow more flexible procedures when awarding concessions notably reflecting national legal traditions and permitting the award process to be organised in the most efficient way. However, the proposal establishes a number of clear procedural safeguards to be applied to the award of concessions notably during negotiations. These safeguards aim at ensuring that the process is fair and transparent.

The proposal provides for an extension of the scope of application of the Remedies Directive 2007/66/EC to all concession contracts above the threshold in order to guarantee effective channels for challenging the award decision in court and provide minimal judicial standards which have to be observed by contracting authorities or entities.

7 The Public-Public Partnership

PUBLIC-PUBLIC CO-OPERATION IN DELIVERING PUBLIC SERVICES

EU law does not restrict the freedom of a contracting authority to perform the public interest tasks conferred on it by using its own administrative, technical and other resources. As such, contracting authorities may choose not to interface with private entities, which are not a part of their own structures.[1] If a contracting authority performs a public task by using its own resources in such a way that no contract for pecuniary interest is concluded, EU public procurement law does not apply. Moreover, the possibility to perform public tasks using its own resources may also be exercised in cooperation with other contracting authorities. Several contracting authorities may mutually assist each other. If such arrangements are not based on remuneration or any exchange of reciprocal rights and obligations, there is no contractual interface within the meaning of EU public procurement law. However, there are significant parameters which must be observed for such a discretion of Member States to function.

First, dependency in terms of overall control of an entity by the state or another contracting authority presupposes a control similar to that which the state of another contracting authority exercises over its own departments. The 'similarity' of control denotes lack of independence with regard to decision making. The Court in *Teckal* concluded that a contract between a contracting authority and an entity, which the former exercises control similar to the control that it exercises over its own departments, and at the same time that entity carries out the essential part of its activities with the contracting authority, is not a public contract, irrespective of that entity being a contracting authority or not.[2] The similarity of control as a reflection of dependency reveals the thrust of the discretion of contracting authorities to engage in in-house relationships.

Secondly, service contracts which are awarded by Member States to an entity that is itself a contracting authority on the basis of an exclusive right that is granted to the contracting authority by a law, regulation or administrative provision of the Member State[3], are exempted from any competitive requirements for their award. Similarly, in the utilities sectors certain contracts between contracting authorities and affiliated undertakings[4] are also excluded from competitive tendering. An affiliated undertaking is one which its annual accounts are consolidated with those of the contracting entity in accordance with the requirements of the Seventh Company Law Directive.[5] There are service contracts awarded to a service provider affiliated with the contracting entity, and there are service contracts awarded to a service provider affiliated with a contracting entity participating in a joint venture, formed for the purpose of carrying out an activity covered by the Directive. The explanatory memorandum accompanying the text amending the Utilities Directive states that this provision relates, in particular, to three types of service provisions within groups. These categories, which may or may not be distinct, are: (i) the provision of common services such as accounting, recruitment and management; (ii) the provision of specialised services embodying the know-how of the group, and; (iii) the provision of a specialised service to a joint venture. The exclusion of contracts to affiliated undertakings is subject, however, to two conditions: first, the service provider must be an undertaking affiliated with the contracting authority and, second, at least 80 per cent of its average turnover arising within the European Union for the preceding three years, must be derived from the provision of the same or similar services to undertakings with which it is affiliated.

Similarity of Control and Dependency between Public Actors

The notion of control[6] for in-house relations and the *similarity* requirement merit a comprehensive approach, which should not be based solely on either company law features or on the level of the contracting authority's shareholding. Normally, corporate control indicates decisive influence over management actions, operational and strategic decisions in a similar manner to the concept of majority shareholder control found in company laws of Member States. Nevertheless, any appraisal of the legal position of a majority shareholder in order to assert control must be taken in conjunction with the statutes governing the relevant entity over which the control is exercised and not by sole reference to national company law provisions, as often minority shareholdings provide for rights of decisive influence, such as specific oversight and blocking rights.

The notion of control for the purposes of in-house contracts, as developed by the Court, entails much more than the ingredients of 'dominant influence' as a company law notion, or as a public procurement notion, which defines certain bodies as contracting authorities. In particular, control is extended beyond the 'dominant influence' notion found in the Utilities Directive.[7] For the purposes of in-house relations, the object of such control should not be confined to strategic market decisions or procurement decisions, but should embrace individual management and operational decisions as well. Corporate control is exercised by conclusive influence on both strategic objectives and significant decisions. Therefore, the concept of control must be understood in functional, not formal terms. There is nothing to prevent it from being applied to the relationship between a contracting authority and legal persons governed by private law, such as a limited liability company. The use of the term *departments* derives from the original reason for setting up autonomous bodies, which was to entrust particular departments with a function or the delivery of a specific public service.[8] The control exercised over an entity or an undertaking by a public authority must be similar to that which the authority exercises over its own departments, but not identical in every respect and must be effective. But, it is not essential that it be exercised individually.[9]

However, the existence of private capital, participating in an entity which has corporate links with a contracting authority, negates the similarity of control requirement. *Stadt Halle* held that private sector participation cannot emulate the pursuit of public interest objectives entrusted to public sector entities.[10] The relationship between a public authority and its own departments is governed by considerations and requirements proper to the pursuit of objectives in the public interest. Any private capital investment in an undertaking follows considerations appropriate for private interests and pursues objectives of a different kind.[11] The participation, even as a minority, of a private undertaking in the capital of a company in which the awarding public authority is also a participant excludes the possibility that the public authority will exercise control that is similar to that which it exercises over its own departments over such a company.[12]

The category of semipublic entities or undertakings, which in their own rights are regarded as contracting authorities, could not be viewed as entities upon which a contracting authority can exercise similar control to that over its own departments.

A contracting authority cannot exercise in-house control over an entity when one or more private undertakings also participate in the ownership of that entity.[13] That is the case even if the contracting authority is able to independently make all decisions regarding that entity, regardless of the private holding. The Court reasoned that the relationship between a contracting authority and its own departments is governed by considerations and requirements proper to the pursuit of objectives in the public interest.

By contrast, any private capital investment in an undertaking follows considerations proper to private interests and pursues objectives of a different kind. This is also relevant for pure capital injections by a private company into the in-house entity (e.g. the buying of shares, not the provision of standard loans), even if this does not involve any operational contribution. As a general rule, the determination of the existence of a private holding in the capital of the company to which the public contract at issue is awarded must be undertaken at the time of the award.[14] Exceptionally, special circumstances may require events occurring after the date on which the contract was awarded to be taken into consideration. Such is the case, in particular, when shares in the contracting company, previously wholly owned by the contracting authority, are transferred to a private undertaking shortly after the contract at issue has been awarded to that company by means of an artificial device designed to circumvent the relevant EU rules.[15] The future opening of the company's capital is taken into account only if there is a real prospect of such opening in the short term at the time of the award of a contract to the company.[16]

The mere theoretical possibility of a private party participating in the capital of an in-house entity does not in itself undermine the in-house relationship between the contracting authority and its company. However, if a contract were to be awarded to the company without being put out to competitive tender on the basis of the in-house exception, the subsequent acquisition of a stake in the company by private investors at any time during the period of validity of the contract would constitute an alteration of a fundamental condition of the award of the contract. Under these circumstances, the contract has to be put out to competitive tender. Conversely, the sole ownership by contracting authorities should be regarded as an indication of the existence of the control required for the in-house exception, but not as a factor that is decisive per se.[17] This indication is rebutted where contracting authorities establish a profit-making company that is fully independent of them. This is also illustrated by the *Parking Brixen* case, in which the entity was, at the time of the award, owned by one contracting authority but enjoyed a degree of independence, which led the Court to deny the in-house status.[18]

If a company's capital is wholly owned by the contracting authority, alone or together with other public authorities, when the contract in question is awarded to that company, the potential opening of the company's capital to private investors may not be taken into consideration unless there is a real prospect in the short term of such an opening. Therefore, when the capital of the contracting company is wholly public and in which there is no actual sign of any impending opening of that company's capital to private shareholders, the mere fact that private undertakings, at some point in time, may hold capital in the company does not support the conclusion that the condition relating to the control by the public authority over that company is not present. That conclusion is not contradictory to *Coname,* which indicated that the fact that a company is open to private capital prevents it from being regarded as a structure for the 'in-house' management of a public service on behalf of the municipalities that form part of it.[19] In this case, a public service was awarded to a company in which not all, but most, of the capital was public at the time of that award. *Sea* clarifies that when a contract is awarded to a public capital company, without subjection to competitive tender, the fact that subsequent to the award but during the contract's period of validity, private shareholders were permitted to hold capital in the company constitutes an alteration of a fundamental condition of the contract. The above parameters do not regard the contract as an in-house arrangement.

Another parameter which determines in-house arrangements specifies that an essential part of the controlled entity's activities must be carried out for the benefit of the controlling contracting authority or authorities.[20] *Sea* held that the control exercised over that company by the shareholder authorities may be regarded as similar to that which they exercise over their own departments when the company's activity is limited to the territory of those authorities and is carried on essentially for its benefit.[21] The Court maintained, in *Parking Brixen,* that the essential part of the controlled entities' activities cannot be carried out for the benefit of the controlling public authority if the geographical area has been extended to the entire country and abroad.[22]

The 'essential part' criterion relates to a certain minimum proportion of the total activities performed by the controlled body.[23] However, not only quantitative elements must be taken into account in determining the term *essential.* While it could be convenient to define the essential part criterion in line with a provision governing awards to undertakings affiliated with the contracting authority, namely the 80 per cent criterion, the Court has rejected such an approach on the grounds that a transposition of an exceptional provision from the Utilities Directive to the Public Sector Directive is of questionable *vires.*[24] *Carbotermo* revealed interesting insights on operational dependency.[25] The Court declared that the 80 per cent rule of affiliated operational dependency cannot be imported into the public sector procurement because such provision is regarded as being a restrictively interpreted exception applicable only to supply contracts covering affiliated undertakings.[26]

So, although an 'essential part' indicates a quantitative measure in relation to turnover or financial quantum of the volume of activities performed by the controlled entity, qualitative factors such as strategic services, organisational planning, market analysis, the profitability of the entity in pursuit of the activities for the controlling authority, and also the market dynamics under which the controlled entity operates should be taken into account. *Carbotermo* also ruled that to determine whether an undertaking carries out the essential part of its activities with the controlling authority account must be taken of all the activities that the undertaking carries out on the basis of an award made by the contracting authority, regardless of who pays for those activities.[27] If the public authority that receives an essential part of an entity's activities controls that entity through another company, the control criterion is still present, provided that control is demonstrable at all levels of the contracting authority's corporate interface.

Public–Public Partnerships

A public authority may perform public interest tasks conferred to it by using its own administrative, technical and other resources, without being obliged to call on outside entities that are not a part of its own departments.[28] The possibility for public authorities to use their own resources to perform the public interest tasks conferred on them may also be exercised in co-operation with other public authorities.[29]

Commission v. Germany provided for a demonstration of flexibility in the hands of contracting authorities in relation to their freedom to organise and deliver public services.[30] Co-operation between independent contracting authorities in the form of establishing an entity upon which no similar control is exercised to that over their own departments, resulting in the entrustment of a contract on behalf of the participant contracting authorities, can be deemed to meet the criteria for an in-house exception. Such a classification is warranted provided a variety of conditions are satisfied: (i) the remit of such public co-operation exists in relation to a public task or service specified under Community law, (ii) there is no intention to circumvent public procurement rules, and (iii) the contractual relation is based on neither a pecuniary interest consideration nor payments between the entity and the participant contracting authorities. The Court used an analogy with *Coditel Brabant* where contractual relations between intermunicipal co-operative societies whose members are contracting authorities and a jointly controlled entity can be deemed in-house.[31]

The Court also accepted public-public cooperation outside the concept of jointly controlled in-house entities. The Court stressed that EU law does not require contracting authorities to use any particular legal form in order to jointly carry out their public service tasks. For the purposes of this document, this type of cooperation is qualified as 'noninstitutional' or 'horizontal', involving different contracting authorities. Until now this has been the only judgment of the Court on public-public cooperation that has not involved jointly controlled in-house entities. The Court appears to have relied on many individual circumstances that were relevant to this particular case in order to arrive at its conclusion.[32] Nevertheless, considering the aspects of the judgement that could be of general relevance, it appears reasonable to conclude that contracting authorities may establish horizontal co-operation among themselves (without creating a jointly controlled 'in-house' entity). In order to do so, they must conclude agreements not covered by EU public procurement law. Such a conclusion is reasonable only if, at a minimum, the following conditions are met: (i) the arrangement involves only contracting authorities, and there is no participation of private capital; (ii) the character of the agreement is that of real co-operation aimed at the joint performance of a common task, as opposed to a normal public contract; and (iii) their cooperation is governed only by considerations relating to the public interest.[33]

The aim of public-public cooperation is to jointly ensure the execution of a public task that all of the cooperating partners have to perform. Such joint execution is characterised by the participation and mutual obligations of the contractual partners, which lead to mutual synergy effects. This does not necessarily mean that each of the co-operating partners participates equally in the actual performance of the task—the co-operation may be based on a division of tasks or on a certain specialisation. Nevertheless, the contract needs to address a common aim, namely the joint performance of the same task. Case law also suggests that the character of the agreement needs to be that of real co-operation, as opposed to a normal public contract where one party is performing a certain task against remuneration.[34] Such a unilateral assignment of a task by one contracting authority to another cannot be considered as co-operation.

Co-operation is governed by considerations relating to the pursuit of objectives in the public interest. Thus, while it may involve mutual rights and obligations, it must not involve financial transfers between the public co-operating partners, other than those corresponding to the reimbursement of actual costs of the works/services/supplies: service provision against remuneration is a characteristic of public contracts subject to the EU public procurement rules.

Restrictions on Public–Public Co-operation

Public-public co-operation should only be governed by public interest considerations. Thus, it would not be exempt if it were guided, that is, principally determined, by other considerations, especially commercial ones. Therefore, in principle, the co-operating partners should not perform activities on the market as part of the co-operation. In other words, the co-operation agreement should not include activities to be offered on the open market.

It can be established that normal public contracts between contracting authorities continue to be subject to the procurement obligations (e.g. the purchase of certain services from another contracting authority). However, contracting authorities can establish structures to cooperate with each other, whether they are institutional or not.[35]

One of the relevant amendments introduced by the Lisbon Treaty is the acknowledgement of local and regional self-governance.[36] Furthermore, Article 1 of Protocol 26 on Services of General Interest of the Lisbon Treaty acknowledges the essential role, and wide discretion, of national, regional and local authorities in providing, commissioning and organising services of general economic interest as closely as possible to the needs of the users.[37] These provisions confirm authorities' right to decide how to execute the services that they are obliged to provide to the public. On the other hand, while the existence of this right was not disputed, even in the past, it is clear that it needs to be exercised in accordance with other provisions of EU law. Accordingly, certain choices made by contracting authorities might imply the need to comply with EU public procurement law. EU law does not seek to force contracting authorities to externalise, but to ensure that if contracting authorities decide to involve a separate entity—public or private—on a commercial basis, this is done in a transparent and nondiscriminatory manner. In view of the Commission services, the two forms of vertical and horizontal public-public cooperation are two equally available means for contracting authorities to organise the performance of their public tasks outside the scope of application of EU public procurement law. The Court has clearly confirmed that EU law does not require contracting authorities to use any particular legal form in order to carry out jointly their public service tasks. While there are structurally two different types of public–public cooperation outside EU public procurement law, they share some common characteristics.

A contracting authority may perform the public interest tasks with its own resources, without recourse to entities outside its own departments, and it may do so in co-operation with other contracting authorities, either in an institutional co-operation through a jointly controlled in-house entity or without establishing such an institutional form. Second, it seems clear from the case law of the Court that in order to be exempted from the application of the EU public procurement rules, any public-public cooperation must remain purely public.[38] The participation of private capital in one of the co-operating entities will thus prevent the co-operation from being exempted from public procurement rules.

If the co-operating entities are market oriented, they are in direct competition with private operators having the same or similar commercial objectives and instruments. Co-operation which is exempt from the procurement rules and aimed at fulfilling a public task should only involve entities which are principally not active on the market with a commercial purpose. This results primarily from the fact that the co-operation partners must be contracting authorities. The status of public authorities entails limits to their activities, while bodies governed by public law have to be 'established for the specific purpose of meeting needs in the general interest, not having an industrial or commercial character'.[39] Furthermore, in vertical co-operation, the in-house entity has to perform the essential part of its activities for the contracting authorities that control it. Any activity performed on the market has to remain incidental to these core activities, because a possible market orientation would weaken the joint control required in vertical cooperation.

In relation to horizontal cooperation, the Court stated that, where co-operation between public authorities is governed solely by considerations and requirements relating to the pursuit of objectives in the public interest, it does not undermine the principal objective of the EU rules on public procurement, namely the free movement of services and the opening up of undistorted competition in all the Member States This is the case if the co-operation does not involve any commercial considerations. EU law does not require contracting authorities to use any particular legal form in order to carry out jointly their public service tasks. Although there is no such requirement, looking at the two forms of vertical and horizontal public-public cooperation it should be noted that the type of connection between the co-operating entities is different and needs to be addressed.

In an institutional co-operation, it is the presence of a (joint) in-house control that could lead even an agreement to being exempted from the scope of the procurement regime that would normally be covered by it. In other words, the in-house exception relates to an otherwise covered public procurement contract for the performance of a task against remuneration. By contrast, in the case of noninstitutional co-operation, in order to distinguish it from a normal public contract, it seems to be important that the character of the former is that of co-operation involving mutual rights and obligations going beyond 'performance of a task against remuneration' and that the aim of the co-operation is not of a commercial nature.[40]

Externalisation of Public Co-operation

The public interest task conferred on a contracting authority might be ultimately carried out by resources external to the contracting authority. This can be the case where the competence for the given public task is transferred as such to another public authority. The performance of a given task may also be entrusted to another entity. This may be achieved without establishing contractual links, or by calling on another contracting authority which enjoys an exclusive right, or through joint procurement with other contracting authorities or through central purchasing bodies. Legal competence for a public task could be understood as the exclusive obligation and right to fulfil this task by own administrative, technical and other means or by calling upon external entities. The term *competence* for a given public task includes the official authority necessary to establish the regulatory framework for fulfilling the task at the level of the authority concerned. The organisation of national administrations as such does not fall within the competence of the EU. Consequently, it is the discretion of Member States to organise its administration and as part of such re-organisation to allow for the transfer of competences for certain public tasks from one public authority to another.

The transfer of competence for a given public task from one contracting authority to another is not governed by public procurement rules. Transferring competence for a given public task from one public body to another involves transferring both the official authority and any associated economic activities. In the area of waste management, for example, the transfer of all competences means transferring the right to set tariffs, to fix rules for collecting, sorting, storing and treating waste, as well as the right to manage and ultimately to carry out the task according to these rules. All these rights constitute official authority. Part of these rights is the right to determine how the actual economic activities which need to be performed in order to fulfil the public task are to be performed: either by the public body itself or by a third party mandated by it.

Although situations where competence is transferred occur in Member States, neither EU legislation nor the case law of the Court of Justice explicitly recognised such situations. The Court has referred[41] to the transfer of official authority when a Member State invoked the transfer of competences from a public body to a third person. According to this case law, a transfer of competences has not taken place if i) the public entity that is originally competent remains primarily responsible for a project, because it has a legal obligation not to withdraw from its task; ii) the new entity may only take legally relevant actions after the public entity that is originally competent has given its approval, and iii) the new entity is financed by the public entity that is originally competent to fulfil its tasks, with the result that it has no room for manoeuvre. On this basis, the distinctive feature of transferring competences from one public body to another as part of the re-organisation of public administration is the comprehensive nature of the transfer. The body transferring competence does not retain any responsibility. The beneficiary of the transfer must exercise the competence independently and on its own responsibility.

In particular, the transferring body does not retain the right to determine the performance of economic activities undertaken in the context of the respective public task. Such economic tasks are performed under the authority of the beneficiary of the transfer. However, this does not exclude the possibility that the transferring body might have some influence on the practical organisation of the performance of the public task in question. In fact, officials of the transferring public body could be members of the executive or management bodies of the authority to which competence for the public task in question was transferred. The transferring authority may also retain the right to receive certain information.

The Noncontractual Attribution of Tasks

The EU Public Procurement Directives presuppose the existence of a contract, which necessitates at least two, legally distinct entities which are independent of each other in regard to decision making. A contract is essentially a meeting of wills, whereby the parties to it are able to decide whether they wish to initiate or to terminate the contractual link.[42] Other indications of the existence of a contract are the ability of the parties to negotiate on the actual contents of the services to be rendered and the tariffs of those services. A contract implies a transactional relationship. If there is no contract, the EU Public Procurement Directives do not apply. The Court's case law finds that if an entity carries out an activity on account of its obligations resulting from national legislation, rather than on a contractual basis, it is not covered by the EU Public Procurement Directives.

More specifically, in the *Tragsa* case the Court found that, on the basis of the relevant national law, Tragsa, which was a public undertaking, had no choice as to the acceptance of an assignment, or the tariff for its services, but was obliged by law to execute the demands of the contracting authority, insofar as it was an instrument and technical service of that authority. The Court held that Tragsa's relations with the contracting authorities using its services were not contractual, but internal, dependent and subordinate in every respect. Consequently, the EU Public Procurement Directives did not apply to this relationship.

Exclusive Rights

If a contracting authority enjoys an exclusive right, other contracting authorities can only award the respective services contacts to this entity. The key reason for introducing this provision was to avoid competitive award procedures in cases where, due to the existence of an exclusive right, only one entity could ultimately be awarded the contract in question.

In the general debate, the term *exclusive rights* could refer to quite different phenomena ranging from reserving a whole economic sector to public authorities to the exclusive assignment of one specific task to one specific undertaking. However, not every exclusive right justifies the exemption of the award of a public service contract. The respective exclusive right needs to be granted by a law, regulation or administrative provision which is published and compatible with EU law and Treaty. An exclusive right, which by definition restricts the freedom of other entities to provide services, is justified only under certain conditions.[43] Thus, the exclusive right must be justified either by a derogation expressly provided for by the EU Treaty, exercise of official authority (Article 51 TFEU), grounds of public policy, public security or public health (Article 52 TFEU) or, in accordance with the case law of the Court, by imperative requirements in the general interest, which must be appropriate for achieving the objective which they pursue, not go beyond what is necessary in order to attain it and must in any event be applied without discrimination.[44]

Rights granted to particular public sector bodies to provide certain services, on an exclusive basis, are justified if the justification for the restriction of the freedom to provide services is an imperative requirement in the general interest and the measure in question nondiscriminatory.

8   Regulatory and Legal Trends in Public-Private Partnerships

In this chapter a conceptual forecast of the legal and regulatory mapping of public-private partnerships will be attempted. In ascertaining current and future regulatory trends in public-private partnerships, the role and remit of function of both public and private sectors will be clearer and allow for lawmaking and policy making to effectively establish a blueprint for shaping the public-private interface in the delivery of public services.

The notion of public-private partnerships reveals complex *forms of co-operation* between the state and private actors which exceed the remit of traditional contractual interface, moving into a strategic sphere of public sector management. Public-private partnerships aim at delivering both infrastructure facilities and public services and are regarded as attractive and credible solutions to solve the *infrastructure deficit* of many developed and developing states. The modern state justifies its existence through the provision of *public services*, a concept which encapsulates the pursuit of public interest. A regulatory trend in public-private partnerships which has strongly emerged over the past twenty years reflects the internalisation and externalisation options available to the state in delivering public services. The delivery and regulation of public services are based on two diametrically different models which reflect on internalisation choices or externalisation choices on the part of the state. Firstly, as far as internalisation choices are concerned, the notion of public services often fuses with state ownership of assets or infrastructure and amalgamates the ensuing provision of services to the public. It also refers to functions which underpin essential facilities of the state (i.e. defence, justice, policing) and as a result these functions are sheltered from market forces in order to ensure the integrity of their delivery. Secondly, in relation to externalisation choices of the state, public services regularly capture interests of general needs which are delivered through market-based mechanisms where the public sector interfaces contractually or even competes with private actors. However, the externalised organisation and delivery of public services reveals that their providers interface with the state in a market place which does not correspond to the principles and dynamics of private markets, thus requiring a different type of regulation which could be seen an amalgam of legal, financial and policy attributes reflecting the constant changing of societal needs, expectations and requirements.

A policy-making prism in viewing regulatory trends in public-private partnerships reveals the incentive of the public sector to engage in a partnership mode with the private sector to deliver public services. It has emerged that optimal risk management is the prime advantage to the state from involving private actors through a partnership format in the delivery of public services. This axiom underlines the principle of public accountability for the modern state in a number of ways. Firstly, the private actor partner is obliged to commit its own capital resources for the funding and the delivery of public services. It is not therefore a mere contractor; it is a stakeholder which has a vested interest in the effective and efficient delivery of the relevant public services in order to attain its returns and recoup its investment. This attribute results in an increased certainty of outcomes, both in terms of on-time delivery and in terms of within-budget delivery. Thus, the private actor is strongly motivated to complete the project as early as possible and to control its costs in order that the payment streams emanating from the partnership can commence. In addition, often, the payment schedule of the private sector partner is pre-determined , a fact which helps protect the public sector from exposure to cost overruns.

By transferring the risk of the funding required for the delivery of public services to private actors, the state manages the public finances in a strategic way. Repayment of the private partner investment in a public-private partnership arrangement is often conditional upon meeting pre-determined performance targets. In addition, private actors in public-private partnerships are often financially incentivised to offer value-for-money solutions in the delivery of public services through continuous quality improvement, innovation, management efficiency and effectiveness.

Behavioural elements which underpin private sector entrepreneurship are harnessed by the state to enhance the quality of public services through a transfer of financial and operational risk to private actors; the latter become an essential component of the state's functions, thus revealing a conceptual convergence between public and private sectors in the delivery of public services. Furthermore, and since the private sector provides the financing for the infrastructure and delivery of public services within a public-private partnership, it has emerged that a different accountancy treatment benefits the state in that the debt financing of public-private partnerships is regarded as off-balance sheet borrowing. This indicates that the borrowing of the state to repay the investment of the private actor does not affect the state's public sector borrowing requirements (PSBR) and any measurements or calculations of its indebtedness.

PUBLIC-PRIVATE PARTNERSHIPS AS PUBLIC SERVICE INSTRUMENTS

One of the most pronounced trends in public-private partnerships has been their reflection as *public service instruments*. As such, the state opts for an externalised model in the delivery of public services and heralds a departure from an asset-based to an enabled-based format in public services. Through risk-transfer mechanisms, the public-private partnership is treated as an emanation of the state and reveals a different ethos in public sector management, which possesses a range of characteristics that point to the role of the state as an enabling and facilitating agent in the delivery of public services. However, the strategic role of private actors in financing and delivering infrastructure and public services by providing input into the various phases such as finance, design, construction, operation and maintenance reflect the need for longevity of the relations between public and private sectors. The duration is justified on the basis of affordability for repayment on the part of the public sector and on the basis of the ability of the private sector to recoup its investment profitably. Nevertheless, this would result in market foreclosure. There is a pertinent need to address the *competitiveness* of public-private partnerships before and after the procurement process of the private actor.

Another trend which has emerged from viewing public-private partnerships as public service instruments and as a result of the strategic role of the private sector and its long-term engagement in delivering infrastructure and public services reflects on the treatment of risk distribution between the public and private sectors within public-private partnerships. It is widely accepted that five broad categories of risk migrate to the private sector partner in a public-private partnership. These include *construction or project risk* (risks related to design problems, building cost overruns and project delays), *financial risk* (risk related to variability in interest rates, exchange rates and other factors affecting financing costs), *performance risk* (risk related to the availability of an asset and the continuity and quality of the relevant service provision), *demand risk* (risk related to the ongoing need for the relevant public services) and *residual value risk* (risk related to the future market price of an asset). The above risk categories have shaped the operational types of public-private partnerships which have emerged.

Three operational types of public-private partnerships codify the relations between the state and private actors and draw their origins from the risk treatment in public-private partnerships. All types have as pivotal features asset-ownership and potential transfer to the public sector. The first type of such relations includes legal formats where the private actor designs, builds, owns, develops, operates and manages an asset with no obligation to transfer ownership to the public sector. Secondly, another type of public-private partnerships includes legal formats where the private actor buys or leases an existing asset from the public sector, renovates, modernises, and/or expands it and then operates the asset exclusively, with no obligation to transfer ownership back to the public sector. Thirdly, another legal format of public-private partnerships includes relations where the private sector designs and builds an asset, operates it and then transfers it to the public sector when the operating contract ends, or at some other specified time.

The private partner may subsequently rent or lease the asset from the public sector to deliver the related public services.

The risk transfer exercise within a public-private partnership from the public sector to the private sector reflects and influences the cost and the availability of finance for the project. This has a significant impact on whether a public-private partnership is a more efficient and cost-effective alternative to publicly funded provision of services.[1] The assumption that private sector borrowing generally costs more than government borrowing is balanced by the expectation in efficiency gains from the delivery of public services through public-private partnerships that offset potentially higher private sector borrowing costs. In addition to risk transfer, the sources of finance could also have an impact on the affordability of financing a public-private partnership. The nature of the markets which will be called upon to provide debt or equity finance to a public-private partnership is detrimental to their assessment of risk and the pricing of risk. Sophisticated financial markets which are conducive to spreading risk widely to reduce the cost of capital are more effective than the public sector spreading risk through taxation.

The different approach in pricing risk in public-private partnerships on the part of the public and private sectors respectively reflect the ultimate risk of such interface: *default risk,* which projects the likelihood of the public sector defaulting on its obligation within a public-private partnership and causing the insolvency of the SPV. The public sector's attraction to the use of the social time preference rate (STPR) or other risk-free rate to discount future cash flows when appraising projects for the delivery of public services is contrasted with the private sector's widely used capital asset pricing model (CAPM), which offers a more realistic and market-oriented returns assessment for investments.

A different type of public-private partnerships has emerged through the award and granting of concessions, which are revenue-generating relations, involving an infrastructure or a service, the use of which necessitates the payment of fees borne directly by end-users and any operation or function emanating from the sale, rent or exploitation of public land or buildings. The notion of a concession is based on the assumption that no contractual remuneration is paid by the granting public entity to the concessionaire. The latter must therefore simply be given the right to economically exploit the concession, although this right may be accompanied by a requirement to pay some consideration to the grantor, depending on elements of risk allocation agreed between the parties. There are three main distinctive features in public concessions. First, the beneficiary of the service provided must be third parties (usually the public or end-users of a public service) rather than the awarding public entity itself. Second, the subject of the service upon which the concession is based must concern a matter which is in the public interest. Finally, the concessionaire must assume the economic risk related to the performance of the relevant service.

PUBLIC-PRIVATE PARTNERSHIPS AS INVESTMENT INSTRUMENTS

Public-private partnerships can be viewed as *investment instruments*. The axiom of private financing in the delivery of public services offers a variety of opportunities for the financial industry to facilitate and provide funding to public-private partnerships. Financing public-private partnerships is morphing into an investment market, for both debt and equity instruments. Debt-financing of public private partnerships is levered on the basis of future projected revenue streams resulting from the project's exclusive operation by the private sector partner. Often a high ratio of debt-to-equity is required, as the public-private partnership would have only the minimum equity to issue the debt instruments, which could be either geared or leveraged. The accountancy treatment of debt in a public-private partnership is determined by the controlling party of the special purpose vehicle (SPV) which legally encapsulates the public-private interface. If the private sector partner controls the SPV, its debt is recorded off-balance sheet for public sector borrowing considerations; conversely, if an SPV is controlled by the public sector, it should be consolidated with public sector borrowing. In the event that risk stays with the public sector, even if the SPV is controlled by the private sector partner, the consolidated accounts of the SPV should be recorded in the public sector accounts.

Equity financing is often underpinned by financial guarantees of the private partner to a public-private partnership, usually limited to the respective financial contribution. It is unusual for the public sector to provide any guarantees to lenders for raising equity to public-private partnerships. However, the public sector could guarantee private sector borrowing or make a direct contribution to project costs, in the form of equity (where there is profit sharing), a loan or a subsidy (where social returns exceed private returns).

Both debt and equity financing of public-private partnerships could be raised by securitisation of future cash-flows and projected revenues, backed by either an asset which is transferred by the public sector to the partnership or by the public sector's claim to future project revenues. The public-private partnership (SPV) would issue securities to raise finance and amortise treated interest will be returned to investors. Although on first sight, any investor claims are directed towards the SPV, in fact it is the public sector which finances the public-private partnership. The accountancy treatment of securitised debt of public-private partnerships is dependent on the asset transfer conditions from the public sector to the partnership special purpose vehicle (SPV). If the transferred assets which will back the securitisation of the SPV's debt are below market value, the securitised debt should be treated as public borrowing, as insufficient risk has been transferred from the public sector to the private sector within the public-private partnership.

PUBLIC-PRIVATE PARTNERSHIPS AS GROWTH INSTRUMENTS

Public-Private Partnerships can be viewed as *growth instruments*. The European Union 2020 Growth Strategy has approved a series of measures designed to increase investment in the infrastructure of the trans-European transport networks (TENs) and also in the areas of research, innovation and development, as well as the delivery of services of general economic interest. The European Union has envisaged the utilisation of public-private partnerships as sustainable growth instruments which attempt to build a resource efficient, sustainable and competitive economy through two initiatives, namely a *'resource-efficient Europe'* and *'an industrial policy for the globalisation era'*. Both initiatives aim to increase certainty for investment and innovation by forging an agreement on long-term relations between public and private sectors.

TRENDS IN REGULATION OF PUBLIC-PRIVATE PARTNERSHIPS

Procurement Regulation of Public-Private Partnerships

Considerable emphasis has been placed on observing the public sector management principles such as transparency and accountability, competitiveness and value for money during the procurement process of public-private partnerships. When a transaction creating a mixed-capital entity is accompanied by the award of tasks through an act which can be designated as a public contract, or even a concession, it is important that there be compliance with the principles of transparency and accountability, as well as the principle of nondiscrimination. The selection of a private partner called on to undertake such tasks while functioning as part of a mixed entity can therefore not be based exclusively on the quality of its capital contribution or its experience, but should also take account of the characteristics of its offer in terms of the specific services to be provided. The conditions governing the creation of the entity must be clearly laid down when issuing the call for competition for the tasks which one wishes to entrust to the private partner. Also, these conditions must not discriminate against or constitute an unjustified barrier to the freedom to provide services or to freedom of establishment.

In many jurisdictions, legislation allows for mixed entities, in which the participation by the public sector involves the contracting body, to participate in a procedure for the award of a public-private partnership or a concession, even when these entities are only in the process of being incorporated. In this scenario, the entity will be definitively incorporated only after the contract has actually been awarded to it. In many jurisdictions a practice has been developed which tends to confuse the phase of incorporating the entity and the phase of allocating the public services tasks. Thus the purpose of the procurement procedure is to create a mixed entity to which certain tasks are entrusted.[2]

Such solution does not appear to offer satisfactory outcomes. First, there is a risk that the effective competition will be distorted by a privileged position of the company being incorporated, and consequently of the private partner participating in that company. Secondly, the specific procedure for selecting the private partner also poses many problems. The contracting authorities encounter certain difficulties in defining the subject matter of the contract or concession in a sufficiently clear and precise manner in this context, as they are obliged to do. This in turn raises problems not only with regard to the principles of transparency and equality of treatment, but even risks prejudicing the general interest objectives which the public authority wishes to attain.

Structure Regulation of Public-Private Partnerships

Two legal structures/models will assist the evolution and delivery of public-private partnerships. First, the contractual model, where the interface between the state and the private actors reflects on a relation which is based solely on contractual links. Under this model and structure, it is unlikely that there would be any element of exclusive asset exploitation or end-user payments levied by the private actor. However, mechanisms of profit sharing, efficiency gain sharing as well as risk allocation between the public and private partners distinguish contractual public-private partnerships from traditional public contracts for works or services. The contractual model of public-private partnerships assumes that the private sector partner will provide the financing for completing the project and the public sector partner will pay back by way of 'service or unitary charges' which reflect payments based on usage volumes or demand (i.e. payments in lieu of fees or tolls for public lighting, hospitals, schools, roads with shadow tolls).

Secondly, the institutional model of public-private partnerships involves the establishment of a separate legal entity held jointly by the public partner and the private partner. The joint entity has the task of ensuring the raising of finance and the delivery of a public service or an infrastructure project for the benefit of the public. The direct interface between the public partner and the private partner in a forum with a distinctive legal personality allows the public partner, through its presence in the body of shareholders and in the decision-making bodies of the joint entity, to retain a relatively high degree of control over the development and delivery of the project. The joint entity could also allow the public partner to develop its own experience of running and improving the public service in question, while having recourse to the support of a private partner. An institutional public-private partnership can be established either by creating an entity controlled by the public and private sector partners, or by the private sector taking control of an existing public undertaking or by the participation of a private partner in an existing publicly owned company which has obtained public contracts or concessions.

Risk Treatment and Its Regulation in Public-Private Partnerships

A number of criteria have been devised to assess the degree of risk treatment in public-private partnerships and again these criteria involve asset ownership as an essential feature. The extent of risk transfer between the parties and the quantum for such transfer can be assessed by reference to separable contractual relations in a public-private partnership, where a distinction between asset ownership and delivery of public service elements or nonseparable contracts, where asset ownership fuses with public service delivery.[3] For nonseparable contracts, the base line for the assessment rests on the balance of demand risk and residual value risk borne by the public sector and the private operator. Demand risk, which is an operating risk and is the dominant consideration, is borne by the public sector if service payments to a private operator are independent of future need for the service. Residual value risk, which is an ownership risk, is borne by the public sector if an asset of a public-private partnership is transferred to the public sector for less than its true residual value. Residual value risk is borne by the public sector because the private operator reflects the difference between the expected residual value of the asset and the price at which the asset will be transferred to the public sector in the price it charges the public sector for services, or the revenue the public sector receives from a project. If the asset ends up being worth more or less than the amount reflected in the service payment or government revenue, any resulting gain benefits the public sector and any or loss is borne by the public sector. Reference can also be made to various qualitative indicators, including government guarantees of private sector liabilities, and the extent of government influence over asset design and operation.[4]

Future Trends in Regulation

Future trends in regulation for public-private partnerships will reflect on the current regulatory deficit, and in particular, the conceptual limitations of antitrust to intervene in and regulate such complex relations between public and private sectors. Such limitations have set a new paradigm which has established that public services and the modality of public-private partnerships function in a *sui generis* market place, where state intervention in the organisation, structure and delivery of public services reveals a type of regulation based on public law.

As a result of the importance of public-private partnerships to close the infrastructure deficit in developed and developing countries, the public law type of regulation mentioned above should be standardised.[5] Three regulatory actors emerge with competence to accomplish such task of standardisation. Firstly, the United Nations, through the specific task of achieving the Millennium Development Goals by the modality of public-private partnerships. Secondly, the European Union, through its advanced legal framework[6] which produces extraterritorial effects in third countries. Lastly, the World Trade Organisation, which as a result of its globalised agenda in improving trade and liberalising its patterns across its member signatories, could develop standardised legal and regulatory formats for the procurement of public-private partnerships, their legal interface and corporate structure as vehicles in public service delivery and the risk treatment in relations between the state and private actors.

It is worth noting that the public law type of regulation will present national and transnational features in a way that jurisdictional and enforcement characteristics will emerge not only within national markets but also within regional trading blocs. The national/transnational regulation will pave the way towards international norms of coherent and standardised dimensions with a view to establishing not only standardisation of law and policy but uniformity of application and implementation of public-private partnerships and an increased and enhanced legal certainty for both the state, private actors and the public as end-users of public services.

A new trend in societal needs which will emerge out of the route of national towards international regulation of public-private partnerships will reflect on competing models for the delivery of public services. The state will have absolute discretion in engaging with private actors through public-private partnerships to deliver public services or advance models of public-public partnerships, which include intermediary marketisation of public services through mutual societies, social enterprise and in-house arrangements. The competitive dynamics from the interface between public-private partnerships and public-public partnerships will present a valuable benchmark to the state for the ever-increasingly changing background, expectations, standards and needs for the delivery of public services in the twenty-first century.

The concept of public-private partnerships represents a genuine attempt to revolutionise the delivery of public services by introducing the private sector as strategic investor and financier of public services. First, the private sector assumes a direct responsibility in serving the public interest, as part of its contractual obligations vis-à-vis the public sector. The motive and the intention behind such approach focus on the benefits which would follow as a result of the private sector's involvement in the delivery of public services. Efficiency gains, qualitative improvement, innovation, value-for-money and flexibility appear as the most important ones, whereas an overall better allocation of public capital resources sums up the advantages of engaging with the private sector in delivery of public services. Public-private partnerships as a concept of public sector management have changed the methodology of assessing delivery of public services both in qualitative and quantitative terms.

The case for the success of public-private partnerships rests on the relative efficiency of the private sector. However, this efficiency must demonstrate itself in a dynamic mode, reflecting the need for competition in the provision of the relevant services through the public-private partnership. In traditional public contracting, public procurement through tendering secured the repeated competition for a market which is inherently oligopolistic yet contestable by new entries or offerings. However, the scope for competition in the activities undertaken by public-private partnerships is more limited, because they tend to be less contestable for reasons relevant to the longevity of the engagement between public and private sectors, for reasons under which social infrastructure remains undervalued and economic infrastructure involves large sunk costs. For public-private partnerships to operate in a competitive environment globally, safeguard the principles of transparency and accountability in public sector management, incentive-based regulation is paramount. Where a private sector operator can sell public services to the public, but there is little scope for competition, the public sector must regulate prices. However, the challenge is to design well-functioning regulation which increases output towards the social optimum, stabilises prices in a sustainable manner, and limits monopoly profit while preserving the incentive for private sector to be more efficient and reduce costs. The Europe 2020 strategy highlights the importance of public-private partnerships for accelerating growth and boosting innovation. In addition, the Single Market Act[7] announced the adoption of a legislative initiative on concessions in 2011 in order to promote public-private partnerships and to help deliver better value for money for users of services and for contracting authorities, while improving market access for EU undertakings by ensuring transparency, equal treatment and a level playing field across the EU.

The challenges which face both the public and private sectors in public-private partnership arrangements focus on the delivery and the financing of public services respectively from quality and efficiency perspectives. They also reveal a close link with industrial policy at global and national levels and as a result a strategic direction of certain sectors.

These challenges translated in the legal interface of the developed and developing nations pose some considerable questions in relation to the role and scope of private actors in delivering public services, the regulatory compatibility between norms of antitrust and exclusivity of private actors in delivering public services, questions relevant to the expectations of private actors both in financial, operational and strategic perspectives, questions in relation to compliance and enforcement of public-private partnerships relations in the process of delivering public services, and finally, questions in relation to risk treatment arising out of such relations.

The phenomenon of public-private partnerships and the recent developments in public-public co-operation represent a genuine attempt to revolutionise the delivery of public services by a new dimension of public sector management which introduces a new role for the the private sector: as strategic investor and financier of public services.[8] Public-private partnerships as a concept of public sector management have changed the methodology of assessing delivery of public services both in qualitative and quantitative terms. The case for public-private partnerships rests on the relative efficiency of the private sector. However, this efficiency must demonstrate itself in a dynamic mode, reflecting the need for competition in the provision of the relevant services through the public-private partnership. In traditional corporatism, public procurement through tendering secured the repeated competition for a market which is inherently monopolistic yet still contestable by new entries or offerings. However, the scope for competition in the activities undertaken by public-private partnerships is more limited, because they tend to be less contestable for reasons evolving around the longevity of the engagement between public and private sectors, social infrastructure being undervalued and economic infrastructure involving large sunk costs.[9]

Strategically, the future legal and regulatory interface in relation to public-private partnerships will focus on regulatory standardisation which will emit best practice, ensure innovation and quality in the delivery of public service and articulate on issues which are inherently relevant to public-private partnerships such as competitive procurement, structure, financing, investment, control and exit of private actors.

Conclusions

The public sector integration in the European Union has been an integral part to the concept of the Internal Market. It provides for economic and policy justifications for establishing a genuinely competitive environment within which both private and public markets may function and interstate trade patterns flourish.

The economic approach to the regulation of the public sector aims at the integration of public markets across the European Union. Through the principles of transparency, nondiscrimination and objectivity in the award of public contracts which pursue public services, it is envisaged that the regulatory system will bring about competitiveness in the relevant product and geographical markets, will increase import penetration of products and services destined for the public sector, will enhance the tradability of public contracts across the common market, will result in significant price convergence and finally it will be the catalyst for the needed rationalisation and industrial restructuring of the European industrial base.

The regulation of public sector reflects the wish of European institutions to create seamless intra-Community trade patterns between the public and private sectors. The influence of neoclassical economic theories on public sector regulation has taken the relevant regime through the paces of the liberalisation of public markets within the European Union. Antitrust has played a seemingly important role in determining the necessary competitive conditions for the supply side to service the public sector. However, we have seen the emergence of a *sui generis* market place where the mere existence and functioning of antitrust is not sufficient to achieve the envisaged objectives. Public markets require a positive regulatory approach in order to enhance market access. Whereas antitrust and the neoclassical approach to economic integration depend heavily on price competition, public procurement regulation requires a system which primarily safeguards market access. Such regulatory system could be described as public competition law and represents the first departure from the *stricto sensu* neoclassical perspective of public procurement. A policy orientation has emerged mainly through the jurisprudential approach of the regime and the willingness of the Court of Justice of the European Union to expand on the element of inherent flexibility.

The neoclassical versus the ordo-liberal approach reflects the frequently rehearsed debate about the origins of antitrust law and policy per se. The European integration has benefited from a system where the neoclassical approach has contributed to the functioning of an environment of workable competition. However, consistently the rigidity of the neoclassical influence has been diluted with policy considerations, often attributed to national policy requirements. The reflection of the above picture is presented in public sector regulation, although there are certain differences: the Court has allowed for a flexible, policy-oriented application of public procurement, where in antitrust the Commission has eroded its strict neoclassical approach to market integration, the similarity of balancing an economic exercise with policy choice is remarkable.

The phenomenon of public-private partnerships fits within the process of public sector regulation in the European Union and its arrival and application have genuinely revolutionised public services and the way such services are organised, financed and actually delivered to the end-user. It has done so by introducing the private sector as strategic investor and financier of public services and as a direct deliverer in serving the public interest.

The outcome of such development has brought on the forefront of the debate the benefits which would follow as a result of the private sector's involvement. These benefits include efficiency gains, qualitative improvement, innovation, value-for-money and flexibility in the delivery of public services. In addition, an overall better allocation of public capital resources provide for optionality on the part of the public sector in an era of severe budgetary constraints.

The arrival of public-private partnerships as a concept of public sector management has changed the methodology of assessing the delivery of public services both in qualitative and quantitative terms. Not only the price and value of public services are factored in the assessment process, but also their financing and risk allocation. Public-private partnerships rely on the efficiency of the private sector. Its engagement with the public sector is calibrated not only as a result of the appetite for innovation, risk transfer and quality in the delivery of public services, but also as a result of a process which must ensure the competitive environment of the relevant market.

The private sector efficiency in engaging with the public sector in public-private partnerships must also reflect a dynamic mode, demonstrating the need for competition in the provision of the relevant services through the relevant markets. In traditional corporatism, it is the role of public procurement through competitive tendering to secure market equilibrium and a genuinely competitive environment in a market which is inherently restrictive yet contestable by new entries or offerings. However, the scope for competition in the activities undertaken by public-private partnerships is even more limited, as such arrangements between the public and private sectors tend to be less contestable for reasons evolving around the longevity of the engagement, the fact that social infrastructure is often undervalued and economic infrastructure involves large sunk costs.

The final concluding remark of this book offers an assumption that for public-private partnerships to function in a competitive environment within the remit of public sector regulation in the European Union and safeguard the principles of transparency, and accountability in public sector management, it is imperative that incentive-based regulation is introduced. Where a private sector operator can engage with the public sector to offer public services solutions in infrastructure and wider public services for the public, but under such market there is little scope for genuine competition, the public sector has one real alternative; it must regulate the prices which the private sector charges through public-private partnerships in delivering public services. However, the challenge for policy and law makers is to design a system of well-functioning regulation which increases output towards the social optimum, stabilises prices in a sustainable manner, and at the same time limits monopoly profit while preserving the incentive for the private sector to be more efficient and to innovate and improve the quality of public services.

Notes

NOTES TO INTRODUCTION

1. R. Wettenhall and I. Thynne, 'Emerging Patterns of Governance: Synergies, Partnerships and the Public-Private Mix', *International Journal of Public-Private Partnerships* 3, no. 1 (2000), 3–14.
2. R. Rhodes, *Understanding Governance: Policy Networks, Governance, Reflexivity and Accountability* (Buckingham and Philadelphia: Open University Press, 1997).
3. C. Bovis, La notion et les attributions d'organisme de droit public comme pouvoirs adjudicateurs dans le régime des marchés publics, Contrats Publics, Septembre 2003, 26-58. Valadou, La notion de pouvoir adjudicateur en matière de marchés de travaux, Semaine Juridique, 1991, Edition E, No. 3, 35–52.
4. Flamme et Flamme, *Enfin l' Europe des Marchés Publics,* Actualité Juridique—Droit Administratif, 1989.
5. On the issue of public interest and its relation with profit, Cases C-223/99, Agora Srl v. Ente Autonomo Fiera Internazionale di Milano and C-260/99 Excelsior Snc di Pedrotti Runa & C v. Ente Autonomo Fiera Internazionale di Milano, [2001] ECR 3605; C-360/96, Gemeente Arnhem Gemeente Rheden v. BFI Holding BV, [1998] ECR 6821; C-44/96, Mannesmann Anlangenbau Austria AG et al. v. Strohal Rotationsdurck GesmbH, [1998] ECR 73.
6. C. Bovis, *Public Procurement: Case Law and Regulation* (Oxford: Oxford University Press, 2006), chap. 2.
7. A. Sanchez Graells, *Public Procurement and the EU Competition Rules* (Oxford: Hart, 2011).
8. Communication from the Commission Europe 2020, 'A Strategy for Smart, Sustainable and Inclusive Growth', COM (2010) 2020 final. 2010, Brussels.
9. Communication from the Commission to the European Parliament, the Council, the Economic and Social Committee and the Committee of the Regions, *Single Market Act Twelve Levers to Boost Growth and Strengthen Confidence: 'Working Together to Create New Growth'*, COM (2011) 206 final.
10. J. Lunsdgaard, 'Competition and Efficiency in Publicly Funded Services', OECD Economics Department Working Paper, 2002, 7.
11. PricewaterhouseCoopers, London Economics and Ecorys, 'Public Procurement in Europe—Cost and Effectiveness'. A Study on Procurement Regulation prepared for the Commission, March 2011.
12. W. S. Atkins Management Consultants, *The Costs of Non-Europe in Public Sector Procurement, Basic Findings,* Vol 5, Part A and B (Luxembourg: Office for Official Publications of the EC, 1988).
13. P. Cecchini, *The European Challenge, 1992: The Benefits of a Single Market* (Aldershot: Wildwood House, 1988).

14. D. Holland, R. Barrell and T. Fic, 'Global Prospects and Sources of Economic Growth', *National Institute Economic Review*, Volume 212 (2010): Issue 76, Section F, 4–11.

15. F. Ilzkovitz, A. Dierx, V. Kovacs and N. Sousa, *Steps towards a Deeper Economic Integration: The Internal Market in the 21st Century—A Contribution to the Single Market Review* (Brussels: Directorate-General for Economic and Financial Affairs, 2007).

16. European Commission, 'Communication to the European Council and the European Parliament, the European and Economic and Social Committee and the Committee of Regions on Sustainable Consumption and Production and Sustainable Industry Policy Action Plan', 397/3. Brussels: EC, 2008.

17. K. Head, and T. Mayer, 'Non-Europe: The Magnitude and Causes of Market Fragmentation in the EU', *Review of World Economics* 136, no. 2 (2000): 284–314.

18. Report from the Commission Concerning Negotiations Regarding Access of Community Undertakings to the Markets of Third World Countries in Fields Covered by the Directive 2004/17/EC, COM (2009) 592 final 28.10.2009.

19. Communication from the Commission Europe 2020, 'A Strategy for Smart, Sustainable and Inclusive Growth', COM (2010) 2020 final. 3.3.2010, Brussels. Also, European Commission, *The Opening-up of Public Procurement to Foreign Direct Investment in the European Community*, CC 93/79 1995.

20. W. Sauter and H. Schepel, State and Market in the European Union Law: The Public and Private Spheres of the Internal Market before the EU Courts (Cambridge: Cambridge University Press, 2009).

21. J. L. Buendia Sierra, *Exclusive Rights and State Monopolies under EC Law* (Oxford: Oxford University Press, 1999), 330.

22. T. Prosser, *The Limits of Competition Law* (Oxford: Oxford University Press, 2005); also C. Graham, 'Essential Facilities and Services of General Interest', *Diretto e Politiche dell'Unione Europea* Volume 1 (2007): 29.

23. A. Moriceau, 'Services d'intérêt économique general et valeurs communes', *Revue du Marché Commun et de l'Union Europénne*, no. 519 (2008): 358.

24. M. Ross, 'Article 16 E.C. and Services of General Interest: From Derogation to Obligation?', *European Law Review* (2000): 22–38.

25. C. Bovis, 'Competition and Telecommunications', chap. 18 in *Encyclopaedia of Competition Law*, ed. R. Merkin (London: Sweet and Maxwell, 2007); also C. Bovis, 'The Application of Competition Rules to the European Union Transport Sectors', *Columbia Journal of European Law* 11, no. 5 (2005): 1–49.

26. In the context of air transport, public service obligation is defined in Council Regulation 2408/92 as amended by Regulation 1008/2008 as *any obligation imposed upon an air carrier to take, in respect of any route which it is licensed to operate by a Member State, all necessary measures to ensure the provision of a service satisfying fixed standards of continuity, regularity, capacity and pricing, which standards the air carrier would not assume if it were solely considering its economic interest.*

27. W. Sauter, 'Services of General Economic Interest and Universal Service in EU Law', *European Law Review* (2008): 172.

28. In the context of the Universal Services Directive EC 2002/22, universal service obligations are services made available to the public at the quality specified to all end-users in their territory, independently of geographical location, and, in the light of specific national conditions, at an affordable price.

29. Art 16 EC reads 'Without prejudice to Articles 77, 90 and 92 [now Articles 93, 106, and 107 TFEU], and given the place occupied by services of general economic interest in the shared values of the Union as well as their role in

promoting social and territorial cohesion, the Community and the Member States, each within their respective powers and within the scope of application of this Treaty, shall take care that such services operate on the basis of principles and conditions which enable them to fulfil their missions'.

30. P. Craig and G. De Búrca, *EU Law—Text, Cases and Materials,* 5th ed. (Oxford: Oxford University Press, 2011).

31. Communication to the European Council and the European Parliament, the European and Economic and Social Committee and the Committee of Regions—Partnering in Research and Innovation. European Commission, COM (2011) 572 final, Brussels.

32. European Commission, *Green Paper on Services of General Interest,* COM (2003) 270 final. 21.5.2003.

33. European Commission, Communication from the Commission to the European Parliament, the Council, the European Economic and Social Committee and the Committee of the Regions, 'A Single Market for 21st Century Europe—Services of General Interest, Including Social Services of General Interest: A New European Commitment', COM (2007) 725. Also, C. Joerges and F. Rödl, '"Social Market Economy" as Europe's Social Model?' *EUI Working Paper LAW No. 2004/8,* European University Institute, 2004.

34. Case C-360/96, *Gemeente Arnhem Gemeente Rheden v. BFI Holding BV,* [1998] ECR 6821.

35. Communication to the European Council and the European Parliament, the European and Economic and Social Committee and the Committee of Regions of 16 July 2008, Public Procurement for a Better Environment. European Commission, COM (2008) 400 final, Brussels.

36. Case C-223/99, C-223/99, Agora Srl v. Ente Autonomo Fiera Internazionale di Milano and C-260/99 Excelsior Snc di Pedrotti Runa & C v. Ente Autonomo Fiera Internazionale di Milano, [2001] ECR 3605.

37. R. Mangabeira Unger, *Free Trade Re-imagined: The World Division of Labour and the Method of Economics* (Princeton, NJ: Princeton University Press, 2007).

38. C. Bovis, 'Financing Services of General Interest, Public Procurement and State Aids: The Delineation between Market Forces and Protection', *European Law Journal* 11, no. 1 (2005): 79–109.

39. The term *industrial and commercial character* features in the public procurement *acquis* and corresponds to the presence of market competitiveness supported through the factors of profitability and demand substitutability; C. Bovis, 'Redefining Contracting Authorities under the EC Public Procurement Directives: An Analysis of the Case C-44/96, *Mannesmann Anlangenbau Austria AG et al. v. Strohal Rotationsdurck GesmbH*', *Common Market Law Review* 39 (1999): 41–59.

40. Services of general economic interest and public service obligations conceptually merge through the medium of *public service contract.* Regulation 1893/91, OJ L 169, 1991 as amended by Regulation 1008/2008. The concept of public service contracts, which covers contractual relations between competent authorities of Member States and undertakings and encapsulates contractualised obligations to provide adequate services to the public, introduces the need of the principles of transparency and accountability in the selection process and methods of the entrusted undertaking to provide such services. A public service contract in the transport sector may cover: i) transport services satisfying fixed standards of continuity, regularity, capacity and quality; ii) additional transport services; iii) transport services at specified rates and subject to specified conditions, in particular for certain categories of passenger or on certain routes; iv) adaptation of services to actual requirements.

41. European Commission XXIII Competition Report, point 534.
42. Case C-412/96, *Kainuun Liikenne Oy,* [1998] ECR 1515. The case elaborated on the ability of transport undertakings which are subject to a public service obligation to apply for the termination of such an obligation in whole or in part, under Article 4 of Regulation 1191/69. There is discretion on the part of Member States to grant such request, which entails that they can refuse even in cases that the pursuit of public service obligations entails economic disadvantages for the relevant transport operator. However, such a refusal can only be based on the necessity of maintaining the provision of adequate transport services. The Court maintained that such necessity must be assessed having regard to the public interest; the possibility of having recourse to other forms of transport and the ability of such forms to meet the transport needs under consideration; the transport rates and conditions which can be quoted to users. The Court implied that the competent authorities will choose the service that secures the lowest costs for the community if other services can be offered for equivalent conditions.
43. Communication to the European Council and the European Parliament, the European and Economic and Social Committee and the Committee of Regions— Pre-commercial Procurement: Driving Innovation to Ensure Sustainable High Quality Public Services in Europe, European Commission, COM (2007) 799 final, Brussels.
44. The concept of public service obligation within the context of the air transport regime is defined in Regulation 2408/92 as amended by Regulation 1008/2008 on access for air carriers to intra-Community air routes as *any obligation imposed upon an air carrier to take, in respect of any route which it is licensed to operate by a Member State, all necessary measures to ensure the provision of a service satisfying fixed standards of continuity, regularity, capacity and pricing, standards which the air carrier would not assume if it were solely considering its economic interest.*
45. Community rules on public procurement contracts do not apply to the awarding by law or contract of exclusive concessions, which are exclusively ruled by the procedure provided for pursuant to Article 4(1) of Regulation 2408/92 as amended by Regulation 1008/2008.
46. The implementation of public service obligation must be transparent and the selected transport operators are expected to account annually for the relevant costs, including fixed costs and revenues attributed to the relevant routes.
47. Although Article 4(1)(f) of Regulation 2408/92 as amended by Regulation 1008/2008 refers to the compensation required as just one of the criteria to be taken into consideration for the selection of submissions, the Commission considers that the level of compensation should be the main selection criterion, as other elements such as adequacy, fare prices and standards are constituent elements of the public service obligations themselves.
48. Cases C-301/87 *France v. Commission,* [1990] ECR I, p. 307; Case C-142/87 *Belgium v. Commission* [1990] ECR I, p. 959.
49. Case 173/73, *Italy v. Commission,* [1974] ECR, p. 709.
50. For example, reimbursement for public services to the Atlantic islands (Azores) are excluded from the scope of Regulation 2408/92 as amended by Regulation 1008/2008, but are subject to Articles 107 and 108 TFEU. Commission Decision of 6 July 1994, Case C-7/93 on reimbursement of the deficit sustained by TAP on the routes to the Atlantic islands, OJ C178, 30. 6. 1993.
51. Article 4(1)(i) of Regulation 2408/92 as amended by Regulation 1008/2008 obliges the Member States to take the measures necessary to ensure that any decision to award public service obligations can be reviewed effectively. The Commission may carry out an investigation and take a decision in case the

development of a route is being unduly restricted under Article 4(3) of the Regulation. However, the Commission's powers under the Regulation are without prejudice to its exclusive powers under the state aid rules of the Treaty. In case there is clear evidence that the Member State has not selected the best offer, the Commission may request information from the Member State in order to examine whether the award of a public service obligation includes, in addition to their compensation, state aid elements. Such elements are likely to occur where a Member State has selected not the lowest offer in relation to the financial compensation to be paid to the air carrier.

NOTES TO CHAPTER 1

1. Green Paper on Modernisation of Public Procurement Policy: Towards a more Efficient European Procurement Market, COM (2011) 15 final.
2. B. De Witte, 'Direct Effect, Primacy and the Nature of the Legal Order', in *The Evolution of EU Law*, 2nd ed., ed. P. Craig and G. De Burca (Oxford: Oxford University Press, 2011): 323–362.
3. Cases 286/82 & 26/83 *Luisi & Carbone v. Ministero del Tesoro*, [1984] ECR 377, 308/86 *Ministere Public v. Lambert*, [1988] ECR 478.
4. The famous Case 26/62, NV Algemene Transport-en Expeditie Onderneming Van Gend en Loos v. Nederlandse Administrtie der Belastigen, [1963] ECR 1.
5. M. Kumm, 'The Jurisprudence of Constitutional Conflict: Constitutional Supremacy in Europe before and after the Constitutional Treaty', *European Law Journal* 11 (2005): 262. Also, A. Dashwood, 'The Relationship between the Member States and the EU/EC', *Common Market Law Review* 41 (2004): 355.
6. Kapteyn van Themaat and VerLoren van Themaat, *The Law of the European Union and the European Communities*, 4th ed. (Deventer: Kluwer, 2009), chap. 1, 34–37.
7. The first transitional period covers the time period from the establishment of the European Communities until 31/12/1969. For more details, see P. Oliver, 'Some Further Reflections on the Scope of Articles 28–30 (ex 30–36) EC', *Common Market Law Review* 36 (1999): 783.
8. European Commission, *White Paper for the Completion of the Internal Market*, (COM) 85 310 final, 1985.
9. The completion of the internal market required the adoption at Community level and the implementation at national level of some three hundred Directives on the subjects specified in the Commission's White Paper. Also the *Third Report of the Commission to the European Parliament on the Implementation of the White Paper*, (COM) 1988, 134 final.
10. Lord Cockfield's quotation in the Cechinni Report, *The European Challenge 1992, The Benefits of a Single Market* (Aldershot: Wildwood House, 1988).
11. W. S. Atkins Management Consultants, *The Cost of Non-Europe, Basic Findings, Vol 5, Part A; The Cost of Non-Europe in Public Sector Procurement* (Luxembourg: Official Publications of the European Communities, 1988). Also the Cechinni Report *The European Challenge 1992, The Benefits of a Single Market* (Aldershot: Wildwood House, 1988).
12. European Commission, *White Paper for the Completion of the Internal Market*, (COM) 85 310 final, 1985.
13. Commission of the European Communities, *The Cost of Non-Europe, Basic Findings, Vol 5, Part A; The Cost of Non-Europe in Public Sector Procurement* (Luxembourg: Official Publications of the European Communities, 1988).

Also the Cechinni Report *The European Challenge 1992, The Benefits of a Single Market* (Aldershot: Wildwood House, 1988).

14. The European Commission has claimed that the introduction of competition in the relevant markets and the regulation of public procurement could bring substantial savings of ECU 20 bn or 0.5 per cent of GDP to the (European) public sector. European Communities, *The Cost of Non-Europe*, op. cit.

15. Commission of the European Communities, 'Statistical Performance for Keeping Watch over Public Procurement', 1992. Also *The Cost of Non-Europe, Basic Findings, Vol. 5, Part A; The Cost of Non-Europe in Public Sector Procurement,* op. cit. Also, M. Dowdle, ed., *Public Accountability: Designs, Dilemmas and Experiences* (Cambridge: Cambridge University Press, 2006); Also R. Anderson and W. Kovacic, 'Competition Policy and International Trade Liberalisation: Essential Complements to Ensure Good Performance in Public Procurement Markets', *Public Procurement Law Review* (2009): Volume 2, 67–101, 71.

16. C. Bovis, 'Public Procurement in the EU: Jurisprudence and Conceptual Directions', *Common Market Law Review* 49 (2012): 1–44. Also, C. Bovis, 'Recent Case Law Relating to Public Procurement: A Beacon for the Integration of Public Markets', *Common Market Law Review* 39 (2002): 42–79.

17. The term *national champion* implies a firm with more than a third of its turnover made in its own country and has enjoyed formal or informal government protection. The term has been defined by R. Abravanel and D. Ernst, 'Alliance and Acquisition Strategies for European National Champions', *The McKinsey Quarterly,* no. 2 (1992): 45–62 and has been used subsequently by policy makers.

18. P. Nicolaides, ed., *Industrial Policy in the European Community: A Necessary Response to Economic Integration* (Deventer: Martinus Nijhoff, 1993). Also, European Commission, 'The EU Industrial Policy and the 2020 Vision for Growth', COM (2011) 642 final, Brussels 14/10/2011.

19. H.C.H. Hofmann, 'Negotiated and Non-Negotiated Administrative Rule-Making: The Example of EC Competition Policy', *Common Market Law Review* 43 (2006): 153-178. Also, O. A. Stefan, 'European Competition Soft Law in European Courts: A Matter of Hard Principles', *European Law Journal* 14 (2008): 753–772.

20. Communication from the European Commission to the Council, the European Parliament, the Economic and Social Committee, and the Committee of the Regions, 'Working Together to Maintain Momentum', Review of the Internal Market Strategy, Brussels, 11 April 2001, COM (2001) 198 final. Also European Commission, Commission Communication, 'Public Procurement in the European Union', Brussels, 11 March 1998, COM (98) 143.

21. European Commission, Communication to the European Parliament, the Council, the Economic and Social Committee and the Committee of the Regions, *Towards a Single Market Act,* COM (2010) 608 final.

22. Green Paper on the Modernisation of Public Procurement Policy: Towards a More Efficient European Procurement Market COM (2011) 15 final.

23. 'Proposal for a Directive of the European Parliament and of the Council on Public Procurement', COM (2011) 896 final.

24. O. Odudu, *The Boundaries of EC Competition Law: The Scope of Article 81* (Oxford: Oxford University Press, 2006).

25. O. Dekel, 'The Legal Theory of Competitive Bidding for Government Contracts', *Public Contract Law Journal* 37 (2008): 237; B. Mukhopadhyay, 'Evaluating Public Procurement', *Review of Market Integration* 3, no. 1 (2011): 21; P. Chirulli, 'Public Contracts', *International Journal of Public Administration* 34, no. 1–2 (2011): 134. Also, A. Konstadacopoulos, 'The Linked Oligopoly Concept in the Single European Market', *Public Procurement Law Review* 4 (1995): 213.

26. W.K. Viscusi, J. Harrington and J. Vernon, *Economics of Regulation and Antitrust*, 4th ed. (Cambridge, MA: MIT Press, 2005).

27. G. S. Ølykke, 'How Does the Court of Justice of the European Union Pursue Competition Concerns in a Public Procurement Context?', *Public Procurement Law Review* 6 (2011): 179.

28. O. Black, *Conceptual Foundations of Antitrust* (Cambridge: Cambridge University Press, 2005).

29. G. S. Ølykke, C. Risvig and C. Tvarnø, eds., *EU Public Procurement— Modernisation, Growth and Innovation* (Copenhagen: DJØF, 2012).

30. W. Sauter and H. Schepel, *State and Market in the European Union Law* (Cambridge: Cambridge University Press, 2009).

31. Case *Cooperative Vereniging 'Suiker Unie' UA v. Commission,* [1975] ECR 1663, in which the European Court of Justice recognised the adverse effects of concerted practices in tendering procedures on competition in the common market. This case appears to have opened the way for the application of competition law on public procurement in the Community. The applicability of Competition Law provisions of the Treaty in controlling collusive tendering and anticompetitive behaviour of suppliers was also the subject of Commission Decision 92/204, O.J. 1992 L92/1. It could be argued that competition law and policy applies equally to private as well as public markets, but the explicit provisions of the Directives on consortia participation in tendering procedures might limit the scope of applying antitrust provisions in public procurement.

32. OECD, *Public Procurement: The Role of Competition Authorities in Promoting Competition* (2007).

33. E. Szyszczak, *The Regulation of the State in Competitive Markets in the EU* (Oxford: Hart, 2007).

34. C. Bovis, 'Public Procurement and the Internal Market of the 21st Century: Economic Exercise versus Policy Choice', chap. 17 in *EU Law for the 21st Century: Rethinking the New Legal Order,* ed. P. Nebia and T. Tridimas (Oxford: Hart, 2005).

35. The thresholds laid down by Article 7 of the Public Sector Directive 2004/17 and Article 6 of the Utilities Directive 2004/18 are as follows: 6,242,000 euro for all work and construction projects, 249,000 euro for supplies contracts within the European Union and 162,000 euro for supplies contracts from third countries which participate in the WTO Government Procurement Agreement, 242,000 euro for services contracts, 600,000 euro for supplies of telecommunication equipment under the Utilities Directive and 400,000 euro for all other supplies contracts awarded by public utilities.

36. Commission Interpretative Communication on the European law applicable to contract awards not or not fully subject to the provisions of the Public Procurement Directives, [2006] OJ C 179/2.

37. Case C-27/86, Constructions et Enterprises Indusrtielles S.A (CEI) v. Association Intercommunale pour les Autoroutes des Ardennes; Case C-28/86, Ing.A. Bellini & Co. S.p.A. v. Regie de Betiments; Case C-29/86, Ing.A. Bellini & Co. S.p.A. v. Belgian State, [1987] ECR 3347.

38. T. Lawton, ed., *European Industrial Policy and Competitiveness: Concepts and Instruments* (London: Macmillan, 1998). Also, W. Sauter, *Competition Law and Industrial Policy* (Oxford: Clarendon Press, 1997).

39. Case 76/81, SA Transporoute et Travaux v. Minister of Public Works, [1982] ECR 457; Case 103/88, Fratelli Costanzo S.p.A. v. Comune di Milano, [1989] ECR 1839; Case 296/89, Impresa Dona Alfonso di Dona Alfonso & Figli s.n.c. v. Consorzio per lo Sviluppo Industriale del Comune di Monfalcone, [1991] ECR 2967; Case C-285/99 & 286/99, Impresa Lombardini SpA v. ANAS, [2001] ECR 9233.

40. Case 76/81 *Transporoute*, [1982] ECR 417, op. cit.
41. Case C-285/99 & 286/99, *Impresa Lombardini SpA v. ANAS,* judgement of 27 November 2001.
42. Case C-94/99, *ARGE Gewässerschutzt,* [2000] ECR I-11037.
43. Paragraphs 26 *et seq.* of the Court's judgement in *ARGE.*
44. Graells A. Sanchez, *Public Procurement and the EU Competition Rules* (Oxford: Hart, 2011), chap. 4.
45. Commission Communication, Public Procurement, September 22 1989, C 311 89.
46. The Commission's arguments in the *Beentjes* (Case 31/87, *Gebroeders Beentjes B.V. v. State of Netherlands* [1988] ECR 4635), Nord-Pas-de-Calais (Case C-225/98, *Commission v. French Republic,* [2000] ECR 7445) and the Concordia (Case C-513/99, *Concordia Bus Filandia v. Helsingin Kaupunki et HKL-Bussiliikenne,* [2002] ECR 7213).
47. Case C-45/87, *Commission v. Ireland,* [1988] ECR 4929; Also Case C-359/93, *Commission v. The Netherlands,* [1995] ECR 151.
48. Case 76/81, SA Transporoute et Travaux v. Minister of Public Works, [1982] ECR 457; Case 103/88, Fratelli Costanzo S.p.A. v. Comune di Milano, [1989] ECR 1839; Case 296/89, Impresa Dona Alfonso di Dona Alfonso & Figli s.n.c. v. Consorzio per lo Sviluppo Industriale del Comune di Monfalcone, [1991] ECR 2967; Case C-285/99 & 286/99, Impresa Lombardini SpA v. ANAS, [2001] ECR 9233.
49. R. Posner, *Economic Analysis of Law* (Deventer: Kluwer, 2007).
50. G.L. Albano et al., 'Preventing Collusion in Public Procurement', in *Handbook of Procurement,* ed. N. Dimitri, G. Piga, and G. Spagnolo (Cambridge: Cambridge University Press, 2006).
51. M. Monti, 'Article 81 EC and Public Policy', *Common Market Law Review* 39 (2002), 1057–1099, where it is argued that public policy considerations balance the legality test of *ab initio* illegal restrictive agreements by virtue of Art 81(1)(2) EC with a set of requirements contained in Art 81(3) EC and also developed by the EC Commission in its jurisdictional capacity to provide individual exemptions.
52. M.M. Bazex, *Le droit public de la concurrence,* RFDA (Revue de réflexion et d'approfondissement en droit public), Paris, 1998; A. Arcelin, *L'enterprise en droit interne et communautaire de la concurrence* (Paris: Litec, 2003); O. Guézou, *Droit de la concurrence et droit des marches publics: vers une notion transverale de mise en libre concurrence,* Contrats Publics, Paris, Mars 2003.
53. A. Jacquemin and W.D. de Jong, *European Industrial Organization* (London: Macmillan, 1997); W. Möschel, 'Competition Law from an Ordo Point of View', in *German Neo-Liberals and the Social Market Economy,* ed. A. Peacock and H. Willgerodt (London: Macmillan, 1989).
54. Commission Interpretative Communication on the European Law Applicable to Public Procurement and the Possibilities for Integrating Social Considerations into Public Procurement, COM (2001) 566, 15 October 2001. Also, Commission Interpretative Communication on the European Law Applicable to Public Procurement and the Possibilities for Integrating Environmental Considerations into Public Procurement, COM (2001) 274, 4 July 2001. Also, Commission Communication—Implementing the Community Lisbon Programme: Social Services of General Interest in the European Union, COM (2006) 177 final. 26.4.2006 Brussels. Also, Commission Communication to the European Parliament, the Council, the European Economic and Social Committee and the Committee of the Regions, Accompanying the Communication on 'A Single Market for 21st Century Europe' Services of General Interest, Including Social Services of General Interest: A New European Commitment, COM (2007) 725 final. 20.11.2007 Brussels.

55. Green Paper on Services of General Interest, COM (2003) 270 final. Brussels 21.5.2003. Also, Communication from the Commission—Implementing the Community Lisbon Programme: Social Services of General Interest in the European Union, Brussels COM (2006) 177 final. 26.4.2006. Also, Commission Communication to the European Parliament, the Council, the European Economic and Social Committee and the Committee of the Regions, Accompanying the Communication on 'A Single Market for 21st Century Europe' Services of General Interest, Including Social Services of General Interest: A New European Commitment, COM (2007) 725 final. 20.11.2007, Brussels. Also, Commission Communication to the European Parliament, the Council, the European Economic and Social Committee and the Committee of the Regions—Reform of the EU State Aid Rules on Services of General Economic Interest, COM (2011) 146 final. 23.3.2011, Brussels.
56. Commission Communication, 'Europe 2020, A Strategy for Smart, Sustainable and Inclusive Growth', COM (2010) 2020 final.
57. Commission, 'Guide to the Application of the European Union Rules on State Aid, Public Procurement and the Internal Market to Services of General Economic Interest, and in Particular to Social Services of General Interest', SEC (2010) 1545 final. Commission, 'Buying Social: A Guide to Taking Account of Social Considerations in Public Procurement', SEC (2010) 1258, final.
58. The legislation on public procurement in the early stages clearly allowed for 'preference schemes' in less favoured regions of the common market which were experiencing industrial decline. Articles 29(4) and 29(a) of the EC Public Works Directive 71/305; also Article 26 of EC Public Supplies Directive 77/62. Such schemes required the application of award criteria based on considerations other than the lowest price or the most economically advantageous offer, subject to their compatibility with European law inasmuch as they did not run contrary to the principle of free movement of goods and to competition law considerations with respect to state aid. Since the completion of the Internal Market (1992) they have been abolished, as they have been deemed capable in contravening directly or indirectly the basic principle of nondiscrimination on grounds of nationality stipulated in the Treaties.
59. Case C-380/98, The Queen and H.M. Treasury, ex parte University of Cambridge, judgement of 3 October 2000 at paragraph 17; Case C-44/96, C-44/96, Mannesmann Anlangenbau Austria AG et al. v. Strohal Rotationsdurck GesmbH, judgement of 15 January 1998, paragraph 33; Case C-360/96, Gemeente Arnhem Gemeente Rheden v. BFI Holding BV, judgement of 10 November 1998 at paragraphs 42 and 43; C-237/99, Commission v. France, judgement of 1 February 2001, at paragraphs 41 and 42.
60. C. Bovis, 'The Compatibility of Compulsory Tendering with Transfer of Undertakings: The Case of Contract Compliance and the Acquired Rights Directive', chap. 21 in *Legal Regulation of the Employment Relations,* ed. H. Collins, A. Davies and R. Rideout (Deventer: Kluwer, 2000).
61. C. McCurdden, *Buying Social Justice: Equality, Government Procurement and Legal Change* (Oxford: Oxford University Press, 2007).
62. In particular in the US, Case 93–1841, *Adarand Constructors v. Pena,* 1995 Annual Volume of US Supreme Court. The United States Supreme Court questioned the constitutionality in the application of contract compliance as a potential violation of the equal protection component of the Fifth Amendment's Due Process Clause and ordered the Court of Appeal to reconsider the employment of socioeconomic policy objectives in the award of federal public procurement contracts.
63. For an overview of the social policy in North American systems, see C. Cnossen and C. Bovis, 'The Framework of Social Policy in Federal States: An

Analysis of the Law and Policy on Industrial Relations in USA and Canada', *International Journal of Comparative Labour Law and Industrial Relations* 12, 7–23 (1996).

64. For example, in United Kingdom, every initiative relating to contract compliance has been outlawed by virtue of the Local Government Act 1988. Contract compliance from a public law perspective has been examined by T. Daintith, 'Regulation by Contract: The New Prerogative', *Current Legal Problems* 32 (1979): 41.

65. Case 31/87, *Gebroeders Beentjes B.V v. The Netherlands*, [1989] ECR 4365. Also Case C-360/89, *Commission v. Italy*, judgement of 3 July 1992.

66. There are a number of legal instruments relevant to social policy at Community level that may apply to public procurement. They include, in particular, Directives on safety and health at work (e.g. Council Directive 89/391 as amended on the introduction of measures to encourage improvements in the safety and health of workers at work, and Directive 92/57 as amended on the implementation of minimum safety and health requirements at temporary or mobile construction sites), working conditions and the application of employment law (e.g. Directive 96/71/EC of the European Parliament and of the Council concerning the posting of workers in the framework of the provision of services, OJ L 18/1 of 21.1.1997, and Directive 2001/23 as amended on the safeguarding of employees' rights in the event of transfers of undertakings, businesses or parts of undertakings or businesses, OJ L 82/16 of 22.3.2001, codifying Directive 77/187/EEC), Directive 2000/43/EC of 29.6.2000 implementing the principle of equal treatment between persons irrespective of racial or ethnic origin (OJ 2000 L 180/22) and Directive 2000/78/EC of 27.11.2000 as amended establishing a general framework for equal treatment in employment and occupation (OJ 2000 L 303/16).

67. It should be mentioned that adherence to health and safety laws has been considered by a British court as part of the technical requirements specified in the Works Directive for the process of selection of tenderers; *General Building and Maintenance v. Greenwich Borough Council*, [1993] IRLR 535. Along these lines, the Commission's Interpretative Communication on the European Law Applicable to Public Procurement and the Possibilities for Integrating Social Considerations into Public Procurement, COM (2001) 566, 15/10/01. Also, Commission Communication to the European Parliament, the Council, the European Economic and Social Committee and the Committee of the Regions—Reform of the EU State Aid Rules on Services of General Economic Interest, COM (2011) 146 final. 23.3.2011, Brussels.

68. K. Kruger, R. Nielsen, and N. Brunn, *European Public Contracts in a Labour Law Perspective* (Copenhagen: DJOF, 1997).

69. C. Bovis, 'Social Policy Considerations and the European Public Procurement Regime', *International Journal of Comparative Labour Law and Industrial Relations* 3 (1998):137–163.

70. See, European Commission, Communication to the European Council and the European Parliament, the European and Economic and Social Committee and the Committee of Regions on Sustainable Consumption and Production and Sustainable Industry Policy Action Plan, (2008) 397/3. Brussels.

71. Communication to the European Council and the European Parliament, the European and Economic and Social Committee and the Committee of Regions—Pre-Commercial Procurement: Driving Innovation to Ensure Sustainable High Quality Public Services in Europe, European Commission, COM (2007) 799 final. Brussels.

72. An example of such approach is the views of the UK Government in relation to the involvement of the private sector in delivering public services. The so-called

Private Finance Initiative (PFI) has been utilized as a procurement and contractual system in order to create a framework between the public and private sectors working together in delivering public services.

73. Of interest is the case *ARGE* (paragraphs 26 *et seq.* of the Court's judgement), where even the receipt of aid or subsidies incompatible with the Treaty by an entity may be a reason for disqualification from the selection process, as an obligation to repay an illegal aid would threaten the financial stability of the tenderer in question. Case C-94/99, *ARGE Gewässerschutzt v. Bundesministerium für Land-und Forstwirtschaft,* judgement of 7 December 2000, where the Court concluded that if the legislature wanted to preclude subsidized entities from participating in tendering procedures for public contracts, it should have said so explicitly in the relevant Directives.

74. *White Paper on Services of General Interest* [COM (2004) 374], the Communication on Developing PPPs [COM (2009) 615 final].

75. *Green Paper on the Modernization of EU Public Procurement Policy: Towards a More Efficient European Procurement Market,* COM (2011) 15/47. Also, European Commission, White Paper for the Completion of the Internal Market, (COM) 85 310 final, 1985. Also Commission of the European Communities, The Cost of Non-Europe, Basic Findings, Vol. 5, Part A; The Cost of Non-Europe in Public Sector Procurement, Official Publications of the European Communities, Luxembourg, 1988. Also Paolo Cecchini, *The European Challenge 1992, The Benefits of a Single Market* (Aldershot: Wildwood House, 1988).

76. Commission Communication to the European Parliament, the Council, the Economic and Social Committee and the Committee of the Regions, *Towards a Single Market Act,* COM (2010) 608 final.

77. European Commission, *Public Procurement: Regional and Social Aspects* COM (89) 400.

78. J.M. Fernadez-Martin and O. Stehmann, 'Product Market Integration versus Regional Cohesion in the Community', *European Law Review* 16 (1991): 216–243.

79. C. Bovis, *The Liberalisation of Public Procurement in the European Union and Its Effects on the Common Market* (Dartmouth: Ashgate 1998).

80. European Commission, *Public Procurement: Regional and Social Aspects* (COM (89) 400).

81. Commission of the European Communities, *Statistical Performance for Keeping Watch over Public Procurement,* 1992.

82. Case 84/86, *Commission v. Hellenic Republic,* not reported; Case C-21/88, *Dupont de Nemours Italiana S.p.A v. Unita Sanitaria Locale No.2 di Carrara,* judgement of 20 March 1990, [1990] ECR 889; Case C-351/88, *Lavatori Bruneau Slr. v. Unita Sanitaria Locale RM/24 di Monterotondo,* judgement of 11 July 1991; Case C-360/89, *Commission v. Italy,* [1992] ECR I 3401; Case C-362/90, *Commission v. Italy,* judgement of 31 March 1992.

83. Case C-74/76, *Ianelli & Volpi Spa v. Ditta Paola Meroni,* [1977] 2 CMLR 688.

84. Case C-18/84, *Commission v. France,* 1985, ECR 1339; Case 103/84, *Commission v. Italy,* 1986, ECR 1759; also, Case C-244/81, *Commission v. Ireland,* 1982, ECR 4005.

85. C. Bovis, 'Public Procurement as an Instrument of Industrial Policy in the European Union', chap. 7 in *European Industrial Policy and Competitiveness: Concepts and Instruments,* ed. T. Lawton (London: Macmillan, 1998); J. M. Fernadez Martin and O. Stehmann, *Product Market Integration versus Regional Cohesion in the Community,* op. cit.

86. Conclusions of the European Council of 14 and 15 December 2001, paragraph 26; Conclusions of the Internal Market, Consumer Affairs and Tourism Council

meeting of 26 November 2001 on Services of General Interest; Commission Report to the Laeken European Council on Services of General Interest of 17 October 2001, COM (2001) 598; Communication from the Commission on the Application of the State Aid Rules to Public Service Broadcasting, OJ 2001 C 320, p. 5; also the two general Commission Communications on Services of General Interest of 1996 and 2000 in OJ 1996 C 281, p. 3 and OJ 2001 C 17, p. 4.

87. C. Bovis, 'Public Procurement and Services of General Economic Interest', in *The Changing Legal Framework of Services of General Interest—Between Competition and Solidarity*, ed. M. Krajewski, U. Neergaard and J. van de Gronden (The Hague, T.M.C. Asser Press, 2009): 150–178.

88. Case C-387/92 [1994] ECR I-877; Case T-106/95, *FFSA and Others v. Commission* [1997] ECR II-229; Case C-174/97 P [1998] ECR I-1303; Case T-46/97 [2000] ECR II-2125.

89. Article 107(1) TFEU defines state aid as 'any aid granted by a Member State or through State resources in any form whatsoever which distorts or threatens to distort competition by favoring certain undertakings or the production of certain goods . . . , in so far as it affects trade between Member States'.

90. Article 106(2) TFEU stipulates that 'Undertakings entrusted with the operation of services of general economic interest . . . shall be subject to the rules contained in this Treaty, in particular to the rules on competition, insofar as the application of such rules does not obstruct the performance, in law or in fact, of the particular tasks assigned to them. The development of trade must not be affected to such an extent as would be contrary to the interests of the Community'.

91. Case 240/83 [1985] ECR 531; Case C-53/00, judgement of 22 November 2001; Case C-280/00, judgement of 24 July 2003.

92. Jens Hilger, 'The Award of a Public Contract as State Aid within the Meaning of Article 87(1) EC', *Public Procurement Law Review* vol. 12, no. 3 (2003): 109–30.

93. Case C-280/00, Altmark Trans GmbH, Regierungsprösidium Magdeburg et Nahverkehrsgesellschaft Altmark GmbH, Oberbundesanwalt beim Bundesverwaltungsgericht, (third party), judgement of 24 July 2003.

94. Opinion of Advocate General Jacobs in Case C-126/01, *Ministre de l'economie, des finances et de l'industrie v. GEMO SA*, 30 April 2002.

95. N. Tosics and N. Gaal, 'Public Procurement and State Aid Control—The Issue of Economic Advantage', *Competition Policy Newsletter* 3 (2007): 15–18.

96. For example the form in which the aid is granted (Cases C-323/82, *Intermills v. Commission* [1984] ECR 3809, paragraph 31; Case C-142/87, *Belgium v. Commission*, cited in note 18, paragraph 13; and Case 40/85, *Belgium v. Commission* [1986] ECR I-2321, paragraph 120), the legal status of the measure in national law (Commission Decision 93/349/EEC of 9 March 1993 concerning aid provided by the United Kingdom Government to British Aerospace for its purchase of Rover Group Holdings over and above those authorised in Commission Decision 89/58/EEC authorizing a maximum aid to this operation subject to certain conditions (OJ 1993 L 143, p. 7, point IX)), the fact that the measure is part of an aid scheme (Case T-16/96, *Cityflyer Express v. Commission*, [1998] ECR II-757), the reasons for the measure and the objectives of the measure (Case C-173/73 *Italy v. Commission* [1974] ECR 709; *Deufil v. Commission*, [1987] ECR 901; Case C-56/93, *Belgium v. Commission*, [1996] ECR I-723; Case C-241/94, *France v. Commission* [1996] ECR I-4551;Case C-5/01, *Belgium v. Commission* [2002] ECR I-3452) and the intentions of the public authorities and the recipient undertaking (Commission Decision 92/11/EEC of 31 July 1991 concerning aid provided by the Derbyshire County Council to Toyota Motor Corporation, an undertaking producing motor vehicles (OJ 1992 L 6, p. 36, point V)).

97. Case C-173/73, *Italy v. Commission* [1974] ECR 709, paragraph 27; *Deufil v. Commission,* [1987] ECR 901; Case C-56/93, *Belgium v. Commission,* [1996] ECR I-723 paragraph 79; Case C-241/94, *France v. Commission* [1996] ECR I-4551, paragraph 20; and Case C-5/01, *Belgium v. Commission* [2002] ECR I-3452, paragraphs 45 and 46.

98. Communication of the Commission to the Member States concerning public authorities' holdings in company capital (*Bulletin EC* 9–1984, point 3.5.1). The Commission considers that such an investment is not aid where the public authorities authorized it under the same conditions as a private investor operating under normal market economy conditions. Also Commission Communication to the Member States on the Application of Articles 92 and 93 of the EEC Treaty and of Article 5 of Commission Directive 80/723/EEC to Public Undertakings in the Manufacturing Sector (OJ 1993 C 307, p. 3, point 11).

99. In particular Case 234/84, *Belgium v. Commission* [1986] ECR 2263, paragraph 14; Case C-142/87, *Belgium v. Commission* (*'Tubemeuse'*) [1990] ECR I–959, paragraph 26; and Case C-305/89, *Italy v. Commission* (*'Alfa Romeo'*) [1991] ECR I–1603, paragraph 19.

100. For example where the public authorities contribute capital to an undertaking (Case 234/84, *Belgium v. Commission* [1986] ECR 2263; Case C-142/87, *Belgium v. Commission* [1990] ECR I–959; Case C-305/89, *Italy v. Commission* [1991] ECR I–1603), grant a loan to certain undertakings (Case C-301/87, *France v. Commission* [1990] ECR I–307; Case T-16/96, *Cityflyer Express v. Commission* [1998] ECR II–757), provide a state guarantee (Joined Cases T-204/97 and T-270/97, *EPAC v. Commission* [2000] ECR II–2267), sell goods or services on the market (Joined Cases 67/85, 68/85 and 70/85 *Van der Kooy and Others v. Commission* [1988] ECR 219; Case C-56/93, *Belgium v. Commission* [1996] ECR I–723; Case C-39/94, *SFEI and Others* [1996] ECR I-3547), or grant facilities for the payment of social security contributions (Case C-256/97, *DM Transport* [1999] ECR I–3913), or the repayment of wages Case C-342/96, *Spain v. Commission* [1999] ECR I–2459).

101. Case C-303/88, *Italy v. Commission* [1991] ECR I–1433, paragraph 20; Case C-261/89, *Italy v. Commission* [1991] ECR I–4437, paragraph 15; and Case T-358/94, *Air France v. Commission* [1996] ECR II–2109, paragraph 70.

102. For example where the public authorities pay a subsidy directly to an undertaking (Case 310/85, *Deufil v. Commission* [1987] ECR 901), grant an exemption from tax (Case C-387/92, *Banco Exterior* [1994] ECR I–877; Case C-6/97, *Italy v. Commission* [1999] ECR I–2981; Case C-156/98, *Germany v. Commission* [2000] ECR I–6857) or agree to a reduction in social security contributions (Case C-75/97, *Belgium v. Commission* [1999] ECR I–3671; Case T-67/94, *Ladbroke Racing v. Commission* [1998] ECR II–1)

103. The analysis in the Joined Cases C-278/92 to C-280/92, *Spain v. Commission* [1994] ECR I–4103.

104. Case C-360/96, *Gemeente Arnhem Gemeente Rheden v. BFI Holding BV,* op. cit.

105. Cases C-223/99, Agora Srl v. Ente Autonomo Fiera Internazionale di Milano and C-260/99, Excelsior Snc di Pedrotti Runa & C v. Ente Autonomo Fiera Internazionale di Milano, op. cit.

106. E. Szyszczak, J. Davies, M. Andenaes, and T. Bekkedal, eds., *Developments in Services of General Interest* (The Hague: TMC Asser Press/Springer, 2011). Also, A. Arcelin, *L'enterprise en droit interne et communautaire de la concurrence* (Paris: Litec, 2003); O. Guézou, *Droit de la concurrence et droit des marchés publics: vers une notion transverale de mise en libre concurrence,* Contrats Publics, Mars 2003 and M.M. Bazex, *Le droit public de la concurrence* (RFDA (Revue de réflexion et d'approfondissement en droit public), Paris, 1998).

107. According to Advocate General Léger in his Opinion on the *Altmark* case, the apparent advantage theory occurs in several provisions of the Treaty, in particular in Article 92(2) and (3), and in Article 77 of the EC Treaty (now Article 73 EC). Article 92(3) of the Treaty provides that aid may be regarded as compatible with the common market if it pursues certain objectives such as the strengthening of economic and social cohesion, the promotion of research and the protection of the environment.

108. According to the Public Procurement Directives, two criteria provide the conditions under which contracting authorities award public contracts: *the lowest price* or the *most economically advantageous offer*. The first criterion indicates that, subject to the qualitative criteria and financial and economic standing, contracting authorities do not rely on any other factor than the price quoted to complete the contract. The Directives provide for an automatic disqualification of an 'obviously abnormally low offer'. The term has not been interpreted in detail by the Court and serves rather as an indication of a 'lower bottom limit' of contracting authorities accepting offers from the private sector tenderers. Case 76/81, *SA Transporoute et Travaux v. Minister of Public Works,* [1982] ECR 457; Case 103/88, *Fratelli Costanzo S.p.A. v. Comune di Milano,* [1989] ECR 1839; Case 296/89, *Impresa Dona Alfonso di Dona Alfonso & Figli s.n.c. v. Consorzio per lo Sviluppo Industriale del Comune di Monfalcone,* judgement of 18 June 1991. In Case C-94/99, *ARGE Gewässerschutzt* the Court ruled that directly or indirectly subsidised tenders by the state or other contracting authorities or even by the contracting authority itself can be legitimately part of the evaluation process, it did not elaborate on the possibility of rejection of an offer, which is appreciably lower than those of unsubsidised tenderers by reference to the of abnormally low disqualification ground, paragraphs 26 *et seq.* of the Court's judgement.

109. The meaning of the most economically advantageous offer includes a series of factors chosen by the contracting authority, including price, delivery or completion date, running costs, cost-effectiveness, profitability, technical merit, product or work quality, aesthetic and functional characteristics, after-sales service and technical assistance, commitments with regard to spare parts and components and maintenance costs, security of supplies. The above list is not exhaustive.

110. Community framework for state aid for research and development and innovation, OJ C 323, 30.12.2006, p. 1–26, paragraph 2.1.

111. Case C-44/96, *Mannesmann Anlangenbau Austria AG et al. v. Strohal Rotationsdurck GesmbH,* op. cit. also the analysis of the case by C. Bovis, 'Redefining Contracting Authorities under the EC Public Procurement Directives: An Analysis of the Case C-44/96, *Mannesmann Anlangenbau Austria AG et al. v. Strohal Rotationsdruck GesmbH*' in *Common Market Law Review* 36(1) (1999): 205–25.

112. Case 127/73, *BRT v. SABAM* [1974] ECR 313, paragraph 20; Case 66/106, *Ahmed Saeed Flugreisen v. Commission* [1989] ECR 803, paragraph 55.

113. The standard assessment criterion applied under Article 106(2) EC only requires for the application of Article 87(1) EC to frustrate the performance of the particular public service task, allowing for the examination being conducted on an *ex post facto* basis. Also the reasoning behind the so-called electricity judgements of the ECJ of 23 October 1997; Case C-157/94, *Commission v. Netherlands* [1997] ECR I–5699; Case C-158/94, *Commission v. Italy* [1997] ECR I–5789; Case C-159/94, *Commission v. France* [1997] ECR I–5815 and C-160/94, *Commission v. Spain* [1997] ECR I–5851; a great deal of controversy exists as to whether the material standard of the frustration of a public service task under Article 106(2) EC had lost its strictness. S. Magiera, *Gefährdung der öffentlichen Daseinsvorsorge durch das EG-Beihilfenrecht?* (Köln, Berlin, Bonn und München, FS für Dietrich Rauschning, 2000).

114. Opinion of Advocate General Lenz, delivered on 22 November 1984 in Case 240/83, *Procureur de la République v. ADBHU* [1985] ECR 531 (536). Advocate General Lenz in his opinion held that the indemnities granted must not exceed annual uncovered costs actually recorded by the undertaking, taking into account a reasonable profit. However, the Court in the *ADBHU* case did not allow for the permissibility of taking into account such a profit element. Interestingly, the approach of the Court of First Instance on Article 106(2) EC has never allowed any profit element to be taken into account, but instead focussed on whether without the compensation at issue being provided the fulfillment of the specific public service tasks would have been jeopardised.
115. 'Community Guidelines on State Aid to Promote Risk Capital Investments in Small and Medium-sized Enterprises OJ C 194, 18.8.2006', p. 2–21.
116. 'Community Guidelines on State Aid for Environmental Protection, OJ C 82, 1.4.2008', p. 1–33.
117. Commission Communication, 'Community Guidelines for the Application of State Aid Rules in Relation to Rapid Deployment of Broadband Networks, OJ C 235, 30.9.2009', p. 7–25.
118. Communication to the European Council and the European Parliament, the European and Economic and Social Committee and the Committee of Regions—Partnering in Research and Innovation, European Commission, COM (2011) 572 final. Brussels.
119. H. Demsetz, 'Why Regulate Utilities?', *Journal of Law and Economics* 11, no. 1 (1968): 50–62.
120. European Commission, SME TASK FORCE: SMEs and Public Procurement, Brussels 1988; European Commission, Pan European Forum on Sub-Contracting in the Community, Brussels 1993. Also, D. Mardas, 'Subcontracting, Small and Medium Sized Enterprises (SMEs) and Public Procurement in the European Community', *Public Procurement Law Review* 3 (1994): CS 19. Also, see, Communication from the Commission Europe 2020: A Strategy for Smart, Sustainable and Inclusive Growth, COM (2010) 2020 final. 3.3.2010, Brussels.
121. Proposal for a Directive of the European Parliament and of the Council on the Award of Concession Contracts (which includes an explanatory memorandum and brief justification), COM (2011) 897 final. Also *Green Paper on Public-Private Partnerships and European Law on Public Contracts and Concessions,* COM (2004) 327 final. Also, OECD-Sigma, Brief 18: Public Procurement-Concessions and PPPs, August 2011.
122. C. Doyle and R. Inderst, 'Some Economics on the Treatment of Buyer Power in Antitrust', *European Competition Law Review* 28, no. 3 (2007): 210–19.
123. Communication to the European Council and the European Parliament, the European and Economic and Social Committee and the Committee of Regions of 16 July 2008, Public Procurement for a Better Environment. European Commission, COM (2008) 400 final. Brussels.
124. M. Trybus, *European Union Law and Defence Integration* (Oxford: Hart, 2005).
125. M. Trybus and N. White, eds., *European Security Law* (Oxford: Oxford University Press, 2007).
126. Directive 2009/81/EC.

NOTES TO CHAPTER 2

1. Case C-44/96, *Mannesmann Anlagenbau Austria and Others,* [1998] ECR I–73, paragraphs 20 and 21; Case C-470/99, *Universale-Bau and Others* [2002] ECR I-11617, paragraphs 51 to 53; Case C-214/00, *Commission v. Spain*

[2003] ECR I–4667, paragraphs 52 and 53; and Case C-283/00, *Commission v. Spain* [2003] ECR I–11697, paragraph 69.

2. Article 1(9) of the Public Sector Directive and Article 2(1)(a) of the Utilities Directive. A body governed by public law indicates any organization which satisfies the following conditions in a cumulative manner. First, the organization must be established for the specific purpose of meeting needs in the general interest which do not have an industrial or commercial character; secondly, it must have legal personality; and thirdly, it must be financed, for the most part, by the state, regional or local authorities, or other bodies governed by public law. Alternatively and as part of the third criterion, a body governed by public law must be subject to management supervision by the state, regional or local authorities, or other bodies governed by public law or it must have an administrative, managerial or supervisory board, more than half of whose members are appointed by the state, regional or local authorities, or by other bodies governed by public law. Nonexhaustive lists of bodies and categories of bodies governed by public law which fulfil the three cumulative criteria for a body governed by public law are set out in Annex III of the Directive.

3. Article 2(1)(b) of the Utilities Directive. Contracting authorities exercise dominant influence upon public undertakings when directly or indirectly, in relation to an undertaking, hold the majority of the undertaking's subscribed capital, or control the majority of the votes attaching to shares issued by the undertaking, or can appoint more than half of the undertaking's administrative, management or supervisory body.

4. Article 2(3) of the Utilities Directive.

5. The determination of a genuinely competitive regime is left to the utilities operators themselves. Case C 392/93, *The Queen and H.M. Treasury, ex parte British Telecommunications PLC*, O.J. 1993, C 287/6. This is perhaps a first step towards self-regulation which could lead to the disengagement of the relevant contracting authorities from the public procurement regime.

6. C. Bovis, 'Public Entities Awarding Procurement Contracts under the Framework of EC Public Procurement Directives', *Journal of Business Law* 1 (1993): 56–78.

7. Case 31/87, *Gebroeders Beentjes B.V. v. State of Netherlands* [1988] ECR 4635.

8. The formality test and the relation between the state and entities under its control was established in Cases C-249/81, *Commission v. Ireland*, [1982] ECR 4005 and C-36/74 *Walrave and Koch v. Association Union Cycliste International et al.*, (1974) ECR 1423.

9. Cases C-353/96, *Commission v. Ireland* and C-306/97, *Connemara Machine Turf Co Ltd v. Coillte Teoranta*, judgement of 17 December 1998, [1998] All ER (D) 765.

10. Case C 323/96, *Commission v. Kingdom of Belgium*, [1998] ECR I–5063.

11. For a similar approach, also Case C-144/97, *Commission v. France*, [1998] ECR I–613.

12. Article 1(b) of Directive 93/37.

13. This type of dependency resembles the Court's definition in its ruling on state-controlled enterprises in Case 152/84, *Marshall v. Southampton and South West Hampshire Area Health Authority*, [1986] ECR 723.

14. Case C-237/99, *Commission v. France*, [2001] ECR I–939.

15. Case C-380/98, *The Queen and H.M. Treasury, ex parte University of Cambridge*, [2000] ECR I-8035.

16. Paragraph 25 of the Court's judgement as well as the Opinion of the Advocate General, in paragraph 46.

17. Case C-107/98, *Teckal Slr v. Comune di Viano*, [1999] ECR I–8121.

18. Case C-380/98, *The Queen and H.M. Treasury, ex parte University of Cambridge*, [2000] ECR 8035, paragraph 20, and Case C-237/99, *Commission v. France*, [2001] ECR 934, paragraph 44.
19. Case C-237/99, *Commission v. France*, paragraphs 48 and 49.
20. Case C-373/00, *Adolf Truley GmbH and Bestattung Wien GmbH*, [2003] ECR I-1931.
21. Cases C-223/99, Agora Srl v. Ente Autonomo Fiera Internazionale di Milano, and C-260/99, Excelsior Snc di Pedrotti runa & C v. Ente Autonomo Fiera Internazionale di Milano, [2001] ECR I-3605; C-360/96, Gemeente Arnhem Gemeente Rheden v. BFI Holding BV, [1998] ECR I-6821. C-44/96, Mannesmann Anlangenbau Austria AG et al. v. Strohal Rotationsdurck GesmbH, [1998] ECR I-73.
22. Opinion of Advocate General Léger, point 65 of the *Strohal* Case C-44/96, above.
23. Case C-179/90, *Merci Convenzionali Porto di Gevova*, [1991] ECR 1-5889; General economic interest as a concept represents 'activities of direct benefit to the public'; point 27 of the Opinion of Advocate General van Gerven.
24. P. Valadou, 'La notion de pouvoir adjudicateur en matière de marchés de travaux', *Semaine Juridique* E, no. 3 (1991): 33.
25. Case C-44/96, *Mannesmann Anlangenbau Austria*, op. cit.
26. For example Case 118/85, *Commission v. Italy* [1987] ECR 2599 paragraph 7, where the Court had the opportunity to elaborate on the distinction of activities pursued by public authorities.
27. Case C-364/92, *SAT Fluggesellschafeten* [1994] ECR 1-43; also Case C-343/95, *Diego Cali et Figli* [1997] ECR 1-1547.
28. Case C-360/96, *Gemeente Arnhem Gemeente Rheden v. BFI Holding BV*, op. cit.
29. Case C-223/99, Agora Srl v. Ente Autonomo Fiera Internazionale di Milano, op. cit.
30. Case C-44/96, Mannesmann Anlangenbau Austria v. Strohal Rotationsdurck GesmbH, op. cit.
31. For a comprehensive analysis of the case, see analysis by C. Bovis, 'Redefining Contracting Authorities under the EC Public Procurement Directives: An Analysis of the Case C-44/96, *Mannesmann Anlangenbau Austria AG et al. v. Strohal Rotationsdruck GesmbH*' in *Common Market Law Review* 36(1) (1999): 205–25.
32. In particular, Working Together—Private Finance and Public Money, Department of Environment, 1993. Private Opportunity, Public Benefit—Progressing the Private Finance Initiative, Private Finance Panel and HM Treasury, 1995.
33. Case C-107/98, *Teckal Slr v. Comune di Viano*, op. cit.
34. Case C-300/07, Hans & Christophorus Oymanns GbR, Orthopädie Schuhtechnik, v. AOK Rheinland/Hamburg, judgement of 11 June 2009.
35. Case C-337/06, *Bayerischer Rundfunk et al. V. GEWA* [2007] ECR I-11173.
36. Case C-84/03, *Commission of the European Communities, v. Kingdom of Spain*, [2005] ECRI-139.
37. Case C-44/96, *Mannesmann Anlagenbau Austria*, [1998] ECR I-73, paragraphs 17 to 35.
38. Case 31/87, *Beentjes* [1988] ECR 4635 and Case C-360/96, *BFI Holding* [1998] ECR I-6821.
39. Case C-26/03, Stadt Halle, RPL Recyclingpark Lochau GmbH v. Arbeitsgemeinschaft Thermische Restabfall- und Energieverwertungsanlage TREA Leuna, [2005) ECR I-1.
40. Case C-283/00, *Commission of the European Communities, v. Kingdom of Spain*, [2003] ECR I-11697.

41. Case C-44/96, *Mannesmann Anlagenbau Austria,* [1998] ECR I–73, paragraphs 20 and 21.
42. Case C-237/99, *Commission v. France* [2001] ECR I–939, paragraphs 41 to 43, and Case C-470/99, *Universale-Bau and Others* [2002] ECR I–11617, paragraphs 51 to 53.
43. Case C-373/00, *Adolf Truley* [2003] ECR-1931, paragraph 43.
44. In particular, *Mannesmann Anglagenbau Austria and Others,* paragraphs 6 and 29; Case C-360/96, *BFI Holding* [1998] ECR I–6821, paragraphs 61 and 62; and Case C-237/99, *Commission v. France,* paragraphs 50 and 60.
45. Case C-44/96, *Mannesmann Anlagenbau Austria,* [1998] ECR I–73, paragraphs 17 to 35.
46. Case C-214/00, *Commission v. Spain* [2003] ECR I-4667, paragraphs 54, 55 and 60; and Case C-283/00, *Commission v. Spain* [2003] ECR I–11697, paragraph 75.
47. Case C-373/00, *Adolf Truley* [2003] ECR-193, paragraph 66, and C-18/01 *Korhonen and Others* [2003] ECR I–5321, paragraphs 48 and 59.
48. Case C-470/99, *Universale-Bau and Others* [2002] ECR I–11617, paragraphs 51 to 53.
49. Case C-26/03, Stadt Halle, RPL Recyclingpark Lochau GmbH v. Arbeitsgemeinschaft Thermische Restabfall- und Energieverwertungsanlage TREA Leuna [2005] ECR I–1.
50. Case C-283/00, *Commission v. Spain,* [2003] ECR I–11697. Cases C-373/00, *Adolf Truley* [2003] ECR-193, paragraph 42, and C-18/01, *Korhonen and Others* [2003] ECR I–5321, paragraphs 51 and 52.
51. Case C-470/99, Universale-Bau AG, Bietergemeinschaft Hinteregger & Söhne Bauges.mbH Salzburg, ÖSTU-STETTIN Hoch- und Tiefbau GmbH, and Entsorgungsbetriebe Simmering GesmbH, [2002] ECR I–11617.
52. Case C-18/01, Arkkitehtuuritoimisto Riitta Korhonen Oy, Arkkitehtitoimisto Pentti Toivanen Oy, Rakennuttajatoimisto Vilho Tervomaa and Varkauden Taitotalo Oy, [2003] ECR I–12.

NOTES TO CHAPTER 3

1. Article 1(2)(a) of the Public Sector Directive. Public contracts are contracts for pecuniary interest concluded in writing between one or more economic operators and one or more contracting authorities and having as their object the execution of works, the supply of products or the provision of services. Article 1(2)(b) of the Public Sector Directive specifies as public works contracts, contracts which have as their object either the execution or both the design and execution, of works, or the completion, by whatever means, of a work corresponding to the requirements specified by the contracting authority. A work means the outcome of building or civil engineering works taken as a whole which is sufficient of itself to fulfill an economic or technical function. Article 1(2)(c) of the Public Sector Directive specifies as public supply contracts, contracts having as their object the purchase, lease, rental or hire purchase, with or without option to buy, of products. A public contract having as its object the supply of products and which also covers, as an incidental matter, placement and installation operations must be considered as a public supply contract. Article 1(2)(d) of the Public Sector Directive specifies as public service contracts, contracts other than public works or supply contracts having as their object the provision of services referred to in Annex II of the Directive. A public contract having as its object both products and services within the meaning of Annex II must be considered as a 'public service contract' if the

value of the services in question exceeds that of the products covered by the contract.

2. Case C-536/07, *Commission v. Germany,* ECR I–10355.
3. Case C-399/98, *Ordine degli Architetti and Others* [2001] ECR I–5409.
4. Case C-264/03, *Commission v. France* [2005] ECR I–8831.
5. Case C-220/05, *Jean Auroux and Others v. Commune de Roanne,* ECR [2007], p. I–385.
6. Case C-480/06, *Commission v. Germany,* [2009] ECR I–04747.
7. The European Commission in its Interpretative Communication on Public-Private Partnerships COM (2007) 6661 is against double tendering requirements in the case of Institutional Public Private Partnerships, by encouraging contracting authorities to consider *en bock* the selection of a private partner and the subsequent award of works or services as a single contractual interface.
8. Case C-451/08, *Helmut Müller v. Bundesanstalt für Immobilienaufgaben,* [2010] 3 CMLR 18.
9. Joined Cases C-147/06 and C-148/06, *SECAP SpA* and *Santorso Soc. coop. arl,* [2008] ECR I–3565; Case C-412/04, *Commission v. Italy* [2008] ECR I–0000, paragraph 65.
10. Case C-59/00, *Vestergaard* [2001] ECR I–9505.
11. Case C-324/98, *Telaustria and Telefonadress* [2000] ECR I–10745, paragraph 60.
12. Case C-6/05, *Medipac-Kazantzidis AE v. Venizelio-Pananio (PE.S.Y. KRITIS),* [2007] ECR I–4557.
13. Case C-324/98, *Telaustria and Telefonadress* [2000] ECR I–10745, paragraphs 60 and 61; Case 59/00, *Vestergaard,* paragraphs 20 and 21; Case C-231/03, *Coname* [2005] ECR I–7287, paragraphs 16 and 17; and Case C-458/03, *Parking Brixen* [2005] ECR I–8585, paragraphs 46 to 48.
14. Case C-324/98, *Telaustria and Telefonadress,* paragraph 60; Case C-50/00, *Vestergaard,* paragraphs 20 and 21; Case C-264/03, *Commission v. France* [2005] ECR I–8831, paragraph 32; and Case C-6/05, *Medipac-Kazantzidis* [2007] ECR I-4557, paragraph 33.
15. Case C-220/06, Asociación Profesional de Empresas de Reparto y Manipulado de Correspondencia v. Administración General del Estado, [2007] ECR I–12175.
16. Case C-458/03, *Parking Brixen* [2005] ECR I–8585, paragraph 48, and Case C-410/04, *ANAV* [2006] ECR I–3303, paragraph 20.
17. Case C-458/03, *Parking Brixen* [2005] ECR I–8612, paragraph 49, and Case C-410/04, *ANAV,* paragraph 21.
18. Case C-507/03, *Commission v. Ireland* [2007] ECR I-0000, paragraph 29, and *Commission v. Italy,* paragraphs 66 and 67.
19. Case C-231/03, *Coname* [2005] ECR I–7287, paragraph 20.
20. Case C-79/01, *Payroll and Others* [2002] ECR I–8923, paragraph 26; Case C-442/02, *CaixaBank France* [2004] ECR I–8961, paragraphs 12 and 13; and Case C-452/04, *Fidium Finanz* [2006] ECR I-9521, paragraph 46.
21. Case C-507/03, *Commission v. Ireland,* (An Post) [2007] ECR I–9777.
22. Case C-324/98, *Telaustria and Telefonadress,* [2000] ECR I–10745, paragraphs 60 and 61, and Case C-231/03, *Coname* [2005] ECR I–7287, paragraph 17.
23. Case C-231/03, *Coname* [2005] ECR I–7287, paragraph 19.
24. Case C-380/98, *University of Cambridge* [2000] ECR I–8035, paragraph 16; Case C-19/00, *SIAC Construction* [2001] ECR I–7725, paragraph 32; and Case C-92/00, *HI* [2002] ECR I-5553, paragraph 43.
25. Case C-324/98, *Telaustria and Telefonadress,* [2000] ECR I–10745.
26. Case C-231/03, *Consorzio Aziende Metano (Coname). v. Comune di Cingia de' Botti* [2005] ECR I–7287.

27. Case C-458/03, *Parking Brixen* [2005] ECR I-8612.
28. Case C-324/98, *Telaustria and Telefonadress* [2000] ECR I–10745, paragraph 60, and Case C-231/03, *Coname* [2005] ECR I–7287, paragraph 16.
29. Case C-3/88, *Commission v. Italy* [1989] ECR 4035, paragraph 8.
30. Case 810/79, *Überschär* [1980] ECR 2747, paragraph 16.
31. Case C-87/94, *Commission v. Belgium* [1996] ECR I–2043, paragraphs 33 and 54.
32. Case C-324/98, *Telaustria and Telefonadress*, op. cit., paragraphs 61 and 62.
33. C. Bovis, 'The State, Competition and Public Services', chap. 11 in *The European Union Legal Order after Lisbon*, ed. P. Birkinshaw and M. Varney (Alphen aan den Rijn, The Netherlands: Kluwer, 2010).
34. Case C-382/05, *Commission v. Italy* [2007] ECR I–6657, paragraph 34, and Case C-437/07, *Commission v. Italy* [2008] ECR I–0000, paragraph 29; also European Commission Interpretative Communication on Concessions under Community Law, OJ 2000 C 121, p. 2.
35. Case C-206/08, *WAZV Gotha v. Eurawasser Aufbereitungs* [2009] ECR I–8377.
36. Case C-31/87, *Beentjes* [1988] ECR 4635, paragraph 11; and Case C-360/96, *BFI Holding* [1998] ECR I–6821, paragraph 62.
37. Case C-126/03, *Commission of the European Communities v. Federal Republic of Germany*, judgement of 18 November 2004 and the Opinion of Advocate General paragraph 28.
38. Cases C-107/98, *Teckal* [1999] ECR I–8121, and C-399/98, *Ordine degli Architetti and Others* [2001] ECR I–5409.
39. Case C-360/96, *BFI Holding*, and Joined Cases C-223/99 and C-260/99, *Agorà and Excelsior* [2001] ECR I–3605.
40. Case C-44/96 [1998] ECR I–73.
41. Case C-18/01, *Korhonen and Others* [2003] ECR I–5321, paragraph 51.
42. Article 1(a)(ii) of the Public Services Directive 92/50 and the equivalent Articles in Council Directive 93/36 coordinating procedures for the award of public supply contracts (OJ 1993 L 199, p. 1) and Directive 93/37 coordinating procedures for the award of public works contracts (OJ 1993 L 199, p. 54).
43. Case C-126/03, *Commission of the European Communities v. Federal Republic of Germany*, judgement of 18 November 2004.
44. Case C-176/98, *Holst Italia*, [1999] ECR-I–8607.
45. Case C-314/01, Siemens AG Österreich, ARGE Telekom & Partner and Hauptverband der österreichischen Sozialversicherungsträger, judgement of 18 March 2004.
46. Case C-176/98, *Holst Italia*, [1999] ECR-I–8607, paragraphs 26 and 27.
47. Case C-176/98, *Holst Italia*, [1999] ECR-I–8607, paragraph 29.
48. Case C-314/01, Siemens AG Österreich, ARGE Telekom & Partner and Hauptverband der österreichischen Sozialversicherungsträger, judgement of 18 March 2004.
49. Case C-84/03, *Commission of the European Communities, v. Kingdom of Spain,* [2005] ECRI–139.
50. Case C-237/99, Commission v. France, Case C-380/98, The Queen and H.M. Treasury, ex parte University of Cambridge, Case C-107/98, Teckal Slr v. Comune di Viano, [1999] ECR I–8121.
51. Case C-107/98, *Teckal,* op. cit.
52. Case C-107/98, *Teckal,* op. cit.
53. Article 2(1)(b) of the Utilities Directive.
54. Case C-458/03, *Parking Brixen* [2005] ECR I-8612, paragraph 65.
55. Case C-340/04, Carbotermo SpA, Consorzio Alisei v Comune di Busto Arsizio, AGESP SpA, [2006] ECR I–4137.

56. Case C-340/04, *Carbotermo and Consorzio Alisei,* paragraph 37, and Case C-295/05, *Asemfo* [2007] ECR I–2999, paragraph 57.
57. Case C-324/07, *Coditel Brabant SA v. Commune d'Uccle, Région de Bruxelles-Capitale,* [2009] 1 CMLR 29.
58. Case C-458/03, *Parking Brixen,* [2005] ECR I–8612, paragraph 62.
59. Case C-26/03, *Stadt Halle and RPL Lochau* [2005] ECR I–1.
60. Case C-26/03, *Stadt Halle and RPL Lochau,* op. cit., paragraph 50.
61. Case C-26/03, *Stadt Halle and RPL Lochau,* op. cit., paragraph 49.
62. Case C-29/04, *Commission v. Austria* [2005] ECR I–563.
63. Case C-410/04, Associazione Nazionale Autotrasporto Viaggiatori (ANAV) v. Comune di Bari, AMTAB Servizio SpA, [2006] ECR, I–3303.
64. Case C-29/04, *Commission v. Austria* [2005] ECR I–563, paragraph 48.
65. Case C-573/07, *Sea Srl. v. Comune di Ponte Nossa* [2009] ECR I–08127.
66. Case C-26/03, *Stadt Halle and RPL Lochau,* op. cit., paragraphs 15 and 52.
67. Case C-458/03, *Parking Brixen* [2005] ECR I–8612, paragraphs 67 and 72.
68. Case C-29/04, *Commission v. Austria* [2005] ECR I–9705, paragraphs 38 to 41.
69. Case C-231/03, *Coname* [2005] ECR I–7287, paragraphs 5 and 28.
70. Case C-340/04, *Carbotermo Spa v. Comune di Busto Arsizio* [2006] ECRI 4137.
71. Case C-26/03, *Stadt Halle and RPL Lochau* [2005] ECR I–1, paragraph 48.
72. Case 295/05, Asociación Nacional de Empresas Forestales (Asemfo) v. Transformación Agraria SA (Tragsa) and Administración del Estado, [2007] ECR I-2999, paragraph 65.
73. Case C-480/06, *Commission v. Germany,* [2009] ECR I–04747.
74. Case C-324/07, *Coditel Brabant SA v. Commune d'Uccle, Région de Bruxelles-Capitale,* [2009] 1 CMLR 29.

NOTES TO CHAPTER 4

1. United States General Accounting Office (GAO), Commercial Activities Panel, Improving the Sourcing Decisions of the Government: Final Report (April 2002).
2. M. Trebilcock, *The Prospects for Reinventing Government* (Toronto: C.D. Howe Institute, 1994).
3. T. Daintith, 'The Executive Power Today: Bargaining and Economic Control', in *The Changing Constitution,* ed. J. Jowell and D. Oliver (Oxford: Oxford University Press, 19851), where reference is made to the distinction between *dominium* and *imperium* (the use of force by way of regulatory or criminal law) as two ways of policy implementation by the state.
4. The industrial or commercial character of an organisation depends much upon a number of criteria that reveal the thrust behind the organisation's participation in the relevant market. The state and its organs may act either by exercising public powers or by carrying economic activities of an industrial or commercial nature by offering goods and services on the market. for example, Case 118/85, *Commission v. Italy* [1987] ECR 2599 paragraph 7, where the European Court of Justice had the opportunity to elaborate on the distinction of activities pursued by public authorities and activities of commercially oriented undertakings. The key issue is the organisation's intention to achieve profitability and pursue its objectives through a spectrum of commercially motivated decisions. The distinction between the range of activities which relate to public authority and those which, although carried out by public persons, fall within the private domain is drawn most clearly from case law and

judicial precedence of the ECJ concerning the applicability of competition rules of the Treaty to the given activities. Cases C-364/92, *SAT Fluggesellschaften* [1994] ECR 1–43 and C-343/95, *Diego Cali et Figli* [1997] ECR 1–1547).

5. L. Salamon, ed., *The Tools of Government: A Guide to the New Governance* (New York: Oxford University Press, 2002).

6. The origins of such activities can be found in J. J. Rousseau, *The Social Contract,* 1762, where a core range of obligations is undertaken by the state on behalf of its subjects. This is perhaps the first attempt to contractualise the state/society relationship.

7. M. Harrison, *Corporatism and the Welfare State,* chap. 1 (Aldershot: Gower, 1984).

8. M. Flamme et M. Flamme, *Enfin l'Europe des Marchés Publics,* Actualité Juridique—Droit Administratif, 20 November 1989, p. 653.

9. The concept 'public interest' denotes the requirements of a community (local or national) in its entirety which should not overlap with the specific or exclusive interest of a clearly determined person or group of persons. P. Valadou, 'La notion de pouvoir adjudicateur en matière de marchés de travaux', *Semaine Juridique* E, no. 3 (1991): 33. Also, the European Court of Justice has approached the above concept of public interest by a direct analogy of the concept 'general economic interest', as defined in Article 90(2) EC, which refers to public undertakings. Case C-179/90, *Merci Convenzionali Porto di Gevova,* [1991] ECR 1–5889, where the notion general economic interest as a concept represents 'activities of direct benefit to the public'.

10. Apart from the above fundamental differentiating factor, a number of striking variances distinguish private from public markets. These variances focus on structural elements of the relevant market place, competitiveness, demand conditions, supply conditions, the production process, and finally pricing and risk. They also provide for an indication as to the different methods and approaches employed in their regulation. See, C. Bovis, *The Liberalisation of Public Procurement and Its Impact on the Common Market* (Ashgate: Dartmouth, 1998), 5–11.

11. J.J. Laffont and J. Tirole, *A Theory of Incentives in Procurement and Regulation* (Cambridge, MA: MIT Press, 1993).

12. Corporatism has been deemed as an important instrument of industrial policy of a state, in particular where procurement systems have been utilised with a view to promoting structural adjustment policies and favour 'national champions'. C. Bovis, 'The Choice of Policies and the Regulation of Public2 Procurement in the European Community', in *European Industrial Policy and Competitiveness: Concepts and Instruments,* ed. T. Lawton (London, Macmillan, 1998).

13. Although antitrust rules are of negative nature, by no means they can be deemed static. Perceptions concerning cartels and abusive dominant behaviour change in line with contemporary socioeconomic parameters.

14. C. Bovis, 'The Regulation of Public Procurement as an Element in the Evolution of European Economic Law', *European Law Journal* 4, no. 2 (June 1998): 220 *et seq.*

15. The adverse effects of concerted practices in tendering procedures on competition in the common market were recognised by the European Court of Justice in Case *Cooperative Vereniging 'Suiker Unie' UA v. Commission,* [1975] ECR 1663.

16. European Commission, *The Cost of Non-Europe, Basic Findings, Vol. 5, Part A; The Cost of Non-Europe in Public Sector Procurement,* Official Publications of the European Communities, Luxembourg, 1988. The European Commission has claimed that the regulation of public procurement through the newly established regime and the resulting elimination of nontariff barriers arising from discriminatory and preferential purchasing patterns of Member

Sates could bring about substantial savings of 20 euro bn or 0.5 per cent of GDP to the (European) public sector.

17. R. Hoogland DeHoog and L. Salamon, 'Purchase-of-Service Contracting', in Lester M. Salamon, ed., *The Tools of Government: A Guide to the New Governance* (New York: Oxford University Press, 2002), 319–340.

18. E. Savas, *Privatization in the City: Successes, Failures, Lessons* (Washington, DC: CQ Press, 2005).

19. E. Cheung, A. Ping-Chuen Chan and S. Kajewski, 'Reasons for Implementing Public Private Partnership Projects: Perspectives from Hong Kong, Australian and British Practitioners', *Journal of Property Investment and Finance* 27, no. 1 (2009), 81–95.

20. P. Cook and C. Kirkpatrick, 'Assessing the Impact of Privatisation in Developing Countries', in *International Handbook on Privatization*, ed. D. Parker and D. Saal (Cheltenham, Edward Elgar, 2003): 341–387.

21. S. Kelman, 'Contracting', in *The Tools of Government: A Guide to the New Governance*, ed. Lester M. Salamon (New York: Oxford University Press, 2002), 282–319.

22. M. Trebilcock and E. Iacobucci, 'Privatization and Accountability', *Harvard Law Review* 116, no. 5 (March 2003), 145–167.

23. D. Andrew, C. Smith and Michael J. Trebilcock, 'State-Owned Enterprises in Less Developed Countries: Privatization and Alternative Reform Strategies', *European Journal of Law and Economics* 12 (2001), 240–258.

24. S. Osborne, ed., *Public–Private Partnerships: Theory and Practice in International Perspective* (London: Routledge, 2001).

25. A. Ghobadian, D. Gallear, H. Viney and N. O'Regan, 'The Future of Public–Private Partnership', in *Public–Private Partnerships: Policy and Experience*, ed. A. Ghobadian, D. Gallear, N. O'Regan and H. Viney (Basingstoke: Palgrave Macmillan, 2004), 271–302.

26. N. Khanom, 'Conceptual Issues in Defining Public Private Partnerships (PPP)', *International Review of Business Research Papers* 6, no. 2 (2010), 254–278.

27. E. Yescombe, *Public-Private Partnerships: Principles of Policy and Finance* (Oxford: Butterworth-Heinemann, 2007).

28. E. Dannin, 'Crumbling Infrastructure, Crumbling Democracy: Infrastructure Privatization Contracts and Their Effects on State and Local Governance', *Northwestern Journal of Law and Social Policy* 6 (2011), 46–104.

29. D. Andrew, C. Smith and Michael J. Trebilcock, 'State-Owned Enterprises in Less Developed Countries: Privatization and Alternative Reform Strategies', *European Journal of Law and Economics* 12 (2001), 220–245.

30. D. Grimsey and M. Lewis, *Public–Private Partnerships: The Worldwide Revolution in Infrastructure Provision and Project Finance* (Cheltenham: Edward Elgar, 2004).

31. D. Hall, *Public-Private Partnerships (PPPs) Summary Paper*, A Report Commissioned by the European Federation of Public Service Unions (EPSU) (2008).

32. M. Minow, 'Public and Private Partnerships: Accounting for the New Religion', *Harvard Law Review* 116, no. 5 (March 2003), 1229-1284.

33. G. A. Hodge and C. Greve, 'Public-Private Partnerships: An International Performance Review', *Public Administrative Review* 67 (2007), 545–558.

34. C. Harris, *Private Participation in Infrastructure in Developing Countries: Trends,* Impacts, and Policy Lessons (Washington, DC: World Bank, March 2003).

35. J. Freeman, 'Extending Public Law Norms through Privatization', *Harvard Law Review* 116, no. 5 (March 2003), 1285–1302.

36. For an analysis of the concept, see C. Bovis, *The Liberalisation of Public Procurement and Its Impact on the Common Market*, 4–20, op. cit.

37. J. Freeman, 'Extending Public Law Norms through Privatization', *Harvard Law Review* 116, no. 5 (March 2003), 1285–1302.
38. P. Birkinshaw, 'Corporatism and Accountability', in *Corporatism and the Corporate State*, ed. N. O'Sullivan and A. Cox (Cheltenham: Edward Elgar, 1988), 178–210.
39. International Monetary Fund, *Public-Private Partnerships, Government Guarantees and Fiscal Risk* (Washington, DC: International Monetary Fund, 2006).
40. P. Vaillancourt Rosenau, 'Strengths and Weaknesses of Public-Private Policy Partnerships', in *Public-Private Policy Partnerships*, ed. Pauline Vaillancourt Rosenau (Cambridge, MA: MIT Press, 2000), 217–242.
41. D. Grimsey and M. Lewis, *Public Private Partnerships: The Worldwide Revolution in Infrastructure Provision and Project Finance* (Cheltenham: Edward Elgar, 2004).
42. For example, defence, policing or other essential or core elements of governance. It is maintained here that activities related to *imperium* (the use of force by way of regulatory or criminal law) could not be the subject of contractualised governance. A useful analysis for such argument is provided in Case C-44/96, *Mannesmann Anlangenbau Austria AG et al. v. Strohal Rotationsdurck GesmbH,* (judgement of 15 January 1998), where the notions of public security and safety are used to described a range of activities by the state which possess the characteristic of 'public service obligations'. For a commentary of the case, see C. Bovis, 'Redefining Contracting Authorities under the EC Public Procurement Directives: An Analysis of the Case C-44/96, *Mannesmann Anlangenbau Austria AG et al. v. Strohal Rotationsdurck GesmbH*', *Common Market Law Review* 36, 1999, 205–25.
43. United Nations Economic Commission for Europe, *Guidebook on Promoting Good Governance in Public Private Partnerships*, ECE/CECI/4, United Nations, 2008.
44. United Nations Millennium Declaration, Resolution 55/2 adopted by the General Assembly, 8th Plenary Meeting, 8 September 2000.
45. HM Treasury, *Public Private Partnerships: The Government's Approach* (London: Her Majesty's Stationery Office, 2000). Also, HM Treasury, *PFI: Meeting the Investment Challenge* (London: Her Majesty's Stationery Office, 2003).
46. L. De Pierris, 'Improving the Infrastructure', *PFI Journal* 40 (2003): 44–45.
47. M. Spackman, 'Public-Private Partnerships: Lessons from the British Approach', *Economic Systems* 26 (2002): 283–301.
48. Department of Treasury and Finance, *Partnerships Victoria* (Melbourne: 2000). Also, Department of Treasury and Finance, *Practitioners' Guide* (Melbourne: 2001).
49. See, Office of Management and Budget, 'Preparation, Submission and Execution of the Budget', OMB Circular No. A-11 (2002).
50. D. Grimsey and M. Lewis, *Public Private Partnerships: The Worldwide Revolution in Infrastructure Provision and Project Finance* (Cheltenham: Edward Elgar, 2004).
51. The Canadian Council for Public-Private Partnerships, http://www.pppcouncil.ca/resources/about-ppp/definitions.html
52. U.S. Department of Transportation, Federal Highway Administration, http://www.fhwa.dot.gov
53. National Council for Public Private Partnerships, http://www.ncppp.org
54. Organisation for Economic Co-operation and Development, 'Public-Private Partnerships for Research and Innovation: An Evaluation of the Australian Experience' (Paris: OECD, 2004).
55. Infrastructure Australia, http://www.infrastructureaustralia.gov.au
56. Partnerships Victoria, http://www.partnerships.vic.gov.au

57. These are End Poverty and Hunger; Universal Education; Gender Equality; Child Health; Maternal Health; Combat HIV/AIDS; Environmental Sustainability; and Global Partnership. See United Nations, http://www.un.org/millenniumgoals/

58. Organisation for Economic Co-operation and Development, 'Encouraging Public Private Partnerships in Utilities Sector: The Role of Development Assistance', A NEPAD/OECD Investment Initiative (OECD, 2005).

59. A. Akintoye, A. Ngowi, P. A. Bowen, *Development in Public Private Partnership for Construction-based Projects in the Developing Countries* (Baghdad: Institute for Integrated Economic Research [IIER], 2009).

60. A. Akintoye and M. Beck, *Policy, Finance and Management for Public Private Partnerships* (Chichester: Wiley-Blackwell, 2009), 130.

61. D. Moss, *When All Else Fails: Government as the Ultimate Risk Manager* (Cambridge, Massachusetts: Harvard University Press, 2002).

62. H. Polackova-Brixi and A. Schick, eds., *Government at Risk: Contingent Liabilities and Fiscal Risk* (Washington, DC: World Bank Publications, 2002).

63. K. Arrow and R. Lind, 'Uncertainty and the Evaluation of Public Investment Decisions', *American Economic Review* 60 (1970): 364–78.

64. International Monetary Fund Department of Fiscal Affairs, *Public-Private Partnerships* (Washington, DC: IMF Publications, 2004).

65. C. Bovis, 'Future Directions in Public Private Partnerships', in *The Law of the Future and the Future of the Law,* ed. S. Muller, S. Zouridis, M. Frishman and L. Kistemaker (Oslo: Torkel Opsahl, 2012), 782.

66. M. Hammami, J.F. Ruhashyankiko, and E. Yehue, 'Determinants of Public Private Partnerships in Infrastructure', IMF Working Paper, WP/06/99, 2006.

67. A. Malik, 'Effects of Private Initiatives in Infrastructure on the Macro Economy of Asia', *European Journal of Economics, Finance and Administrative Sciences* 16 (2009), 50–65.

68. M. Hammami, et al., 'Determinants of Public Private Partnerships in Infrastructure', IMF Working Paper, WP/06/99, 2006.

69. D. Grimsey and M. Lewis, *Public Private Partnerships: The Worldwide Revolution in Infrastructure Provision and Project Finance* (Cheltenham: Edward Elgar), 2012.

70. A. Akintoye and M. Beck, *Policy, Finance and Management for Public Private Partnerships* (Chichester: Wiley-Blackwell, 2009), 129.

71. M. Hammami et al., 'Determinants of Public-Private Partnerships in Infrastructure', IMF Working Paper, WP/06/99, 2006, 12.

72. HM Treasury, *Public Private Partnerships: The Government's Approach* (London: Her Majesty's Stationery Office, 2000). Also, HM Treasury, *PFI: Meeting the Investment Challenge* (London: Her Majesty's Stationery Office, 2003).

73. L. De Pierris, 'Improving the Infrastructure', *PFI Journal* 40 (2003): 44–45.

74. The UK National Audit Office has commented on PFI: 'Most private finance projects are built close to the agreed time, price and specification. 69 per cent of PFI construction projects between 2003 and 2008 were delivered on time and 65 per cent were delivered at the contracted price. Of those delivered late, 42 per cent were delivered within six months of the agreed time, and under half experienced price increases. Public bodies using private finance are normally satisfied with the services provided by contractors. High levels of satisfaction are normally reflected in our reports, case studies and surveys. Whilst we recognise that contract managers may be biased in their response, they are likely to also be the most informed individuals for a project'. National Audit Office, *Private Finance Projects: A Paper for the Lords Economic Affairs Committee,* October 2009.

75. L. Salamon, 'The New Governance and the Tools of Public Action: An Introduction', in *The Tools of Government: A Guide to the New Governance,* ed. Lester M. Salamon (Oxford: Oxford University Press, 2002).
76. National Audit Office (NAO), *Managing the Relationship to Secure a Successful Partnership in PFI Projects* (London: Stationery Office, 2001).
77. See P. Thomas, 'Private Finance Initiative—Government by Contract', *European Public Law* 3, no. 4 (December 1997): 519 *et seq.*
78. L. De Pierris, 'Improving the Infrastructure', *PFI Journal* 40 (2003): 44–45.
79. HM Treasury, *PFI: Meeting the Investment Challenge* (London: Her Majesty's Stationery Office, 2003).
80. HM Treasury, *Infrastructure Procurement. Delivering Long-term Value* (London: Her Majesty's Stationery Office, 2008).
81. A. Pollock, D. Price and S. Playe, 'An Examination of the UK Treasury's Evidence Base for Cost and Time Overrun Data in UK Value-for-Money Policy and Appraisal', *Public Money and Management* 27 (2007): 2.
82. A. Pollock, J. Shaoul and N. Vickers, 'Private Finance and Value for Money in NHS Hospitals: A Policy in Search of a Rationale?', *British Medical Journal* (2002): 324.
83. The structure of public markets reveals that in the supply/demand equation, the dominant part appears to be the demand side (the state and its organs as purchasers), which initialises demand through an institutionalised purchasing system, whereas the supply side (the industry) fights for access to the relevant markets. Although this is normally the case, one should not exclude the possibility of market oligopolisation and the potential manipulation of the demand side. These advanced market structures can occur more often in the future, as a result of the well-established trends of industrial concentration. See C. Bovis, *The Liberalisation of Public Procurement and Its Impact on the Common Market,* op. cit. p. 7; Also, A. Konstadacopoulos, 'The Linked Oligopoly Concept in the Single European Market', *Public Procurement Law Review* 4 (1995): 213.
84. Normally a public contract risk assessment includes contractual elements which are associated with the design or construction of a project, the required investment and financing, planning and operational matters, maintenance, residualisation, obsolescence, political/legal aspects, industrial relations, usage volumes and finally currency transactions.
85. M. Pollitt, 'The Declining Role of the State in Infrastructure Investment in the UK', in *Private Initiatives in Infrastructure: Priorities, Incentives and Performance,* ed. S. V. Berg, M. G. Pollitt and M. Tsuji (Cheltenham: Edward Elgar, 2002), 239–273.
86. A number of impact assessment studies of the procurement regime upon the demand and supply sides have revealed the disproportionate risk allocation amongst the parties. See, European Commission, *The Use of Negotiated Procedures as a Non-Tariff Barrier in Public Procurement,* Brussels, CC 9364, 1995. In this study, the author investigated on behalf of the European Commission the award patterns of public contracts in six EC Member States. The results showed the overall preference of contracting authorities towards *the lowest price* award criterion. Even in cases where *the most economically advantageous offer* was used for the award of a public contract, contracting authorities prioritised the price given by tenderers amongst the other parameters (technical reasons, aesthetic reasons, quality of deliverables, after-sales service or maintenance).
87. In another impact assessment study undertaken on behalf of the European Commission (*The Opening-up of Public Procurement to Foreign Direct Investment in the European Community,* Brussels, CC 93/79, 1995), the author examined the impact of the public procurement regime upon foreign direct investment.

Investment patterns towards industries doing business with the public sector showed a considerable link between the 'low-risk' assessments of the public contracts of these industries.

88. In its policy statement *Public Sector Comparators and Value for Money,* February 1998, the HM Treasury Taskforce has set out the role of comparators in public procurement, stressing the importance of the value-for-money principle. The comparators are indices which help to distinguish between the lowest cost and the best value for money for public authorities and also their use as an exercise of financial management and a means of demonstrating savings to public authorities.

89. J. Kay, 'Efficiency and Private Capital in the Provision of Infrastructure', in *Infrastructure Policies for the 1990s* (Paris: Organization for Economic Cooperation and Development, 1993), 55–74.

90. M. Pollitt, 'Learning from the UK Private Finance Initiative Experience', in *The Challenge of Public–Private Partnerships: Learning from International Experience,* ed. G. Hodge and C. Greve (Cheltenham: Edward Elgar, 2005), 123–150.

91. M. Spackman, 'Public-Private Partnerships: Lessons from the British Approach', *Economic Systems* 26 (September 2002): 283–301.

92. P. Grout, 'The Economics of the Private Finance Initiative', *Oxford Review of Economic Policy* 13 (1997): 53–66.

93. Case 76/81, *SA Transporoute et Travaux v. Minister of Public Works,* [1982] ECR 457; Case No. 104/75, *SA SHV Belgium v. La Maison Ideale et Societe Nationale du Longement,* before the Belgian Conseil d'Etat, judgement of 24 June 1986 of the Belgian *Conseil d'Etat.*

94. PricewaterhouseCoopers, *Delivering the PPP Promise. A Review of PPP Issues and Activities* (2005).

95. National Audit Office, *PFI: Construction Performance,* HC 371 (London: Stationery Office, 2003).

96. The structure of public markets often reveals a monopsony/oligopsony character. In terms of its origins, demand in public markets is institutionalised and operates mainly under budgetary considerations rather than price mechanisms. It is also based on fulfilment of tasks (pursuit of public interest) and it is single for many products. Supply also has limited origins, in terms of the establishment of close ties between the public sector and industries supplying it and there is often a limited product range. Products are rarely innovative and technologically advanced and pricing is determined through tendering and negotiations. The purchasing decision is primarily based upon the lifetime cycle, reliability, price and political considerations. Purchasing patterns follow tendering and negotiations and often purchases are dictated by policy rather than price/quality considerations.

97. Department of the Environment, *Working Together—Private Finance and Public Money* (London: DoE Publications, 1993).

98. Private markets are generally structured as a result of competitive pressures originating in the buyer/supplier interaction and their configuration can vary from monopoly/oligopoly to perfect competition. Demand arises from heterogeneous buyers with a variety of specific needs. It is based on expectations and is multiple for each product. Supply, on the other hand, is offered through various product ranges, where products are standardised using known technology, but constantly improved through research and development processes. The production process is based on mass-production patterns and the product range represents a large choice including substitutes, whereas the critical production factor is cost level. The development cycle appears to be short to medium term and finally, the technology of products destined for the private markets is evolutionary. Purchases

are made when an acceptable balance between price and quality is achieved. Purchase orders are multitude and at limited intervals. Pricing policy in private markets is determined by competitive forces and the purchasing decision is focused on the price-quality relation. The risk factor is highly present.

99. J. Shaoul, 'The Private Finance Initiative or the Public Funding of Private Profit', in *The Challenge of Public–Private Partnerships: Learning from International Experience*, ed. G. Hodge and C. Greve (Cheltenham: Edward Elgar, 2005), 210–246.

100. National Audit Office, *Private Finance Projects: A Paper for the Lords Economic Affairs Committee*, London, October 2009.

NOTES TO CHAPTER 5

1. D. Grimsey and M. Lewis, *Public Private Partnerships: The Worldwide Revolution in Infrastructure Provision and Project Finance* (Cheltenham: Edward Elgar, 2007).

2. See European Commission, 'Report to the Laeken European Council: Services of General Interest', COM (2001) 598; European Commission, 'Communication from the Commission to the Council, the European Parliament, the Economic and Social Committee and the Committee of the Regions on the Status of Work on the Examination of a Proposal for a Framework Directive on Services of General Interest', COM (2002) 689; European Commission, 'Green Paper on Services of General Interest', COM (2003) 270; European Commission, 'Communication from the Commission to the European Parliament, the Council, the European Economic and Social Committee and the Committee of the Regions: White Paper on Services of General Interest', COM (2004) 374.

3. See European Commission, 'Green Paper on Public-Private Partnerships and Community Law on Public Contracts and Concessions', COM (2004) 327.

4. See 'Conclusions of the Presidency', Brussels European Council, 12 December 2003, Council of the European Union, Brussels, 5 February 2004, 5381/04. See Communication from the Commission to the Council and to the Parliament 'Public Finances in EMU 2003', published in the European Economy No. 3/2003 (COM (2003) 283 final).

5. See COM (2003) 270.

6. F. Blanc-Brude, H. Goldsmith and T. Valila, *Public–Private Partnerships in Europe: An Update,* Economic and Financial Report, 2007/03 (Luxembourg: European Investment Bank, 2007).

7. Deloitte, *Closing the Infrastructure Gap: The Role of Public–Private Partnerships,* Deloitte Research Study (London: Deloitte, 2006).

8. F. Poschmann, 'Private Means to Public Ends: The Future of Public Private Partnerships', C. D. Howe Institute Commentary No. 183 (June 2003).

9. M. Minow, 'Public and Private Partnerships: Accounting for the New Religion', *Harvard Law Review* 116, no. 5 (March 2003), 1229–1284.

10. See Communication from the Commission of 23 April 2003, 'Developing the Trans-European Transport Network: Innovative Funding Solutions—Interoperability of Electronic Toll Collection Systems', COM (2003) 132, and the Report of the High-level Group on the Trans-European Transport Network of 27 June 2003.

11. Organisation for Economic Co-operation and Development, 'Public–Private Partnerships: In Pursuit of Risk Sharing and Value for Money' (Paris: OECD, 2008).

12. H. Zarco-Jasso, 'Public–Private Partnerships: A Multidimensional Model for Contracting', *International Journal of Public Policy* 1, no. 1/2 (2005), 22–40.

13. Eurostat (Statistical Office of the European Communities), press release STAT/04/18 of 11 February 2004.
14. A. Boardman, F. Poschmann and A. Vining, 'North American Infrastructure P3s: Examples and Lessons Learned', in *The Challenge of Public–Private Partnerships: Learning from International Experience,* ed. G. Hodge and C. Greve (Cheltenham: Edward Elgar, 2005), 290–304.
15. R. Wettenhall, 'The Public–Private Interface: Surveying the History', in *The Challenge of Public–Private Partnerships: Learning from International Experience,* ed. G. Hodge and C. Greve (Cheltenham, Edward Elgar, 2005), 22–43.
16. Communication from the Commission to the Council and to the Parliament, 'Public Finances in EMU 2003', published in the European Economy No. 3/2003 (COM (2003) 283 final).
17. See P. Grout, 'The Economics of the Private Finance Initiative', *Oxford Review of Economic Policy* 13 (1997): 53–66.
18. J. Kay, 'Efficiency and Private Capital in the Provision of Infrastructure', in *Infrastructure Policies for the 1990s* (Paris: Organization for Economic Co-operation and Development, 1993), 55–73.
19. C. Bovis, 'Public-Private Partnerships in the 21st Century', *ERA Forum* 11, no. 3 (2010): 379.
20. In its policy statement, *Public Sector Comparators and Value for Money,* February 1998, the HM Treasury Taskforce in the United Kingdom set out the role of comparators in public procurement, stressing the importance of the value-for-money principle. The comparators are indices that help to distinguish between the lowest cost and the best value for money for public authorities and also their uses as an exercise of financial management and a means of demonstrating savings to public authorities.
21. C. Bovis, *Public Procurement: Case Law and Regulation* (Oxford: Oxford University Press, 2006), chap. 11, 594.
22. J.J. Laffont and J. Tirole, *A Theory of Incentives in Procurement and Regulation* (Cambridge: Massachusetts, MIT Press 1993).
23. Directive 2004/18 Art. 26, OJ L 134, 30.4.2004 (on the coordination of procedures for the award of public works contracts, public supply contracts and public service contracts); see also Directive 2004/17 Art. 30, OJ L 134, 30.4.2004 (coordinating the procurement procedures of entities operating in the water, energy, transport and postal services sectors).
24. G. Teisman and E. Klijn, 'Public–Private Partnerships in the European Union: Official Suspect, Embraced in Daily Practice', in *Public–Private Partnerships: Theory and Practice in International Perspective,* ed. S. Osborne (New York: Routledge, 2001), 165–186.
25. 'Conclusions of the Presidency', Brussels European Council, 12 December 2003.
26. COM (2003) 270 final.
27. The rules on the internal market, including the rules and principles governing public contracts and concessions, apply to any economic activity, that is, any activity which consists in providing services, goods, or carrying out works in a market, even if these services, goods or works are intended to provide a 'public service', as defined by a Member State.
28. See Interpretive Communication of the Commission on Concessions in Community Law, OJ C 121, 29 April 2000.
29. Directive 2004/18/EC of the European Parliament and of Council of 31 March 2004 relating to the coordination of procedures for the award of public works, supply and services contracts, and Directive 2004/17/EC of the European Parliament and of the Council of 31 March 2004 relating to the

coordination of procedures for the award of contracts in the water, energy, transport and postal services sectors. Moreover, in certain sectors, and particularly the transport sector, the organisation of a public-private partnership may be subject to specific sectoral legislation. See Regulation (EEC) No. 2408/92 of the Council on Access of Community Air Carriers to Intra-Community Air Routes, Council Regulation (EEC) No. 3577/92 applying the principle of freedom to provide services to maritime transport within Member States, Council Regulation (EEC) No. 1191/69 on action by Member States concerning the obligations inherent in the concept of a public service in transport by rail, road and inland waterway, as amended by Regulation (EEC) No. 1893/91, and the amended proposal for a Regulation of the European Parliament and of the Council on action by Member States concerning public service requirements and the award of public service contracts in passenger transport by rail, road and inland waterway (COM (2002) 107 final).

30. Interpretative Communication on Concessions under Community Law, OJ C 121, 29 April 2000.
31. M. Spackman, 'Public-Private Partnerships: Lessons from the British Approach', *Economic Systems* 26 (2002): 283–301.
32. HM Treasury, *Public Private Partnerships: The Government's Approach* (London: The Stationery Office, 2000). See also HM Treasury, *PFI: Meeting the Investment Challenge* (London: The Stationery Office, 2003).
33. L. De Pierris, 'Improving the Infrastructure', *PFI Journal* 40 (2003): 44–45.
34. D. Grimsey and M. Lewis, *Public Private Partnerships: The Worldwide Revolution in Infrastructure Provision and Project Finance* (Cheltenham: Edward Elgar, 2007), 2.
35. See A. Kappeler and M. Nemoz, 'Public-Private Partnerships in Europe— Before and during the Recent Financial Crisis', Economic and Financial Report 2010/04, July 2010, European Investment Bank (EIB).
36. Report on the Public Consultation on the Green Paper on Public-Private Partnership and Community Law on Public Contracts and Concessions 11, SEC (2005) 629.
37. Case C-324/98, Telaustria Verlags GmbH and Telefonadress GmbH v. Post & Telekom Austria AG, [2000] ECR I-10745.
38. C. Bovis, 'Future Directions in Public Private Partnerships', in *The Law of the Future and the Future of the Law,* ed. S. Muller, S. Zouridis, M. Frishman and L. Kistemaker (Oslo: Torkel Opsahl, 2012), 782.
39. C. Bovis, 'Public Procurement and Public Services in the EU', in *Regulating Trade in Services in the EU and the WTO: Trust, Distrust and Economic Integration,* ed. I. Lianos and O. Odudu (Cambridge: Cambridge University Press, 2012), 287.
40. Case C-360/96, *Arnhem and Rheden,* [1998] ECR I-6821 paragraph 25. *Arnhem and Rheden* provides a strong indication that the European Court views the requirement to exploit the right ceded in order to obtain remuneration as the core of what constitutes a genuine concession. The Court maintained that an important feature of service concessions in the Community context is that the concessionaire automatically assumes the economic risk associated with the provision and management of the services that are the subject of the concession.
41. European Commission Interpretative Communication of Community Law on Public Procurement Concessions 2 fn.10, OJ 2000, C 21.
42. S. Van Grasse, *De Concessie in het raam van de publiek-private samenwerking* (Antwerp: Die Keure, 2007). See also A. Alexis, Services Publics et Aides d'Etat 63–107 (2002); J. Arnould, Les Contrats de Concession de Privatisation et des Services 'in-house' au Regard des Règles Communautaires, F.F.D. Adm, 2000, 2–23.

43. PricewaterhouseCoopers, 'London Economics and Ecorys, Public Procurement in Europe—Cost and Effectiveness'. A Study on Procurement Regulation prepared for the Commission, March 2011.

44. Directive 2004/18 EC has adopted a special, mitigated regime for the award of concession contracts in its Article 1(3). The provisions of the Directive only apply to concession contracts when the value is at least 6,242,000 million euro. There are no rules given as to the way in which the contract value must be calculated. For the award of concession contracts, contracting authorities must apply similar rules on advertising as the advertising rules concerning open and restricted procedures for the award of every works contract. Also, the provisions on technical standards and on criteria for qualitative selection of candidates and tenderers do apply to the award of concession contracts. The Directive does not prescribe the use of specific award procedures for concession contracts.

45. Article 59 of Directive 2004/18 EC stipulates that the Directive does not provide for a specific award procedure envisaged for public works concession. Contracting authorities are free to select the standard procedures specified for the award of public contracts. However, contracting authorities must allow a time limit not less than fifty-two days from the date of dispatch of the notice for the presentation of applications for the concession.

46. According to Article 1(2)(b) of Directive 2004/18 EC, public works contracts are public contracts which have as their object either the execution or both the design and execution, of works, or the completion, by whatever means, of a work corresponding to the requirements specified by the contracting authority. A work means the outcome of building or civil engineering works taken as a whole which is sufficient of itself to fulfil an economic or technical function. According to Article 1(3) of Directive 2004/18 EC, public works concession is a contract of the same type as a public works contract except for the fact that the consideration for the works to be carried out consists either solely in the right to exploit the work or in this right together with payment. According to Article 1(4) of Directive 2004/18 EC, service concession is a contract of the same type as a public service contract except for the fact that the consideration for the provision of services consists either solely in the right to exploit the service or in this right together with payment.

47. Directive 2004/18, OJ L 134, 30.4.2004 on the coordination of procedures for the award of public works contracts, public supply contracts and public service contracts.

48. See Directive 2007/66/EC of 11 December 2007, OJ L335/31.

49. Directive 2004/17, OJ L 134, 30.4.2004 coordinating the procurement procedures of entities operating in the water, energy, transport and postal services sectors.

50. C. Bovis, 'The Role and Function of Structural and Cohesion Funds and the Interaction of the EU Regional Policy with the Internal Market Policies', chap. 4 in *The Role of the Regions in EU Governance*, ed. C. Panara and A. De Becker (Heidelberg: Springer, 2011).

51. See European Commission, Public Services in the European Union and in the 27 Member States, Mapping of the Public Services, CEEP Managed Project, May 2010.

52. See European Commission, Assessment of an Initiative on Concessions, Brussels, 20.12.2011, SEC(2011) 1588fin.

53. Directive 2004/17, OJ L 134, 30.4.2004 coordinating the procurement procedures of entities operating in the water, energy, transport and postal services sectors.

54. See the Utilities Directive 2004/17, OJ 2004, L 134/1.

55. See Article 15 of the Public Sector Directive and Article 22(a) of the Utilities Directive.
56. See Article 14 of the Public Sector Directive and Article 21 of the Utilities Directive.
57. See Article 13 of the Public Sector Directive.
58. See Article 16 of the Public Sector Directive.
59. See Article 20(1) of the Utilities Directive.
60. See Article 26(a) of the Utilities Directive.
61. See Article 27 of the Utilities Directive.
62. See Article 29(2) of the Utilities Directive.
63. See Article 30(1) of the Utilities Directive.
64. See Article 30(6) third indent of the Utilities Directive.
65. European Commission's XXI Competition Report, point 177.
66. European Commission's XXIII Competition Report, point 534.
67. The concept of public service obligation within the context of the air transport regime is defined in Regulation 1008/2008 on access for air carriers to intra-Community air routes as 'any obligation imposed upon an air carrier to take, in respect of any route which it is licensed to operate by a Member State, all necessary measures to ensure the provision of a service satisfying fixed standards of continuity, regularity, capacity and pricing, standards which the air carrier would not assume if it were solely considering its economic interest'.
68. It should be mentioned that Community rules on public procurement contracts do not apply to the awarding by law or contract of exclusive concessions, which are exclusively ruled by the procedure provided for pursuant to Article 4(1) of Regulation 1008/2008.
69. See Regulation 1008/2008 of the European Parliament and of the Council of 24 September 2008 on common rules for the operation of air services in the Community (Recast), OJ L 293, 31.10.08.
70. Although Article 4(1)(f) of Regulation 1008/2008 refers to the compensation required as just one of the criteria to be taken into consideration for the selection of submissions, the Commission considers that the level of compensation should the main selection criterion, as other elements such as adequacy, fare prices and standards are constituent elements of the public service obligations themselves.
71. Case C-301/87, *France v. Commission,* [1990] ECR I, p. 307; Case C-142/87 *Belgium v. Commission* [1990] ECR I, p. 959.
72. Case 173/73, *Italy v. Commission,* [1974] ECR, p. 709.
73. Article 4(1)(i) of Regulation 2008/2008 obliges the Member States to take the measures necessary to ensure that any decision to award public service obligations can be reviewed effectively. The Commission may carry out an investigation and take a decision in case the development of a route is being unduly restricted under Article 4(3) of the Regulation. However, the Commission's powers under the Regulation are without prejudice to its exclusive powers under the state aid rules of the Treaty. In case there is clear evidence that the Member State has not selected the best offer, the Commission may request information from the Member State in order to examine whether the award of a public service obligation includes, in addition to their compensation, state aid elements. Such elements are likely to occur where a Member State has selected not the lowest offer in relation to the financial compensation to be paid to the air carrier.
74. Regulation (EC) No. 1370/2007 of the European Parliament and of the Council of 23 October 2007 on public passenger transport services by rail and by road and repealing Council Regulations (EEC) No. 1191/69 and 1107/70, OJ L 315, 03/12/2007.
75. M. Kekelekis and I. Rusu, 'The Award of Public Contracts and the Notion of "Internal Operator" under Regulation 1370/2007 on Public Passenger

Transport Services by Rail and by Road', *Public Procurement Law Review* 19 (2010), 6–29.

76. This is the case of a German notion of *Konzession*. Licences or authorisations are acts whereby a public authority authorises the exercise of an economic activity. While certain conditions for carrying out the activity usually need to be met by the licencee, or he might have been assigned certain public service obligations linked to the licenced activity, the authorisation does not principally aim at assigning a given public task to the licencee. See European Commission, Assessment of an Initiative on Concessions, Brussels, 20.12.2011, SEC (2011) 1588fin.

77. European Commission, Green Paper on Public-Private Partnerships and Community Law on Public Contracts and Concessions, COM (2004) 327 final.

78. Case C-203/08, *Sporting Exchange Ltd Betfair v. Minister van Justitie*, Judgement of the Court (Second Chamber) of 3 June 2010.

79. Under the Public Procurement Directives, qualification criteria need to relate to technical, economic and financial capacity, whereas award criteria relate to price or the economically most advantageous tender. These requirements do not concern either work or service concessions. For example in France, until recently the award was to a large extent dependent on the *intuitu personae* or the relation of personal trust between the contracting authority and the concessionaire. In Lithuania, the 'effect of the tender on the social and economic development of the country or an appropriate region' may be used as an award criterion which may give rise, in view of its wide scope, to possible discrimination. See European Commission, Assessment of an Initiative on Concessions, Brussels, 20.12.2011, SEC (2011) 1588fin.

80. Report on the Public Consultation on the Green Paper on Public-Private Partnership and Community Law on Public Contracts and Concessions 11, SEC (2005) 629.

81. Article 47 of the Charter of Fundamental Rights in the EU, OJ. C C 364/1, 18.12.2000.

82. Directive 2007/66/EC of 11 December 2007, OJ L335/31.

83. European Commission, Assessment of an Initiative on Concessions, Brussels, 20.12.2011, SEC (2011) 1588fin.

84. C. Bovis, 'Public Procurement and Public Services in the EU', in *Regulating Trade in Services in the EU and the WTO: Trust, Distrust and Economic Integration*, ed. I. Lianos and O. Odudu (Cambridge: Cambridge University Press, 2012), 287.

85. Commission Interpretative Communication on Concessions under Community Law 2–13, OJ C 121, 29.4.2000 (2000).

86. Case law is still not sufficiently clear, in particular regarding the level of operating risk to be transferred to the economic operator so that a contract can qualify as a concession. It appears that Case C-437/07, *Commission v. Italy* [2008] ECR I-00153 and Case C-300/07, C-300/07, *Hans & Christophorus Oymanns GbR, Orthopädie Schuhtechnik, v. AOK Rheinland/Hamburg*, [2009] ECR I-4779 are difficult to interpret along Case C-206/08, *WAZV. Gotha v. Eurawasser Aufbereitungs*, [2009] ECR I-8377. The uncertainty is increased by lingering doubts on the categories of risk that can be transferred to the concessionaire. While demand risk for services seems to be widely accepted as relevant for the definition of a concession, there is uncertainty as to what other categories of risk (availability, construction, legal, and political) should also qualify. See *Eurawasser* [2009] ECR I-08377, at paragraph 79 (where the Court ruled that 'general risk resulting from amendments to the rules made in the course of performance of the contract cannot be taken into account').

87. Case C-331/92, *Gestion Hotelera Internacional* [1994] ECR I-01329; see also Case C-220/05, *Jean Auroux and Others v. Commune de Roanne*, [2007] ECR I-00385, paragraphs 36–37.

88. Case C-324/98, *Telaustria and Telefonadress*, [2000] ECR I-10745.
89. H. Zarco-Jasso, 'Public–Private Partnerships: A Multidimensional Model for Contracting', *International Journal of Public Policy* 1, no. 1/2 (2005): 22–40.
90. F. Blanc-Brude, H. Goldsmith and T. Valila, *Public–Private Partnerships in Europe: An Update,* Economic and Financial Report, 2007/03 (Luxembourg: European Investment Bank, 2007).
91. Deloitte, *Closing the Infrastructure Gap: The Role of Public–Private Partnerships,* Deloitte Research Study (London: Deloitte, 2006).
92. J. Koppenjan, 'The Formation of Public–Private Partnerships. Lessons from Nine Transport Infrastructure Projects in the Netherlands', *Public Administration* (2005): 83.
93. C. Bovis, 'Future Directions in Public Private Partnerships', in *The Law of the Future and the Future of the Law,* ed. S. Muller, S. Zouridis, M. Frishman and L. Kistemaker (Oslo: Torkel Opsahl, 2012), 782.
94. T. Irwin, *Government Guarantees: Allocating and Valuing Risk in Privately Financed Infrastructure Projects* (Washington, DC: World Bank Publications, 2007).
95. The International Financial Reporting Interpretations Committee (IFRIC) of the International Accounting Standards Board (IASB) identifies four criteria for consolidation: i) SPV operations are decided by the originator; ii) the originator controls the SPV; iii) the originator benefits most from the SPV; and iv) the originator assumes SPV risk. See International Public Sector Accounting Standards (IPSASs) and Statistical Bases of Financial Reporting: An Analysis of Differences and Recommendations for Governance of Public-Private Partnerships, January 2005.
96. International Monetary Fund, Limits on External Debt or Borrowing in Fund Arrangements—Proposed Change in Coverage of Debt Limits, EBS/00/128 (2000).
97. C. Harris, *Private Participation in Infrastructure in Developing Countries: Trends, Impacts, and Policy Lessons* (Washington, DC: World Bank Publications, March 2003).
98. Eurostat decision on Deficit and Debt Treatment of Public Private Partnerships, STAT/04/18, 11 February 2004.
99. See D. Moss, *When All Else Fails: Government as the Ultimate Risk Manager* (Cambridge, MA: Harvard University Press, 2002).
100. H. Polackova-Brixi and A. Schick, eds., *Government at Risk: Contingent Liabilities and Fiscal Risk* (New York: World Bank/Oxford University Press, 2002).
101. K. Arrow and R. Lind, 'Uncertainty and the Evaluation of Public Investment Decisions', *American Economic Review* 60 (June 1970): 364–78.
102. See International Financial Reporting Interpretations Committee [IFRIC], Consolidation: Special Purpose Entities, Standing Interpretation Committee (SIC) 12 (1999).
103. Organisation for Economic Co-operation and Development, 'Public–Private Partnerships: In Pursuit of Risk Sharing and Value for Money' (Paris: OECD, 2008).
104. Organisation for Economic Co-operation and Development, 'Public–Private Partnerships: In Pursuit of Risk Sharing and Value for Money' (Paris: OECD, 2008).

NOTES TO CHAPTER 6

1. C. Bovis, 'The Effects of the Principles of Transparency and Accountability on Public Procurement Regulation', in *Legal Challenges in EU Administrative Law,* ed. H. Hoffman and A. Turk (Cheltenham: Edward Elgar, 2009), 288–321.

2. For example, national legislation in Spain, Italy, France, Portugal, Germany allows the participation of a mixed-capital entity in public procurement for the award of a service or works contract during their incorporation stages. See C. Bovis, 'Future Directions in Public Private Partnerships', in *The Law of the Future and the Future of the Law,* ed. S. Muller, S. Zouridis, M. Frishman and L. Kistemaker (Oslo: Torkel Opsahl, 2012), 782.

3. In the UK, Sweden, the Netherlands, Austria and Belgium, national legislation allows for the fusion of award of a partnership or a concession contract and the incorporation of the entity which will perform the public service or task allocated as a result of the conclusion of the public-private partnership. See C. Bovis, 'Future Directions in Public Private Partnerships', in *The Law of the Future and the Future of the Law,* ed. S. Muller, S. Zouridis, M. Frishman and L. Kistemaker (Oslo: Torkel Opsahl, 2012), 782.

4. Case C-367/98, *Commission v. Portugal,* ECR I–4731 (2002); Case C-483/99, *Commission v. France,* ECR I–4781 (2002); See also Case C-463/00, *Commission v. Spain,* ECR I–4581 (2003); Case C-98/01, *Commission v. United Kingdom,* ECR I-4641 (2003). On the possible justifications in this framework, see Case C-503/99, *Commission v. Belgium,* ECR I–4809 (2002).

5. M. Bult-Spiering and G. Dewulf, *Strategic Issues in Public-Private Partnerships: An International Perspective* (London: Wiley-Blackwell, 2007).

6. Directive 2004/18, OJ L 134, 30.4.2004 on the coordination of procedures for the award of public works contracts, public supply contracts and public service contracts and Directive 2004/17, OJ L 134, 30.4.2004 coordinating the procurement procedures of entities operating in the water, energy, transport and postal services sectors.

7. Article 27 of Directive 93/37, Article 31 of Directive 93/38 and Article 22 of Directive 92/50.

8. Case 76/81, *SA Transporoute et Travaux v. Minister of Public Works,* [1982] ECR 457.

9. Case C-27/86, Constructions et Enterprises Indusrtielles S.A (CEI) v. Association Intercommunale pour les Autoroutes des Ardennes; Case C-28/86, Ing.A. Bellini & Co. S.p.A. v. Regie de Batiments and Case C-29/86, Ing.A. Bellini & Co. S.p.A. v. Belgian State, [1987] ECR 3347.

10. Case C-89/92, *Ballast Nedam Groep NV v. Belgische Staat,* [1994] 2 CMLR.

11. Case C-5/97, *Ballast Nedam Groep NV v. Belgische Staat,* judgement of 18 December 1997.

12. Case C-176/98, *Holst Italia v. Comune di Cagliari,* judgement of 2 December 1999.

13. *Bellini* case, op. cit.

14. Case C-94/99, *ARGE Gewässerschutzt v. Bundesministerium für Land-und Forstwirtschaft,* paragraph 30, judgement of 7 December 2000.

15. Case 31/87, *Gebroeders Beentjes B.V. v. State of Netherlands* [1988] ECR 4635.

16. *Bellini* Case 28/86, op. cit.

17. Case C-71/92, *Commission v. Spain,* judgement of 30 June 1993. Also, *Beentjes,* op. cit. at paragraphs 15 and 16, where the simultaneous application of selection of tenderes and award procedures is not precluded, on condition that the two are governed by different rules.

18. Case C-31/87, *Gebroeders Beentjes B.V. v. State of Netherlands* [1988] ECR 4635.

19. Case C-28/86, *Bellini* op. cit.

20. Case C-71/92, *Commission v. Spain,* [1993] ECR I–5923. Also, *Beentjes,* op. cit. at paragraphs 15 and 16, where the simultaneous application of selection of tenderes and award procedures is not precluded, on condition that the two are governed by different rules.

21. Case C-199/07, *Commission v. Greece,* judgement of 12 November 2009.
22. Case C-315/01, Gesellschaft für Abfallentsorgungs-Technik GmbH (GAT) and Österreichische Autobahnen und Schnellstraßen AG (ÖSAG), ECR [2003] I-6351.
23. Case 31/87, *Gebroeders Beentjes B.V. v. State of Netherlands* [1988] ECR 4635, paragraphs 15 and 16, where the simultaneous application of selection of tenders and award procedures is not precluded, on condition that the two are governed by different rules; Case C-71/92, *Commission v. Spain,* judgement of 30 June 1993; Case C-28/86 *Bellini,* [1987] ECR 3347.
24. Case C-315/01, Gesellschaft für Abfallentsorgungs-Technik GmbH (GAT) and Österreichische Autobahnen und Schnellstraßen AG (ÖSAG), ECR [2003] I–6351.
25. Article 23(1)(d) of Directive 93/36.
26. Joined cases C-21/03 and C-34/03, *Fabricom SA v. État Belge,* judgement of 3 March 2005.
27. Joined cases C-285/99 and C-286/99, *Lombardini and Mantovani* [2001] ECR I–9233.
28. Case C-324/98, *Telaustria and Telefonadress,* [2000] ECR I–10745.
29. Case C-513/99, *Concordia Bus Finland,* [2002] ECR I–7213, paragraph 81.
30. Case C-434/02, *Arnold André* [2004] ECR I–2902, paragraph 68, and Case C-210/03, *Swedish Match* [2004] ECR I–1620, paragraph 70.
31. Case C-87/94, *Commission v. Belgium,* [1996] ECR I–2043, paragraph 54.
32. Case C-126/03, *Commission v. Germany,* [2004] ECR I–11197.
33. Case C-176/98, *Holst Italia* [1999] ECR I-8607, paragraph 29; Case C-399/98, *Ordine degli Architetti and Others* [2001] ECR I–5409, paragraph 92; and Case C-314/01, *Siemens and ARGE Telekom & Partner* [2004] ECR I–2549, paragraph 44.
34. Case C-176/98, *Holst Italia,* [1999] ECR-I–8607.
35. Case C-314/01, Siemens AG Österreich, ARGE Telekom & Partner and Hauptverband der österreichischen Sozialversicherungsträger, [2004] ECR I–2549.
36. Case C-57/01, *Makedoniko Metro and Mikhaniki* [2003] ECR I–1091.
37. National law allowed for such substitution, subject to approval by the contracting authority, only during the stage after the completion of the contract, but not at a stage prior to award of the contract. See Greek Law No. 1418/1984 (23 A) on public works and related matters and Presidential Decree 609/1985 (223 A).
38. The public procurement Directives prohibit any requirement that consortia assume a particular legal form for the purpose of tendering, but permit such requirement in the event of the award of a contract. See for example Article 21 of the public works Directive 93/37.
39. See Joint Cases C-285/99 and C-286/99, *Impresa Lombardini* [2001] ECR I–9233, paragraph 34; see also Case C-399/98, *Ordine degli Architetti* [2001] ECR I 5409, paragraph 52.
40. See *Impresa Lombardini,* paragraph 38; see also Case C-275/98, *Unitron Scandinavia and 3-S* [1999] ECR I–8291, paragraph 31.
41. See the Opinion of Advocate General in Case C-57/01, *Makedoniko Metro and Mikhaniki* [2003] ECR I–1091, paragraph 65.
42. Case C-213/07, Michaniki AE v. Ethniko Simvoulio Radiotileorasis v. Ipourgos Epikratias and Others, judgement of 16 December 2008.
43. Case C-538/07, *Assitur Srl v. Camera di Commercio, Industria, Artigianato e Agricoltura di Milano,* judgement of 19 May 2009.
44. See Case C-376/08, *Serrantoni Srl and Consorzio stabile edili Scrl v. Comune di Milano* [2009] ECR I–12169.
45. Negotiated procedures without prior publicity are allowed when, for technical or artistic reasons or for reasons connected with the protection of exclusive

rights, the works may only be carried out by a particular contractor; insofar as is strictly necessary when, for reasons of extreme urgency brought about by events unforeseen by the contracting authorities in question, the time limit laid down for the open, restricted or negotiated procedures cannot be kept; for new works consisting of the repetition of similar works entrusted to the undertaking to which the same contracting authorities awarded an earlier contact, provided that such works conform to a project for which a first contract was awarded. This procedure may only be adopted during the three years following the conclusion of the original contract and subject to notice which should be given in the original invitation to tender. See Article 6(3) of Directive 93/36; Article 7(3) of Directive 93/37; Article 20(3) of Directive 93/38; Article 11(3) of Directive 92/50.

46. Case C-71/92, *Commission v. Spain* [1993] ECR I-5923, paragraph 36.
47. Case C-323/96, *Commission v. Belgium* [1998] ECR I–5063, paragraph 34; Case C-57/94, *Commission v. Italy* [1995] ECR I–1249, paragraph 23, and Case C-318/94, *Commission v. Germany* [1996] ECR I–1949, paragraph 13; Case C-84/03, *Commission v. Spain,* not yet reported, where previously unsuccessful award procedures and the procurement of uniform goods were rejected as grounds for negotiated procedures without publicity.
48. Case C-57/94, *Commission v. Italy* [1995] ECR I–1249, paragraph 23. See also Case C-318/94, *Commission v. Germany* [1996] ECR I–1949, paragraph 13. Similarly Advocate General Jacobs at paragraph 64 of his Opinion of 23 March 2000 in Case C-337/98, *Commission v. France* [2000] ECR I–8377, 8379.
49. Case C-199/85, *Commission v. Italy,* [1987] ECR 1039; also Case C-3/88, *Commission v. Italy,* [1989] ECR 4035.
50. Case C-199/85, *Commission v. Italy,* op. cit.
51. In Case C-385/03, *Commission v. Italy,* the Italian government stated that the competent authority wished to forestall any damage to or deterioration of the works already completed, and to avoid difficult questions as to the respective liability of a number of contractors. Those arguments were rejected by the Court.
52. Case C-57/94, *Commission v. Italy* [1995] ECR I–1249, paragraph 23.
53. Case C-513/99, *Concordia Bus Finland* [2002] ECR I-7213, paragraph 57.
54. Joined cases C-20/01 and C-28/01, *Commission v. Germany,* [2003] ECR I–3609.
55. In Cases C-20/01 and C-28/01, *Commission v. Germany,* op. cit., the Commission argued that the principle, provided for in Article 130r(2) of the EC Treaty (now, after amendment, Article 174 EC), that environmental damage should as a priority be rectified at source, should be read in the light of that provision as a whole, according to which environmental protection requirements must be integrated into the definition and implementation of other Community policies. Article 130r(2) does not provide that Community environmental policy is to take precedence over other Community policies in the event of a conflict between them.
56. Case C-513/99, *Concordia Bus Finland* [2002] ECR I–7213, paragraph 63.
57. Case C-107/92, *Commission v. Italy,* [1993] ECR I–4655.
58. Case C-57/94, *Commission v. Italy* [1995] ECR I–1249, paragraph 23; joined cases C-20/01 and C-28/01, *Commission v. Germany* [2003] ECR I–3609, paragraph 58.
59. Case C-107/92, *Commission v. Italy,* [1993] ECR I–4655, paragraph 12, and Case C-318/94, *Commission v. Germany* [1996] ECR I–1949, paragraph 14.
60. Case C-24/91, *Commission v. Spain* [1992] ECR I–1989, paragraph 14; Case C-107/92, *Commission v. Italy,* [1993] ECR I–4655, paragraph 13.
61. Case 199/85, *Commission v. Italy* [1987] ECR 1039, paragraph 14. See also Case C-318/94, *Commission v. Germany* [1996] ECR I–1949, paragraph 13.

62. Case C-199/85, *Commission v. Italy*, [1987] ECR 1039, op. cit.; Case C-3/88, *Commission v. Italy*, [1989] ECR 4035, op. cit. Case C-24/91, *Commission v. Spain*, [1994] CMLR 621; Case C-107/92, *Commission v. Italy*, [1993] ECR I–4655; Case C-57/94, *Commission v. Italy*, [1995] ECR I-1249; Case C-296/92, *Commission v. Italy*, [1994] ECR I–1.
63. Case C-385/02, *Commission v. Italy*, [2004] ECR I–8121.
64. Cases C-296/95, *EMU Tabac and Others* [1998] ECR I–1605, paragraph 36, and C-257/00, *Givane and Others* [2003] ECR I–345, paragraph 36.
65. C. Bovis, 'Developing Public Procurement Regulation: Jurisprudence and Its Influence on Law Making', *Common Market Law Review* 43 (2006): 461–95.
66. Negotiated procedures without prior advertisement are exceptionally allowed 'when for technical or artistic reasons or reasons connected with the protection of exclusive rights the services could only be procured by a particular provider . . . and . . . in cases of extreme urgency brought about by events unforeseeable by the contracting authority'. In Cases C-199/85, *Commission v. Italy*, [1987] ECR 1039 and C-3/88, *Commission v. Italy*, [1989] ECR 4035, the Court rejected the existence of exclusive rights and regarded the abuse of this provision as contrary to the right of establishment and freedom to provide services which are based on the principle of equal treatment and prohibit not only overt discrimination on grounds of nationality, but also all covert forms of discrimination, which, by the application of other criteria of differentiation, lead to the same result. Interestingly, in Case 199/85, *Commission v. Italy*, op. cit., the Court elucidated that exclusive rights might include contractual arrangements such as know-how and intellectual property rights. For urgency reasons brought by unforeseen events to contracting authorities the Court established two tests: i) the need of a justification test based on the proportionality principle, and ii) the existence of a causal link between the alleged urgency and the unforeseen events (see Case C-199/85, *Commission v. Italy*, op. cit.; Case C-3/88, *Commission v. Italy*, op. cit.; Case C-24/91, *Commission v. Spain*, [1994] CMLR 621; Case C-107/92, *Commission v. Italy*, judgement of 2 August 1993; Case C-57/94, *Commission v. Italy*, judgement of 18 May 1995; Case C-296/92, *Commission v. Italy*, judgement of 12 January 1994).
67. The grounds for using this procedure are confined to: i) the nature of the works or services or risks attached thereto do not permit overall pricing and ii) the nature of the services is such that specifications cannot be established with sufficient precision. See Article 7(2)(c) of the Works Directive and Articles 11(2)(b) and 11(2)(c) of the Services Directive.
68. Article 29(1) of the Public Sector Directive.
69. Article 1(11)(c) of the Public Sector Directive.
70. See Article 1(11)(c) second indent of the Public Sector Directive.
71. Article 23(3) of the Public Sector Directive.
72. Article 23(3)(b) of the Public Sector Directive.
73. Article 23(3)(c) of the Public Sector Directive.
74. Article 23(3)(d) of the Public Sector Directive.
75. Articles 44 to 46 of the Public Sector Directive 2004/18 govern the conduct of the procedure for verification of the suitability and choice of participants and award of contracts, criteria for qualitative selection, and suitability to pursue a professional activity.
76. Article 29(2) of the Public Sector Directive.
77. Article 29(8) of the Public Sector Directive.
78. Article 29(3) of the Public Sector Directive.
79. Article 40 of the Public Sector Directive.
80. Article 40(2) of the Public Sector Directive.
81. Article 40(5) of the Public Sector Directive.

82. Article 29(3) second indent of the Public Sector Directive.
83. Article 29(5) of the Public Sector Directive.
84. Article 29(4) of the Public Sector Directive.
85. Article 44(4) of the Public Sector Directive.
86. Article 29(6) of the Public Sector Directive.
87. Article 29(6) second indent of the Public Sector Directive.
88. Article 29(7) of the Public Sector Directive.
89. Article 29(7) second indent of the Public Sector Directive.
90. Article 26 of Directive 93/36, Article 30 of Directive 93/37, Article 34 of Directive 93/38 and Article 36 of Directive 92/50.
91. Case 76/81, *SA Transporoute et Travaux v. Minister of Public Works,* [1982] ECR 457.
92. Case 31/87, *Gebroeders Beentjes v. The Netherlands,* op. cit, paragraph 19.
93. Case C-324/93, *R. v. The Secretary of State for the Home Department, ex parte Evans Medical Ltd and Macfarlan Smith Ltd,* judgement of 28 March 1995, where the national court asked whether factors concerning continuity and reliability as well as security of supplies fall under the framework of the most economically advantageous offer, when the latter is being evaluated.
94. Paragraph 22 of *Beentjes* case, op. cit.
95. Paragraph 37 of *Beentjes.*
96. Cases C-380/98, (*Cambridge University*) at paragraph 17, C-44/96, (*Strohal*), paragraph 33; C-360/96, (*BFI*) paragraphs 42 and 43; C-237/99, (*OPAC*), paragraphs 41 and 42.
97. Case 31/87, *Gebroeders Beentjes B.V v. The Netherlands,* [1989] ECR 4365.
98. To that effect, paragraph 31 of the *Beentje* judgement, where the Court stipulated that an award criterion linked to the campaign against unemployment must be expressly mentioned in the contract notice so that contractors may become aware of its existence.
99. Case C-513/99, Concordia Bus Filandia v. Helsingin Kaupunki et HKL-Bussiliikenne, op. cit.
100. The Opinion of the Advocate General, paragraphs 77 to 123.
101. Article 19 of the Public Works Directive 93/37 and the equivalent provisions in all public procurement Directives.
102. Article 10(2) or by reference to national technical specifications referred to in Article 10(5)(a) and (b) of the Public Works Directive 93/37 and the equivalent provisions in all public procurement Directives.
103. Case 31/87, *Beentjes* [1988] ECR 4635, paragraph 35, and Case C-225/98 *Commission v. France* [2000] ECR I-7445, paragraph 73.
104. Case C-19/00, *SIAC Construction* [2001] ECR I-7725, paragraphs 41 and 42.
105. Case C-421/01, Traunfellner GmbH and Österreichische Autobahnen und Schnellstraßen Finanzierungs-AG (Asfinag).
106. Case C-421/01, Traunfellner GmbH and Österreichische Autobahnen und Schnellstraßen Finanzierungs-AG (Asfinag).
107. Case C-380/98, The Queen and H.M. Treasury, ex parte University of Cambridge, [2000] ECR 8035 at paragraph 17; Case C-44/96, C-44/96, Mannesmann Anlangenbau Austria AG et al. v. Strohal Rotationsdurck GesmbH, [1998] ECR 73 at paragraph 33; Case C-360/96, Gemeente Arnhem Gemeente Rheden v. BFI Holding BV, [1998] ECR 6821 at paragraphs 42 and 43; Case C-237/99, Commission v. France (OPAC), [2001] ECR I–939, at paragraphs 41 and 42.
108. Case C-513/99, *Concordia Bus Finland* [2002] ECR I–7123, paragraph 69; Case C-448/01, *EVN AG, Wienstrom GmbH and Republik Österreich,* [2003] ECR I–14527.

109. Case C-225/98, *Commission v. France*, [2000] ECR I–7445; Case 31/87, *Gebroeders Beentjes B.V v. The Netherlands*, [1989] ECR 4365.
110. See Case 31/87, *Beentjes* [1988] ECR 4635, paragraphs 19 and 26; Case C-19/00, *SIAC Construction* [2001] ECR I–7725, paragraphs 36 and 37; and *Concordia Bus Finland*, [2002] ECR I–7213, paragraphs 59 and 61.
111. Case C-28/86, *Bellini*, [1987] ECR 3347.
112. Case C-379/98, *PreussenElektra* [2001] ECR I-2099, paragraph 73.
113. Case C-513/99, *Concordia Bus Finland* [2002] ECR I–7123, paragraph 55.
114. Case C-448/01, *EVN AG, Wienstrom GmbH and Republik Österreich*, judgement of 4 December 2003, paragraph 70.
115. Case C-448/01, *EVN AG, Wienstrom GmbH and Republik Österreich*, judgement of 4 December 2003.
116. Case C-470/99, *Universale-Bau and Others* [2002] ECR I–11617.
117. Case C-470/99, *Universale-Bau and Others*, op. cit., paragraph 87.
118. Case 31/87, *Beentjes* [1988] ECR 4635, paragraph 21.
119. Case C-324/98, *Telaustria and Telefonadress* [2000] ECR I–10745, paragraph 61, and Case C-92/00 *HI* [2002] ECR I–5553, paragraph 45.
120. Commission Communication, 'The Single Market Act Twelve Levers to Boost Growth and Strengthen Confidence of 13 April 2011'.

NOTES TO CHAPTER 7

1. Case C-26/03, Stadt Halle and RPL Recyclingpark Lochau GmbH v. Arbeitsgemeinschaft Thermische Restabfall- und Energieverwertungsanlage TREA Leuna, [2005] ECR I–00001, paragraph 48.
2. Case C-107/98, *Teckal Slr v. Comune di Viano* [1999] ECR I–8121.
3. This practice resembles the market testing process often employed in the United Kingdom between a contracting authority and an in-house team. I. Harden, 'Defining the Range of Application of the Public Sector Procurement Directives in the United Kingdom', *Public Procurement Law Review* 1 (1992): 362.
4. Article 13 of Directive 2004/17, OJ L 134, 30.4.2004 coordinating the procurement procedures of entities operating in the water, energy, transport and postal services sectors.
5. Directive 83/349/EEC as regards the valuation rules for the annual and consolidated accounts of certain types of companies as well as of banks and other financial institutions as amended by Directive 2001/65/EC of the European Parliament, OJ L283 of 27.10.2001.
6. The *Teckal* first criterion is present when *control similar to that which the contracting entity exercises over one of its own departments* is evident. The notion of control and the *similarity* requirement merit a comprehensive approach, and not one solely based on company law features or one which is based on the level of the contracting authority's shareholding (or, conversely, that of the minority shareholder). Normally, corporate control indicates decisive influence over management, operational and strategic decisions, in a similar fashion to the concept of majority shareholder control found in various company laws of the Member States. Nevertheless, any appraisal of the legal position of a majority shareholder in order to assert control must be taken in conjunction with the statutes governing the relevant entity over which the control is exercised and not by sole reference to national company law provisions, as often minority shareholdings give rights of decisive influence, such as specific oversight and blocking rights. C.H. Bovis, 'Public Procurement in the EU: Jurisprudence and Conceptual Directions', *Common Market Law Review* 49 (2012): 1–44.

7. Utilities Directive 2004/17, OJ L 134, 30.4.2004 coordinating the procurement procedures of entities operating in the water, energy, transport and postal services sectors and in particular Article 2(1)(b) (in relation to public undertakings). A public undertaking is any undertaking over which the contracting authorities may exercise directly or indirectly a dominant influence by virtue of their ownership of it, their financial participation therein, or the rules that govern it. Contracting authorities exercise dominant influence over public undertakings when, directly or indirectly, in relation to an undertaking, they hold the majority of the undertaking's subscribed capital, control the majority of the votes attaching to shares issued by the undertaking, or can appoint more than half of the undertaking's administrative, management or supervisory body.

8. C. Bovis, 'Public Procurement and Public Services in the EU', in *Regulating Trade in Services in the EU and the WTO: Trust, Distrust and Economic Integration*, ed. I. Lianos and O. Odudu (Cambridge: Cambridge University Press, 2012), 287.

9. Case C-458/03, *Parking Brixen, supra* note 111, paragraph 62.

10. Case C-26/03, Case C-26/03, Stadt Halle, RPL Recyclingpark Lochau GmbH v. Arbeitsgemeinschaft Thermische Restabfall und Energieverwertungsanlage TREA Leuna, [2005] ECR I–1.

11. Id. paragraph 50.

12. Id. paragraph 49.

13. 'By contrast, the participation, even as a minority, of a private undertaking in the capital of a company in which the contracting authority in question is also a participant excludes in any event the possibility that the contracting authority exercising over that company a control similar to that which it exercises over its own departments'. *Stadt Halle, RPL Recyclingpark Lochau GmbH v. Arbeitsgemeinschaft Thermische Restabfall und Energieverwertungsanlage TREA Leuna*, [2005] ECR I–1 paragraph 49.

14. Case C-29/04, *Commission v. Austria* [2005] ECR I–9705, paragraphs 24–26.

15. Case C-29/04, *Commission v. Austria* [2005] ECR I–9705, paragraphs 38–41.

16. This position has meanwhile been confirmed by the ECJ in Case C-371/05, *Commission v. Italy,* [2008] ECR I–00110, paragraph 29.

17. Case C-340/04, *Carbotermo SpA and Consorzio Alisei v. Comune di Busto Arsizio and AGESP SpA.,* [2006] ECR I–04137, paragraph 37 ('the fact that the contracting authority holds, alone or together with other public authorities, all of the share capital in a successful tenderer tends to indicate, without being decisive, that that contracting authority exercises over that company a control similar to that which it exercises over its own departments').

18. Case C-458/03, *Parking Brixen GmbH v. Gemeinde Brixen and Stadtwerke Brixen AG.,* [2005] ECR I-08585, paragraph 70.

19. Case C-231/03, *Coname* [2005] ECR I–7287, paragraphs 5, 28.

20. Case C-107/98, *Teckal Slr v. Comune di Viano* [1999] ECR I–;8121.

21. Case C-573/07, *Sea Srl. v. Comune di Ponte Nossa* [2009] ECR I–8127.

22. Case C-458/03, *Parking Brixen GmbH v. Gemeinde Brixen and Stadtwerke Brixen AG,* [2005] ECR I–8612, paragraph 65.

23. C.H. Bovis, 'Public Procurement in the EU: Jurisprudence and Conceptual Directions', *Common Market Law Review* 49 (2012): 1–44.

24. Directive 2004/18, OJ L 134, 30.4.2004 on the coordination of procedures for the award of public works contracts, public supply contracts and public service contracts. Also, Directive 2004/17, OJ L 134, 30.4.2004 coordinating the procurement procedures of entities operating in the water, energy, transport and postal services sectors.

25. Case C-340/04, *Carbotermo Spa v. Comune di Busto Arsizio,* [2006] ECRI 4137.

26. The proposal from the European Commission OJ C 29 E, 30.1.2001, p. 11 and OJ C 203 E, 27.8.2002, p. 210; the opinion of the Economic and Social

Committee OJ C 193, 10.7.2001, p. 7; the opinion of the Committee of the Regions OJ C 144, 16.5.2001, p. 23; the opinion of the European Parliament of 17 January 2002 (OJ C 271 E, 7.11.2002, p. 176), Council Common Position of 20 March 2003 (OJ C 147 E, 24.6.2003, p. 1) and Position of the European Parliament of 2 July 2003. Also the Legislative Resolution of the European Parliament of 29 January 2004 and Decision of the Council of 2 February 2004.

27. Case C-340/04, Carbotermo SpA, Consorzio Alisei v. Comune di Busto Arsizio, AGESP SpA, [2006] ECR I–4137.
28. Case C-26/03, *Stadt Halle and RPL Lochau* [2005] ECR I–1, paragraph 48.
29. Case 295/05, Asociación Nacional de Empresas Forestales (Asemfo) v. Transformación Agraria SA (Tragsa) and Administración del Estado, [2007] ECR I-2999, paragraph 65.
30. Case C-480/06, *Commission v. Germany,* [2009] ECR I–04747.
31. Case C-324/07, Coditel Brabant SA v. Commune d'Uccle, Région de Bruxelles-Capitale, [2009] 1 CMLR 29.
32. The Court eluded that public-public cooperation does itself reflect no similarity of control, rather the remit of such relation to deliver a public task or service specified under Community law; the ultimate tests are no intention to circumvent public procurement rules and not pecuniary contractual relation. Case C-480/06, *Commission v. Germany,* [2009] ECR I–04747; the Court also inferred to intermunicipal co-operative societies whose members are contracting authorities and a jointly controlled entity as a benchmark feature of specific criteria of public-public cooperation. Case C-324/07, *Coditel Brabant SA v. Commune d'Uccle, Région de Bruxelles-Capitale,* [2009] 1 CMLR 29.
33. Case C-480/06, *Commission v. Germany,* [2009] ECR I–04747.
34. Case C-324/07, Coditel Brabant SA v. Commune d'Uccle, Région de Bruxelles-Capitale, [2009] 1 CMLR 29.
35. B. Jan Drijber and H. Stergiou, 'Public Procurement Law and Internal Market Law', *Common Market Law Review* 46 (2009): 805–46; C. Bovis, 'Public Procurement and Public Services in the EU', in *Regulating Trade in Services in the EU and the WTO: Trust, Distrust and Economic Integration,* ed. I. Lianos and O. Odudu (Cambridge: Cambridge University Press, 2012), 287.
36. Article 4(2) TFEU.
37. Article 1 of Protocol (No. 26) on Services of General Interest. This Protocol provides that services of general economic interest are subject to the rules of the Internal Market while noting users' preferences may differ, taking into consideration different geographical, social or cultural situations. Noneconomic services are not covered by the rules of the single market and competition, and are not subject to specific EU legislation.
38. Cases C-26/03, Stadt Halle and RPL Lochau [2005] ECR I–1, paragraph 48; C295/05, Asociación Nacional de Empresas Forestales (Asemfo) v. Transformación Agraria SA (Tragsa) and Administración del Estado, [2007] ECR I–2999, paragraph 65; C-480/06, Commission v. Germany, [2009] ECR I–04747; C-324/07, Coditel Brabant SA v. Commune d'Uccle, Région de Bruxelles-Capitale, [2009] 1 CMLR 29.
39. C.H. Bovis, 'Developing Public Procurement Regulation: Jurisprudence and Its Influence on Law Making', *Common Market Law Review* 43 (2006): 461–95.
40. United Nations Economic Commission for Europe, *Guidebook on Promoting Good Governance in Public Private Partnerships,* ECE/CECI/4, United Nations, 2008.
41. Case C-264/03, *Commission v. France,* [2005] ECR I-08831, paragraph 54. Also the opinion of Advocate General Maduro of 24 November 2004, paragraph 39–41.

42. Case C-295/05, Asociación Nacional de Empresas Forestales (Asemfo) v. Transformación Agraria SA (Tragsa) and Administración del Estado, [2007] ECR I–02999, paragraph 54 and Case C-220/06, Asociación Profesional de Empresas de Reparto y Manipulado de Correspondencia v. Administración General del Estado, [2007] ECR I–12175, paragraph 55.
43. Case 203/08, The Sporting Exchange Ltd, trading as Betfair v. Minister van Justitie, [2010] not yet published, paragraphs 23–25; Case C-124/97, Markku Juhani Läärä, Cotswold Microsystems Ltd and Oy Transatlantic Software Ltd v. Kihlakunnansyyttäjä (Jyväskylä) and Suomen valtio (Finnish State), [1999] ECR I–06067, paragraphs 29–31; Case C-42/07, Liga Portuguesa de Futebol Profissional and Bwin International Ltd v. Departamento de Jogos da Santa Casa da Misericórdia de Lisboa, [2009] ECR I–07633, paragraphs 52–55.
44. Case C-243/01, *Gambelli*, [2003] ECR I–13031, paragraph 65; Case C-288/89, *Stichting Collectieve Antennevoorziening Gouda and Others v. Commissariaat voor de Media*, [1991] ECR I–04007. Furthermore, decisions to award exclusive rights to undertakings can amount to an infringement of the Treaty, where the public service requirements to be fulfilled by the service provider are not properly specified (Case C-66/86, *Silver Line Reisebüro*, [1989] ECR I–803), where the service provider is manifestly unable to meet the demand (Case C-41/90, *Höfner*, [1991] ECR I–1979) or where there is an alternative way of fulfilling the requirements that would have a less detrimental effect on competition (Case T-266/97, *Vlaamse Televisie Maatschappij*, [1999] ECR II–2329). Also, the condition that the granting of the exclusive right is compatible with the Treaty is not fulfilled if the measure by which it is awarded is incompatible with secondary EU legislation, see Case C-220/06, *Correos*, paragraphs 64–66.

NOTES TO CHAPTER 8

1. D. Moss, *When All Else Fails: Government as the Ultimate Risk Manager* (Cambridge, MA: Harvard University Press, 2002).
2. S. Van Grasse, De Concessie in het raam van de publiek-private samenwerking, (Die Keure, 2007). Also, A. Alexis, Services publics et aides d'Etat (Paris: RDUE, 2002), 63–107; J. Arnould, Les contrats de concession de privatisation et des services 'in-house' au regard des règles communautaires, F.F.D. Adm, 2000, 2–23.
3. H. Polackova-Brixi and A. Schick, eds., *Government at Risk: Contingent Liabilities and Fiscal Risk* (New York: World Bank/Oxford University Press, 2002).
4. T. Irwin, *Government Guarantees: Allocating and Valuing Risk in Privately Financed Infrastructure Projects* (Washington, DC: World Bank, 2007).
5. Department of Fiscal Affairs, *Public-Private Partnerships* (Washington, DC: International Monetary Fund, 2004).
6. European Commission, Green Paper on Public-Private Partnerships and Community Law on Public Contracts and Concessions, COM (2004) 327 final.
7. Commission Communication, 'The Single Market Act Twelve Levers to Boost Growth and Strengthen Confidence of 13 April 2011'.
8. C. Bovis, 'The Conceptual Links between State Aid and Public Procurement in the Financing of Services of General Economic Interest', chap. 8 in *The Changing Legal Framework for Services of General Interest in Europe: Between Competition and Solidarity*, ed. M. Krajewski, U. Neergaard and J. van de Gronden (The Hague: ASSER Press, 2009), 149–71.
9. M. Bult-Spiering and G. Dewulf, *Strategic Issues in Public-Private Partnerships: An International Perspective* (London: Wiley-Blackwell, 2007).

Index